Beyond the Storm

A Guide to Emotional Freedom and the Peace that is Always Already Here.

By Ilsa Comte Adair

WAWO Press · Boulder, Colorado

BEYOND THE STORM:
A GUIDE TO EMOTIONAL FREEDOM AND THE PEACE THAT IS
ALWAYS ALREADY HERE.

Copyright Ilsa Comte Adair, 2014

All rights reserved. Except for brief passages quoted in newspaper, magazine, radio, television or online reviews, no portion of this book may be reproduced, distributed, or transmitted in any form by any means, electronic or mechanical, including photocopying, recording, or information storage or retrieval system, without the prior written permission of the author.

WAWO Press
Boulder, Colorado

ISBN 978-0-9905560-0-8

Cover design by Bob Patton

Manufactured in the United States of America
First printing June 2014

Contents

Introduction	1
1. The Imaginary Self	9
Ass Backward	9
A Rough Beginning	13
The Limited and Transient Nature of Change	15
Why Change Doesn't Work	16
Thirsty Fishes	18
Empty your Cup	21
One Last Question	23
Experiential Inquiry: Living the Question	24
2. The Absolute Self – Our Aware Presence	27
Truth and its Many Names	27
The Light of Your Being	29
Life is a Metaphor	30
Experiential Adventure: Exploring your Vastness	35
Closer than Close	37
Dropping our Baggage	39
Experiential Adventure: Meeting the Absolute Self	41
3. A Worthy Compass	43
The Unchanging Truth	43
Finding our Way Home	44
4. Suffering	47

The Intimacy of Conflict	47
All about Nothing	48
A Living Inquiry	50
Wake Up, Wake Up	52
Shifting your Focus	53
Experiential Adventure: Meeting the Conflicted Part	57

5. Our Greatest Longing — 59
Our Common Desire	59
To be Free from Ourselves	63
Changing Direction	65
Experiential Inquiry: Our Selves	67
Beyond the Itch	71
Absolute and Undeniable Awareness	72
Experiential Adventure: The Ease and Eternal Nature of Awareness	73
The Futility of the Search	78
An Important Side Note	82
Experiential Adventure: An In-Depth Meeting with the Absolute Self	84

6. The Unwavering Nature of Change — 87
Great Expectations	87
Experiential Inquiry: Meeting our Expectations	90

7. Mind - The Great Tormentor — 93
The Voice	93
Suffering Revisited	95
The Veil of Reality	97
Experiential Adventure: Experiencing Reality as it Is	100

The Function of Thoughts	102
Seeing our Blindness	105

8. Beliefs - The Lenses of Life — 109
The Truth beyond Right and Wrong	109
Challenging Beliefs	113

9. Emotions – The Misunderstood Energy — 117
Our Emotional Climate	117
Experiential Adventure: The Absolute Self and Emotions	119
The Benevolent Alive Core of Emotions	120
The Prison of Definitions	124
Experiential Adventure: A Four-Step Process to Emotional Freedom	128
Direct Experience	131
Experiential Adventure: Emotions as another Movement of Life	132
Our Innate Freedom	134

10. The Body – Our Intuitive Guide — 137
Experiential Adventure: The Alive Body	137
Our Greatest Ally	141
Experiential Adventure: Recognizing the Voice of Truth	143

11. Energy – The Fuel that Animates Us — 145

The Vitality of an Open Heart	145
Responding over Reacting	147
The Scale - a Tool of Awareness	148
Making Aligned Choices	150

12. Crazy Science - A World Inside Out — 153

Matter Doesn't Matter	154
The Matter of Consciousness	157
The Primordial Nature of Awareness – You are That	159
It's All Inside your Head	161
As Many Worlds as there are Beings	165
From Waves to Particles – From Particles to Waves	166

13. Mirror Mirror – Our Vision of the World — 175

Our Misguided Focus	175
To Believe is to See is to Experience	176
Suffering, Our Greatest Ally	177
The Inside Out World Revisited	179

14. Reality – Our Own Creation — 181

Our Unconscious Invitations	181
The Limitations behind Beliefs	184
The Law of Attraction	186
A Movement of Love	187
Experiential Adventure: Releasing Beliefs and Judgments	188
The Natural Flow of Life	190
The Gift of our Pain	191

15. Awareness – The Ultimate

Subject   193
  Know Yourself as That   193
  Subject versus Object   195
  Who Are You?   197
  A Deeper Exploration of the Body   200
  A Deeper Exploration of our
    Inner World   202
  The Unchanging Nature of Reality   206
  Experiential Adventure: The Bliss
    of this Moment   208
  The Ultimate Subject   209

16. Lucid Living – The Way to Freedom 213
  The Light of Discernment   213
  Living Wide Awake   214
  Shedding the False, Embracing
    the Real   218

17. Staying Put – The Loving Undoing of the False 223
  The Warmhearted Openness of Being   223
  Experiential Adventure: Warmly
    and Openly Noticing what is 226
  Knowing who We Are   227

18. Seeing the Wholeness in Everything 231
  Life through the Eyes of Awareness   231
  The Knots of Resistance   233
  Wholeness Includes the Relative   237
  Answering the Call   239
  Experiential Adventure: The Deep

Dive - Releasing the Knots of
Resistance   **241**
The Loving Expression of the All   **248**
Experiential Inquiry: Seeing
  our Distress through the Light   **251**

19. Love – The Essence of our Being   253

Love is your Birthright   **253**
The Sweetest Remembrance   **255**
Love, our Most Generous Act   **257**
Experiential Adventure: Silly Love
  Meditation #1   **258**
Experiential Adventure: Silly Love
  Meditation #2   **259**
Experiential Adventure: Silly Love
  Meditation #3   **260**
Experiential Adventure: Not so Silly
  Love Meditation #4   **261**

20. Forgiveness – The Spontaneous Movement of Awareness   265

There is Only You   **265**
Infinitely Untouched and Pristine   **269**
Flawless Wholeness   **272**
Do Unto Others   **273**
Experiential Adventure: Spontaneous
  Forgiveness   **276**

21. Acceptance – The Deepest Trust   279

Love in Disguise   **279**
Beyond Our Control   **281**

An Absolute 'Yes'	282
Becoming Whole	284
The Pain that Connects Us	285
The Sweetness of the Whole	287
The Little Self Made of Thoughts	288
The Wide Open Nature of Reality	290
Acceptance is not a Doing but a Being	293
Experiential Adventure: Saying 'Yes' to Life	295
Experiential Inquiry: Locating the One who Resists	297

22. The Art of Meditation: The Embrace of What Is — 299

Staying Open and Vast rather than Focused	299
Experiential Adventure: Being with What Is	302
Falling in Love with Silence	305

23. Awake to the Sweetness of Life — 307

Flipping the Switch	307
Instantaneous and Progressive Path	307
A Never Ending Exploration of Love	309

About The Author	**313**
Reading List	**315**

Introduction

If a man is crossing a river and an empty boat collides with his skiff, even though he is a bad-tempered man he will not become very angry.

But if he sees a man in the boat, he will shout at him to steer clear. If the shout is not heard he will shout again, and yet again, and begin cursing. And all because there is somebody in the boat.

Yet, if the boat were empty, he would not be shouting, and not angry.

If you can empty your own boat crossing the river of the world, No one will oppose you.
No one will seek to harm you...

Such is the perfect man:
His boat is empty.
– "The Way of Chuang Tzu" as translated by Thomas Merton

There are multiple versions of this story. In another version, a fisherman is out early enjoying being on the water. It is foggy that particular morning. As he looks in the distance he sees another boat coming directly toward him. Assuming that the other person has not seen him out of inattention or because of the fog, the fisherman starts to yell warnings. As the boat gets closer and closer without changing direction, the fisherman becomes more and more angry, yelling louder and louder, at first yelling warnings, than yelling insults, and finally yelling threats, as he quickly tries to bring up the anchor. By the time the boat hits him the fisherman is livid. He is ready to jump onto the other boat to throttle whomever is in there, when he notices that the boat is empty. What happens to our sailor's anger at that moment? Almost immediately it vanishes, because who is there to be angry at? Technically, the event is still the same, a boat hit his, but the perception of the event is different. And so this story seems to point to two deep Truths that are directly related to finding peace in our lives. First, to find lasting fulfillment, we must empty ourselves. We must empty our mind of all those incessant thoughts, of all our judgments, beliefs and assumptions. As we will come to see, suffering is directly related to the mind's habit to continually conceptualize our experience. We are so full of the false and of the assumed that we cannot see the Truth and the light that resides prior to and beyond our suffering. We are so full of the false self that we cannot see the light of our own Being.

Secondly, we must come to the understanding that all of life, our entire experience of it, is perception; everything is empty of intrinsic meaning, as we are the ones who give things and situations their meaning. Something is good or pleasant because we say so and something is bad or unpleasant because we say so as well. The whole of life – all events, all people, all circumstances, all states of mind and emotions and all experiences – are at core neutral. It is our minds that decide whether they are good or bad, whether they should bother us or not. But don't worry, this is not a claim I am making without evidence, throughout this book, we will explore the nature of reality and of our own Being, which will show you that who you are at your core, your Essence, is whole and at peace with all of life just as it is, regardless of what your mind has to say about it.

Have you ever seen a storm raging on the surface of the ocean, wind whipping and waves crashing? If you were to dive in rather than stay on the agitated surface, quickly you would discover that beyond the turbulence, in the depth of the ocean, resides a great stillness. It is in fact the stillness at the depth of the ocean that is the foundation and the container for any and all movements on the surface. The quiet core of the ocean holds the turbulence. What is true of the ocean is also true of you. Bellow the movements and storms of your emotions, thoughts and experiences, resides a deep abiding stillness that is the container of and the constant in your life. This book is a guided exploration of the Essence of our own Being and of the peace and happiness that is always already here. As you connect to that inner wellspring, you remember how to live and move through life with ease, openness and joy.

What is emotional freedom exactly? Most people believe that to be emotionally free means never experiencing negative emotions, but is that true freedom? If you read this book, digest what is shared, and practice the explorations, you will find yourself experiencing "negative" emotions less often and with less intensity than before. But true freedom is not freedom from xyz, it is not about experiencing or not experiencing something in particular, if so your freedom is always conditional on this one thing. Freedom with any kind of conditions is just another prison. True freedom is freedom regardless of and within all circumstances, then no matter what, you are free, without conditions. Freedom is about being free within all conditions and all emotions, joy as well as sadness, pleasure as well as pain, disappointment as well as gratitude and anxiety as well as peace. To be free is to realize that you are beyond all and any emotion, condition or circumstance. Your Essence is always already peaceful, whole and complete. When you live your life from that space, you discover the freedom and stillness that is beyond all experiences, all beliefs and all emotions. You are then able to live fully and openly, without fear or resistance. You can remain at peace, happy and whole, in each and every moment, no matter what comes your way.

This is a different type of self-help book, although paradoxically there is no one that actually needs help. What we are, at core, our Essence, needs no help; it is complete and whole as it is. This book is about transformation. Most self-help books talk about bettering ourselves and changing our lives, and they give us techniques to that end. I am not denying that many of these books hold valuable suggestions on our journey to a more peaceful and happy self, but techniques will take you only so far. If the advice they contained truly worked long term, you wouldn't need to keep reading more books, you would already be whoever you wish to be. Don't get me wrong, I love books, but I read for the pleasure of it, the artistry of words weaved into a good story or a fully developed idea, not because of need or the hope that what I read will fill some sort of lack.

Over the years, self-help books have given me great insights, great techniques and all of them brought something to my life. For a while my life would make sense, I would feel lighter, have a clearer direction, and be happier...and then slowly the benefits would wear off, and I would find myself right back where I started, looking for the next great book, the next great teacher and for the technique or insight that would finally bring true and lasting fulfillment. But before we can find a solution to what hails us, we must first understand the cause of our suffering. Many of us have taken different kinds of medicine to try to alleviate the symptoms of our dissatisfaction, our anger, our sadness, our resentment, our loneliness, our shame, our numbness, but we have never stopped long enough to figure out where this suffering comes from. From what disease do those symptoms stem from? And who is it that continually feels like something is not right or lacking? How can we cure what we do not know or understand?

For many, much of what you will read in this book might be foreign. Some of it might even go against everything you have learned to believe is true about yourself and reality, so expect to feel annoyed, overwhelmed, put out and completely confused at different points throughout this book, but please stick it out. Everything I write about stems from my own personal experience as well as from the work I have done with others. This work has transformed my life, and I have seen it transform other people's lives as well. My greatest hope is that it can do the same for you, what have you got to lose? If you give this exploration a genuine open minded try, my experience is that you will come to know and live this new reality. You will find that there are quite a few repetitions throughout the book, no I am not going senile; the repetitions are for your benefit. I try to present this work in many different ways to allow you ample opportunity to absorb, integrate and deepen your understanding of it. The information presented builds on itself while also reviewing key elements. The book is filled with experiential exercises that I have found invaluable in the discovery and experiencing of our Wholeness as well as living a free, wide-open and fearless life, so I encourage you to take the time to practice them. What I ask of you is to suspend your disbelief long enough to journey down this rabbit hole. As Roy Melvyn reminds us in his book, *Disillusionment: The Doorway to Present Moment Clarity,* "You may not be able to change your circumstances, but your attitude can change. Start with a single small step. Be willing to see things differently." Please work through the experiential explorations a few times, as you become more familiar with the work and the theory, they will make more sense and become easier. The experiential component of this work is very important in helping you fully understand, assimilate and live this new reality. The experiential exercises in this book are divided in two formats, the first one I call *experiential adventure,* these exercises tend to be more meditative and include our whole self as much as possible, like going on an adventure. The other format is under the form of inquiries, or questions to ponder and digest. Without the experiential aspects of this book, it will be hard to move from yet another nice philosophy or interesting idea to a felt and lived reality.

While I ask you to suspend your disbelief and give the work an honest effort, I am not asking you to suspend your own intelligence and knowing. On the contrary, I invite you to continually check in with yourself, with your own experience and your own wisdom, for the truth of what I am presenting you. I am convinced that for most of you, some of the information, if not all of it, will resonate. It will be like a part deep inside you remembers a faraway dream. You will sense the Truth of what is written here. This part of you, this deep wellspring within that you have forgotten and locked away, the Essence of your Being, the One that is always already whole and at peace, will recognize the wisdom these words point to. Let's get started, we're entering the burrow.

> *"Who in the world am I? Ah, that's the great puzzle."*
> *"I'm afraid I can't explain myself, sir," said Alice, "because I am not myself, you see?"*
> *"Begin at the beginning," the King said, very gravely, "and go on till you come to the end: then stop."*
> *– Lewis Carroll, "Alice in Wonderland"*

1.
The Imaginary Self

The greatest crime is
The overlooking of
Who you really are
In favor of
The story of
Who you think you are.
This preoccupation with
Your personal drama is
The cloud that masks
The sun.
– Wu Hsin

Ass Backward

Let me tell you a little bit about what I have come to see as the cause of my own and others' suffering. Since childhood, I had been obsessed with becoming happier, wiser, more at peace, simply better in some way shape or form. For some reason, I was not enough, I was not good enough, not kind enough, not smart enough, not pretty enough. I spent my teenage years and my twenties reading every self-help and spiritual book I could find, going to every workshop I could afford, and I loved every minute of it, yet it was never enough. The high would soon wear off and I would veer back to my default setting of dissatisfaction. I always felt like something wasn't quite right with me and with the world, like something was lacking. This is probably the reason I became a therapist, I felt that maybe some in-depth studies of the mind and different theories and systems of healing would not only allow me to help and guide others, but maybe I might finally find my wholeness, my "I am okay, I am enough." Needless to say, years of school and tens of thousands of dollars later, I felt a little smarter, I had had a few more insights, but I was still not whole or complete, and I still didn't have any real answers. Over the next few years, through my work, I started to notice that dissatisfaction is a major epidemic. All my clients felt the same way, regardless of their degree, their looks, their financial accomplishments, none of them felt whole, enough, okay. Whatever we did together, whatever insight they had in therapy, satisfied them for a while, on the surface, but soon enough my clients, just like me, would revert back to this subtle inner dissatisfaction. I was stumped, at a loss for what to do and how to help them and myself.

One day, after a particular disheartening session in which one of my young clients, who had made such progress, had reverted back to self-mutilation during a particularly bad anxiety attack, I went home and sat on my meditation cushion in an attempt to leave the day behind. I was meditating, as I had been doing for years, letting go of thoughts, and trying to calm and focus my mind by counting my breaths, when suddenly I had a thought that revolutionized my life, "I wonder who it is that notices my breathing, notices thoughts come and go and notices the part of me that keeps count of my breaths?" Suddenly it dawned on me that I was not the one who was counting and keeping track of my breaths or the one who was thinking; I was in fact beyond both. I was the one who was aware of both. How was it possible that I had never noticed this Presence in the back of me that was aware of everything? I started playing with this insight and trying to see if this Aware Presence was always there in the background, through every experience, and if so, was it "me" or part of me? Who was I really? Was I the one I had believed I was my entire life, this personality, my thoughts, or was I someone or something else altogether? Could I have been so mistaken all along?

I started to explore this with clients as well, trying to see if they, too, had a quiet still Presence in the back, in the depth of themselves that noticed all their experiences and yet was unaffected by them, and sure enough, with some guidance, clients could connect to this subtle untouched Awareness. This insight was the beginning of my love affair with myself, an in-depth exploration of this quiet, peaceful knowing. I wanted to know all about it, its qualities, its boundaries and its role in my life.

As I connected to this deep part of me that I had overlooked for twenty-some years, I realized that reality is not as it seems and that all my life, my work of trying to change and help myself as well as my clients had been ass backward. I couldn't help myself or anybody else because I had it all wrong. I was trying to change and help an illusion, a superimposition, a thought process, rather than finding out who I was at core and working from essence. With some exploration and some deep work, with myself as well as with clients, it became clear that all our suffering stems from a mistaken identification. We are not who we believe ourselves to be.

You see, I have this person that lives in me, and God knows she creates some trouble. She can be quite a judgy bi***, she complains a lot, she is great at foreseeing worst-case scenarios and feeling betrayed or victimized. One thing that's clear: Whenever I have ever been in some kind of fight or conflict, it is because of her. She feels threatened and alienated from life. Sometimes she is okay – okay on the inside, okay with others, okay with life, but it never lasts long, I call her my imaginary self and she's a problem! In some psychological as well as spiritual settings, this imaginary self is referred to as the ego. We all have one of those selves; he or she talks in our head and has opinions about everything. These selves worry, get pissed off, hold on to bad memories, are critical of themselves and everybody else, create horrible futures in our heads; they just poison our entire lives. I bet you've got one. All these imaginary selves come with slightly different flavors. Some are angry, some are more afraid and prone to worrying, some are more sad and depressed, some eat too much, some drink, some sabotage all our dreams and hard work. One thing that's for sure, they are never satisfied with life or themselves and always in some kind of inner or outer conflict. All our problems and all our unhappiness stem from our identification to this unsatisfied and negative self. As long as we believe that this mind made self is us, we will continue to perpetrate all sorts of misery, for ourselves and others. All my life I had been trying to change and fix problems from that false self's point of view, when in fact it was itself the problem, and as Einstein said, "We cannot solve our problems with the same level of thinking that created them." The good news is there is also a much greater, much more loving and abundant Self that lives within us. This happy, loving and peaceful Presence is our essence, our core, our True Self. We seem to have become so caught up with this imaginary headache that we have forgotten the best part of us, I call this inner depth, the Absolute Self or Aware Presence, and yes we all have it, we are it, it is our true and only nature. As we shall discover, everything else is superimposed on this peaceful Presence, on who we actually are. Everything else fluctuates, comes and goes, but this Absolute Self is always there, unwavering. But like all things of value, like all things real, it is quiet and subtle, it lives deeper within us, and it is radiant without bling, and so we overlook it in favor of the louder, more disruptive drama king and queen that lives on the surface of our mind. Our Absolute Self, our Aware Presence, awaits us in the depth of our being. It is quietly waiting to be rediscovered, remembered and lived. This book is about this discovery, this remembrance and the choice and act of living as the wholeness of that great peaceful Self that we are. But before we jump right into this discovery, let's first explore how we came to loose ourselves and be so mistaken about who we are.

A Rough Beginning

First let's explore a little how the imaginary self comes about. All of us come into this world by being suddenly and brutally pushed and crushed out of our warm and safe environment into a world that is cold, loud and bright, as most hospitals are. We are moved around and slapped awake, forced to take our first painful breath. This is our first experience of life, pain followed by an assault of our senses mixed in with more pain, and that is if it all goes well with the delivery. Some of us are choked by our umbilical cord or after hours of being crushed we are finally cut out of our mother's womb. Is it any real wonder that we come to believe somewhere deep within us that something is not quite right with us and with life. Our first experience of life is an assault, even if you had a blessed childhood, you can never have a different birth.

To make matters worse, most of us don't have blessed childhoods and so our birth followed by our childhood, reinforces this undeniable sense that we are wrong or lacking in some way and that life, at its first chance turned against us. Whatever we experience, our life is lived through and clouded by this sense of distrust and lack. Every experience, including our sense of who we are, is poisoned and tarnished by our belief in our own inadequacy and our wariness and suspicion of what lays outside of us, but as this book will endeavor to show, we are not a mistake, simply mistaken. We have taken on this mistaken identity and forgotten who we are in the depth of our being. We have forgotten the wholeness and undeniable worthiness of our true identity.

In our mistaken identity, we live with this unconscious and underlying fear that no matter what we do and what we accomplish, we will never be good enough and that life is intrinsically unsafe and cannot be trusted. We spend our lives trying to find the safety, warmth and ease of the womb. Jeff Foster, in his amazing book *The Deepest Acceptance*, says, "Perhaps our search for home is also our search for the womb – not the physical location, but the wholeness that was there. We long to feel safe, protected, at one with everything. We long to be deeply okay again." The whole of human suffering lays in the inaccurate assumption that we are unworthy, unloved and unlovable, and that life is cold, dangerous and uncaring. Out of these faulty assumptions, our resistance to life, our search for control, our desire to be and feel better, to be happy, safe and whole begins. As Jeff Foster writes, "Even children who have the most idyllic, loving upbringings do not escape this basic feeling of separation, of lack. It seems to be built into the experience of being an individual." Out of these false assumptions and out of our intrinsic fear, a persona, an identity is born. Its job is to help protect us and find a safe and successful way to deal with and navigate this strange life. This imaginary self is born out of fear, is made out of fear and for most of its life continues to live in fear.

The Limited and Transient Nature of Change

If you are like me and like most people who read these types of books, you've probably been around the spiritual self-help block quite a few times. You've read tons of books on change, on mastering yourself and your life and finding lasting fulfillment, and like most of us, you discovered that whatever insights you had and changes you made were short-lived. Every book, workshop and technique you tried was valuable in its own right and brought something to your life, but they did not truly deliver the lasting transformation you were hoping for. Change cannot last because its very nature is to change; by definition it is transient. Change requires constant maintenance and as we all know, it is common for people to let go of whatever technique they have been using once they are satisfied with their progress. Unfortunately, whatever growth was cultivated slowly seems to disappear along with the technique they were using. It is not unlike a diet, in which the pounds slowly start to come back the moment we stop dieting and exercising.

You might not know this, but what you aspire to is not change but transformation and transcendence. Change needs to be maintained, continually worked on, it takes continuous effort, but transformation and transcendence cannot be undone, it doesn't take effort to maintain. Once the transformation has taken place, once it is done, it is who you are. The butterfly doesn't need to work at remaining a butterfly. Once it is out of the cocoon where it was transformed into a butterfly and transcended the state of a caterpillar, it can never go back to being a caterpillar. It is literally a different species. If you want lasting change, lasting peace and happiness than you have to be willing to leave the person you think you are behind and in some ways become a different species. All techniques help us change, but they cannot reach and bring transformation and transcendence, they lack the necessary spirit, soul and grace needed. The only thing they can offer is a life of continued techniques and practices in an effort to maintain whatever change was reached. How exhausting!

You can never change things by fighting the existing reality. To change something, build a new model that makes the existing model obsolete.
– Buckminster Fuller

Why Change Doesn't Work

Change doesn't seem to stick, and many self-help techniques, exercises and even therapies – including the ones I was practicing – have proven to be futile endeavors in the long term because they work ass backward. They are based on this imaginary self we think we are and trying to change and better it. By definition, imaginary means not real, illusory, transient, you can't make lasting changes to a self that is not lasting. The sense of who you are, this vulnerable separate self, is a lie, a false assumption, a mistaken identification. This "me" is basically created and maintained by a process of thinking that originates from that initial faulty assumption that there is something wrong with you and with life. The belief that you are lacking or inadequate and that you need to protect yourself from this cold world, creates this false and fearful self. You were not born with this mistaken identity; it was born out of you and your experience. You came first and existed prior to it, just like you existed prior to your name. This imaginary self is a defense mechanism that came out of faulty beliefs and out the fear these beliefs generated. It was also reinforced by the way we were raised, by our parents and later by teachers and friends. This false self is superimposed on who you truly are, and that One, who is the real you, is not afraid or damaged in any way.

The origin of the imaginary self is none other than fear itself, and it is maintained by the subtle, or sometimes not so subtle, continuous level of distress we feel throughout our lives. Our thoughts about ourselves and about the world we live in created this imaginary sense of self from an early age. Through our thinking, beliefs, assumptions and fears, we then perceive ourselves, others and the world in such a way that reinforces this illusory sense of self and the suffering it feels. In *Fully Human Fully Divine*, Craig Holliday describes it this way: "The ego is a complex movement of psychological forces; it always thinks in terms of itself, and is constantly defending, upholding, and separating itself from life, even if it doesn't have to."

This entire schema, who we think we are, is created in the mind, it is no more real than a passing thought and feeling. This sense and belief in a "me" that is separate from others and from life and could be harmed or disappear, is not based on the actuality or reality of who you are at the core of your being or on the Truth of how life works. It is a mirage, a habit of the mind, a creation made out of thoughts; it has no more reality and validity than a dream. Because of its illusory nature and the incorrect foundation upon which it is built, any change you try to make to this imaginary, vulnerable "me" cannot bear fruit. It is like waiting for our stuffed dog to finally follow our command and start doing tricks; it is not real, hence it cannot change, move or evolve. No matter how you dress it up, your stuffed pet will never come to life. All these techniques, all this work we do on ourselves, when based on the illusory foundation of the imaginary self, is no other than playing dress up. You can't change something that doesn't exist.

Thirsty Fishes

We spend so much of our lives invested in trying to make this separate person we believe we are, happy, more fit, healthier, more patient, kinder, more successful, wealthier, more spiritual, just better in some way shape or form, but this very individual is a mirage. Since it is built on a foundation of sand, any effort, any work, sticks for a short while and then dissolves back into nothingness. If the foundation of a house is unstable and continuously shifting, then it is doomed before the first brick is ever laid; gold and marble or even steel can be worked into the design, this house can be the most majestic piece of art or the strongest structure ever built, but sooner rather than later it will breakdown. Nothing that is built or created on a faulty foundation, however beautiful or convincing it seems, however much work, time and craftsmanship went into it, can be maintained, nor can it ever truly flourish. We become like the hamster always working hard, running faster to get somewhere that ends up being nowhere, no matter what, we always end up in the same spot we started. All the efforts, time and energy we have put in building and improving ourselves can be likened to gathering water from a mirage. We are like a man, who throughout the day gathers water out of a mirage in an effort to quench his thirst. At the end of the day he finds his bucket empty, realizing that all his hard work has been for nothing. Working on the imaginary self is a little like that, all the effort does nothing but leave us exhausted, frustrated and ever thirstier for the very thing we have been searching for. To push the metaphor a little further, we are working ceaselessly and slowly dying of thirst, when all the while unbeknownst to us, we have been carrying the water we need in the pack on our back. All our suffering and all our hard work is like that, for nothing, since all along we have had with us the one thing we have been searching for. As Kabir would say, we are like thirsty fishes:

> *I laugh when I hear that the fish in the water is thirsty.*
> *You don't grasp the fact that*
> *what is most alive of all*
> *is inside your own house;*
> *And so you walk from one holy city to the next with a confused look!*

The one that you have been working on, the self who has been meditating, attending therapy, trying not to lie or yell, trying to become better or stop drinking, lose weight or be happier, that one is the very one that needs to be transcended. You are like a caterpillar going to therapy because he can't fly. You are not meant to fly in this form. If you want to fly, then just like the caterpillar, you've got to be willing to undo and leave yourself behind and become something else altogether. The state of the butterfly already exists within the caterpillar; similarly, who you are, what you are looking for, already exist within you. Everything you think and feel you are must go, it arose out of ignorance and fear, and it is not who your truly are. You are not who you think, feel and believe yourself to be, so what is the point in trying to fix that one, as it is not you. The recognition that you are not this separate, fragile and limited person with his and her stories and baggage is the premise upon which any and all transformation is built. Stop trying to alter and improve what you are not, it is lunacy and it will only lead to more frustration and pain as well as to ultimate failure; simply discover who you are. What I am talking about and will explore in great detail requires no effort; it is already who you are. Your best Self already exists within you and all it takes to find it and ignite it is a little work and some skillful guidance. I look forward to being your guide on this worthwhile journey.

The goal of this book is to help you discover, remember and live as your true Absolute Self, because the freedom, peace, happiness and wholeness that you seek are byproducts of this transformation, of knowing and living from your essence. In the vastness of your Self (notice the big S), everything is allowed and embraced, even so called negative and destructive emotions, yet it is realized that these emotions are not you and they never did or could define you or harm you. You can allow them to come up and move through you, without ever losing the ease, and harmony that is your essence. In the end, this book is not only about emotions and how to manage them, it is a book about peace and fulfillment, about going from crazy to happy, from fear to freedom and about finding the wholeness and the serenity in the mist of any disturbance. Peace and happiness are what you are, they are the core of what you are and they are your birthright. We have been so busy worrying, fighting, keeping our heads above water that we have forgotten our own essence. We must see the false as false and look for the light that exists hidden beyond the darkness. We must come to know what we are and trust in our boundless Presence, just like we trust that the sun shines beyond the clouds.

*The seed that is to grow
must love itself as seed;
And they that creep
May graduate through
Chrysalis to wings.*

*Wilt thou then, O mortal,
Cling to husks which
Falsely seem to you
The self?*
– Wu Ming Fu

Empty Your Cup

Transcendence and transformation always begins with curiosity. They begin by asking ourselves the questions we either have been too afraid to ask, or not aware enough to ask. Dawna Markova in her spellbinding book, *I Will Not Die an Unlived Life,* talked about the importance of asking questions in our lives, and the significance they have in our evolution. She said, "Questions can be dangerous. They can take us right to the edge of what is known and comfortable. They can require tremendous courage to ask, because we know that new questions can lead to new ways of perceiving, and new perceptions can lead to new explorations of our world." To find meaning, purpose and the essence of one's life, we've got to be willing to honestly and fearlessly ask certain questions and go deep bellow this hollow, busy and divided surface that is our life. We live in a society that is so focused with answers, with understanding, that we forget that discovery, transformation doesn't happen in the answers, it happens in the questions. The wisdom you seek is not in the answers to your questions, but in the questions themselves, in the owning of them, the contemplation of them, in the staying with them and in the living of them. We don't live our answers; we live our questions.

There is a story in which a learned man goes to a master to learn the essence of Zen. The master prepares the tea for the tea ceremony and starts to serve his guest. Tea is poured and poured and starts to overflow. The learned man, tells the master to stop, that the cup is full, to which the master answers, "How can I teach you Zen when your cup is so full? There is no space left in you, you must first empty your cup."

This brings us back to the story I used to open this book, we cannot know the Truth if we remain so full of ourselves. We must empty our boat or in this case our cup of all our notions of true and false, of our opinions, beliefs, stories. The learned man in this story lives in the answers; to him, only the answers have value. He wrongfully believes that wisdom lives in the answers, while the master knows that Truth and wisdom reside in the questions. Answers belong to the domain of filing our cup, while questioning requires that we always empty our cup. If we remain open and empty, then we allow life to fill us in every moment.

By residing and remaining in the profound questions of our lives we become open to the mystery that dwells deep inside us as well as deep inside life. Answers close things down; questions open things up. Here are some of the questions that got my head turning and my heart opening along my own personal exploration. May they propel you forward in this magnificent journey you are about to undertake. May you come back to them often and live with them. May they lovingly guide you as you read this

book, and bring you back to the spectacular mystery that you are. May they help you unravel the false and empty your boat and your cup, to realize the Truth. May they lead you to find your own alive questions to live and love by.
- How do I live undivided, intimately connected with myself, others and life?
- On what do I put my attention and my precious time?
- What would happiness look like? How would I know I was truly happy?
- What does failure look like to me?
- What does success look like to me?
- What does my fear feel like? What different shapes does it take?
- Who would I be without my fear? What could I accomplish?
- What in me is wounded and needs protecting?
- What is wrong, if anything, in this exact present moment?
- Where is this "me" I believe myself to be? Where is it in my body? Is it even in my body?
- Who am I, without my story?
- Who am I, without my purpose and my dreams?
- Who am I, without my past and any future?
- What is here before, throughout and after any sensation or experience?
- What part of me is always at peace?
- Where do I go in deep sleep?
- What experiences my life?
- What sees though my eyes?
- From where do I see? Where am I when I see and perceive the world?
- What or who am I?

One Last Question
- What in me, what part of me is constantly in conflict? There is a part of us that is continually dissatisfied. That part is the essence of the imaginary self. As long as we are identified to it – by that, I mean we believe ourselves to be this false egotistical and conditioned self – we are rarely content. On the contrary, we always wants more or less of something. We want others to be different and for life to obey our every whim. This part of us has judgments about everything, our own self, others, all the way to the weather. It has ingrained beliefs about who and what we are and the way others and the world should be, feel and act. This part of us is our ego, our conditioned self, and it is imaginary and mostly made up of passing thoughts and emotional sensations in the body.

The path to happiness and peace is the undoing of the ego, the emptying of the mind, the loosening of our conditioning and of the traumas we have experienced and that have been passed on to us from generation to generation. These false beliefs, which create our imaginary self, are a hindrance, we are immobilized and dragged down by them and they seem to veil our ability to recognize our essence; our only choice is to see their illusory nature and reach for Truth. It is truly the way to freedom, freedom to be who and what you are without this excess baggage and in turn the freedom for others to be who they are, and for life to take whatever shape it wishes from moment to moment.

This imaginary self, which is built upon the story of me and my beliefs, my thoughts and my emotions, is the barrier that veils us from our True Nature and keeps us from aligning and recognizing the joy, peace and wholeness that is always already here, inside and around us.

~Experiential Inquiry: Living the Question~

Look at the questions above and pick one or two that resonate with you, or make up your own question, one that has been gnawing at you, and one that pushes your edge. Once you have your questions follow one or both of the ensuing guidelines:

- Sit silently, breathe deeply a few times and then slowly and silently ask the question and then fall silent and just stay with the question, stay with the silent intuition of it, the energy of it. Locate in your body where the question resonates. Do that a few times, staying silently with the question for a few breath each times. This is a more intuitive, meditative form of inquiry.

- If you like writing and exploring in a more cerebral way, pick up a pen and paper, sit quietly, calm your mind, slowly and silently ask the question and then fall silent and just stay with the question and see what bubbles up. Every insight that comes up write it down, everything that arises from your core, that feels absolutely true in this moment, write down.

~

2.
The Absolute Self – Our Aware Presence

> *Here is the utter*
> *Simplicity of the matter:*
> *In the absence of identification*
> *With anything.*
> *Who are You?*
> *Or better still,*
> *What are you?*
> *– Wu Hsin*

Truth and its Many Names

I grew up in a relatively nonreligious household. Both my parents believed in something but were not interested in going to church or being part of a more organized movement. Yet, I was sent to Catholic school and outside of a couple nasty nuns, had a relatively good experience with it. Early on, I learned that God was in us, that we all have a spark of God, and that made sense to me. Later I read somewhere that it's not that God lives in us, but it is us who live in God, for as the Bible says, "For in him we live, move and have our being" Acts 17:27-28 NIV. That made sense to me as well, so which was it, was God in us or were we in God. Later, I came to the realization that both are true. The Truth isn't that God is in us, or that we are in God, but simply that there is nothing but God. Everything that exists is God existing in God; nothing exists outside of God. God is nothing but another name for the Ultimate reality of life. Somewhere along this realization, the word God started to feel a little small for me, a little too constrained, and too full of superimposed beliefs and dogma. It is still part of my vocabulary sometimes, but I have found that, unfortunately, it holds too many labels, judgments and bad memories for too many people. But the Alive Spirit that the word "God" speaks to has been called by many names: Absolute, Self, Truth, Consciousness, Awareness, Spirit, Soul, Presence, Reality, Life, Mind and many others. A word is just a word; it has no more meaning than what we give it. Regardless of the meaning we assign it, that which it represents is never sullied. For the purpose of this book, I will refer to the Reality of All That Is, to this indwelling Beingness in which we have our being in a few different terms. All these terms, whether they be the Absolute Self, God, Presence, Awareness or Life...are all interchangeable and synonymous, so feel free to change any name I use for another that you relate to more easily. The word I use is not important; the purpose here is to explore your own nature and to become more receptive and open to the material presented.

What is Real and True, once realized and integrated, requires no effort. What is natural requires no effort. Does it take effort to love your child, to care for your dog, to go to the bathroom, to drive from point A to point B, to open a present, to drink when you are thirsty, or to breathe? No all these things are so ordinary, so authentically part of us that they have almost become us; in some cases they are us. It is the false, the superimposed that doesn't work, that drains us, that always creates conflict and brings chaos, that doesn't seem to fit our lives and that requires effort. No matter how hard we work at it, we can never make the false Truth. Change cannot last without a deep knowing, a deep change of philosophy about who we are, what we are and what life is. All techniques without Soul and Grace are devoid of life, like a plug without juice. They are like a body all dressed up in a suit, but without a beating heart, it is nothing more than a corpse, a shell, going nowhere, inert, devoid of life. It is Spirit that animates this world, humans don't do it. It is Spirit that animates you and your world, you don't do it. What keeps your heart beating, your hair growing, your body fighting and digesting, your cells regenerating, your breath coming and going? What keeps the earth rotating, the grass growing, the seasons coming, certainly you and I don't. Spirit does! Consciousness does! Grace does! The Divine does! It is all the Absolute in its many names.

The Light of Your Being

There is a light inside us, ever present, infinite and limitless, that lights up our life, illuminates our way through life. This inner light illuminates our every step. Every single one of our perceptions and every one of our experiences is lit up with its glow and its warmth, like the sun that still lights and warms our way no matter what storm broods. This Presence that is our very being is like the depths of the ocean, always still, at peace and unaffected regardless of the currents and waves that might rage on the surface. Yet this ocean is primary to any wave, it is the essence as well as the container of all waves. This transformation is about remembering, recognizing and living from this light and from this depth that is the very core of our being, our True Nature, our Aware Presence, our Absolute Self. This inner light and this depth is our grace, our strength and our courage. It is the spark that ignites us and the very life that sustains us. Sense this Spirit, this deep aliveness within you that keeps your body moving, healing and digesting. Sense this peaceful Presence that resides deep within you and all around you. This Presence, the light of your being, sees through your eyes, hears through your ears and flutters in your heart.

This light connects all things. There might be billions of human beings on this planet who seem to be separated and different from one another, but our consciousness is one; we all share the same light that lights up our life and our spirit. All the body of water of the planet, lakes, ocean, pools and so on reflect the light of the sun. In each of these, you see a sun; millions of suns appear throughout the earth at the same time, reflecting the one sun. Each body of water might appear to have its own sun, but all these appearing suns are really a reflection of the one sun appearing as the many. This Universe is a knowing Wholeness, we are intrinsically connected to all other beings and life forms. We are one Spirit, one Whole, appearing as the many. There is nothing that we are not connected to.

To Observe is our birthright. If we utilize our ability to observe, we can free ourselves from the labyrinth of confusions.
– Victoria Boutenko

Life is a Metaphor
Bernardo Kastrup, who is a scientist as well as a philosopher, a truly brilliant mind, uses whirlpools as a metaphor for life. I just love that metaphor and how clearly it describes the nature of existence. Imagine that Reality, all of life, everything that exist, Consciousness, is like a vast body of water, an ocean, in which many things pop up; currents, waves, eddies, bubbles, ripples, foam, swirls and whirlpools, to name a few. Each seems to be its

own localized apparition that can be discerned not only from each other but also from the water that surrounds it, but with a little exploration it becomes clear that there is nothing else to any movement but water. The wave or whirlpool is made of and has its being in water, no matter what it may seem like, it is no other than a localized movement of water happening in water. It started out as water, took on a particular shape or movement and at the end returns to water, without ever being anything else than water. The world is like that, everything that is experienced through our senses is a type of movement in the Ocean of Life, a bubble, a ripple, a whirlpool. Human beings, animals, mountains, and entire planets are localized and distinct apparitions. Sometimes the energy behind a movement might be more powerful, more defined, such as a whirlpool or a strong wave, compared to a ripple, but in the end, regardless of their strength, size or density, they are no other than water appearing in water and returning to water. Human beings are a certain kind of localized energy movement within the Aware Field of Life. As Allan Watts said, "You are a function of what the whole universe is doing in the same way that a wave is a function of what the whole ocean is doing...As the ocean "waves," the universe "peoples." Every individual is an expression of the whole realm of nature, a unique action of the total universe." We are a unique localized process or pattern of Life appearing in Life. A wave is a distinct movement in the ocean, it can be discerned and differentiated from other waves or movements, but upon any kind of investigation, it is clear that all waves appear in the ocean as the ocean. The entire process of the wave, its outside, its inside, its movement, its velocity, its whole being is nothing else than seawater, it can't be removed from the ocean. It was never independent or separate from the ocean itself. Here is a question for you, what if we are not this individual with a body, a mind and a story, but the aware space, in which this seeming person we think we are, appears in? What if we are the eternal limitless ocean, instead of the finite small independent wave? What if all along we have just identified ourselves with the wrong thing?

As the metaphor follows, part of the process, mechanism and activity of a whirlpool or a wave is to send out ripples. These ripples can be compared to human communication and interaction. Human beings, perceive, listen, talk and act, we create movements, ripples in the Field of life. All whirlpools are creating ripples that intersect, connecting one whirlpool to another over the whole body of water, like a net of information about currents and temperature that spreads out to form a collective intelligence, a collective experience.

As human beings, we live and interact in this world, pass on beliefs, stories and apparent knowledge, just like the ripples of the whirlpool that interconnect, we pass on and share information from people to people, nations to nations, but also from generations to generations, which creates a common reality over the whole of life, in which we live. We live in this reality but are also this reality, we shaped it, it arises out of our ripples and our shared experience; we are not separate or different from it. Similarly to waves, we are a movement and process of Life and we have our being in Life. Not only are we not separate from Life itself, but in our essence we are one with each other as well. Remember there is nothing but God, the One appearing as the many. What does this metaphor mean for us? How does it affect us and how we live our lives? There are a few things to consider, which once clearly recognized and understood, can transform the way you look at and live your life.

- First, does a whirlpool or a wave have any personal individuality outside of the water? No, whatever individuality the whirlpool seems to have is only an effect of its process, of its movement; there is nothing to it in its composition and its performance but Ocean. You are nothing other than your source; this is what Jesus meant when he said "The father and I are one." This feeling that you are a separate and vulnerable person, independent from the rest of life is an illusion, part of the process, the mechanism of being a human being. Before and beyond being human, you are life, Awareness, the Absolute Self.

- What was the whirlpool before it appeared, what will it be after it disappears, and what is it while it is appearing? Water. If all there ever was, is or could ever be to the whirlpool is water, can we ever say that it was born or died? Awareness, what you are at core, was here prior to the birth of your body and mind, it is present throughout your life and will remain once your physical shape disappears. There is no such thing as birth and death, only movements of energy, a process, the changing of structure, from one form to another. This body / mind might change and disappear eventually, but you remain as you are, as you have always been.

- Is one whirlpool different from another? Are they separate and independent in any kind of way? No. Some might be larger than others, better formed, with different temperatures and stronger or weaker currents, with different size ripples, but that's all the same stuff. The whirlpools themselves are connected and made of the same water. People are the same way. We might look slightly different, have warmer or colder temperaments, communicate in slightly different ways and slightly different information, but in the end we are made of the same thing and everything that we are and do is part of a greater process called Life or Consciousness.

So to restate, we are life itself, a deep, still knowing and loving creative force in the shape of a human being. We exist as the aware flow of life prior to this shape, during our human incarnation and after the disappearance of this body and mind. We were never born and never will die, just like a whirlpool, we simply take on a particular shape for a short while. We are, our existence is undeniable, both in form and as the formless. If this is true of us, it is true of all beings and of all life forms. We are like snowflakes, each unique, not two exactly the same, and yet each made of the same stuff. There is only one life, one energy in this existence appearing as the many. We are all one Beingness. Once this is truly known, understood and realized, there is nothing left to fear in this life. When it is clearly seen that everything is a movement of One all-encompassing loving intelligence, what is there to worry about? What could possibly go wrong? What mistake could you or another possibly make? You are no other that this Aware Presence, everything and everyone else also is no other than this Aware Presence, which is no other than you. All that is left to do, is to go with the flow and to see yourself everywhere you go, in every seeming other and in every interaction and experience. Where is there space for fear, anger, prejudice or any other form of inner and outer violence with this Realization? Are you really this tiny, fragile, finite, personal self you believe yourself to be? Is your neighbor truly this cold, self-involved, petty personal self, he seems to be? With this understanding, you know the answer to be "No." If you fight with anyone, you fight with yourself, what you do or give to yourself, you do and give to the whole of life. You are life, The Absolute, Awareness appearing in a localized form, living in itself and surrounded by itself, interacting with itself as apparently other localized forms. All that exist is you, by you I mean God, Self, Life, Consciousness, Presence or whatever word you want to use. This transformational path that we are exploring here, has no other purpose but to help you remember yourself, know yourself and to live as That.

~Experiential Adventure: Exploring your Vastness~

This experiential adventure's aim is to help you discover and explore your vastness. Close your eyes, get comfortable, take a few deep breath allowing each breath to help you relax more and more deeply. Let whatever thought come up, and dissipate into stillness through the movement of your breath. Stay with the soothing movement of the breath, feeling it come in and out, the ways waves do. Breathe in and out through your nose, allowing each breath to not only relax you but to open you, to expand you. Breathe in peace and breathe out suffering, yours and the suffering of those around you. As the weight of the world drops away with every breath, see yourself becoming lighter and lighter, less dense, less weighed down, more open. Feel every breath continue to expand you, like a balloon that grows with every breath that is poured into it. Feel the freedom and the peace that lives within you, empty of concerns, confusion and pain. Feel and see the light and the weightlessness that radiates within you.

With every breath feel your Beingness expand slowly, letting go the assumed shape of the body and simply allowing yourself to grow and grow, to become translucent, soft and open. Become wider than your room, as if your Beingness not only fill up the space but contains the space, with every breath allow yourself to grow exponentially, to hold your entire neighborhood, the houses, the people the cars, the pets, trees and birds, all of them being contained within you, as part of you. Feel the space and vastness, the tranquility, love and compassion that exist from this perspective.

Continue to expand so that you are so open, so light, so vast that your city, your state, your country are contained in you. Continue to expand so that our world, all human beings, all species, all fauna and flora, all of the horrors as well as all of the love and beauty, are all contained in you. See that everything is a complete expression of life, of yourself. Feel the clarity, the love, the openness, the compassion and forgiveness that naturally arise for yourself and for all of life, from this expanded perspective. See how all of those aspects, the love, the clarity, the compassion, the openness and forgiveness, are not things you do or give, they are you, they spontaneously radiate out of this vast spacious stillness that you are.

Keep growing, keep expanding, keep opening, to the point that you contain our solar system, then galaxies then the entire universe, the conceivable and unconceivable. Remain as that, just pure openness, pure vastness, with no beginning and no end, with no judgment, just being the stillness that gives life to and contains all movements, the container of all life. Realize that from this position, you and life are one. You are the container, the one infinite, eternal Being that is one with, contains and gives birth to all existence, filled with peace, light and love for all the movements of life, for the whole of creation. Stay with this openness, this vastness and this peace for a few minutes, just allowing it to breathe you, being one with everything.

After a few minutes, gently and slowly, allow yourself to come back to an individual form. Come back to your body, *feel it. Know that this body arises within and is never separate from this vastness that is your Essence, your True Nature. Once back in your body, take a few deep breath and feel the lightness, stillness and vastness that is always within you no matter what. Whenever you feel confused, caught, weighed down by life, reconnect with the Aware Presence within you that is never confused or confined, with the vast aliveness within that is forever free and light, immeasurable, without a beginning or end, infinite, eternal and ever present.*

~

Closer than Close

There is this Zen parable about a room full of people who are slowly starving to death. It just so happens that these people are in a room with a huge buffet filled with delicious food. They are allowed to eat the food, the food is not poisoned or rotten, but no one is eating. Everyone just sits there, slowly starving. It is as if they are under some kind of trance or spell. They do not seem to see the food in front of their eyes or recognize that it is the solution to their hunger, to their suffering. All of their pain would be alleviated if they just saw what is right in front of their eyes and tasted it. We are just like these people, suffering and confused and unable to see what the solution to our suffering is. And just like them the solution is right in front of our eyes, actually in our case it is much closer than that, it is behind our eyes and in our eyes. It is what sees through our eyes, what hears through our ears and touches through our touch. It is our Aware Presence, a clear peaceful seeing, a clear peaceful understanding and experiencing that is prior to our fears and conditioning. It is what we are prior to all the "things" we believe or have been taught we are. We are in total intimacy with the solution to all our suffering, so close to it that it is closer and more intimate than our own breath. It is not in front of our eyes but looking through our eyes. It is so familiar to us, so close to us and so obvious that we have dismissed it and are blind to it.

> *"Life is a banquet. And the tragedy is that most people are starving to death...There's a nice story about some people who were on a raft off the coast of Brazil perishing from thirst. They had no idea that the water they were floating on was fresh water. The river was coming out into the sea with such force that it went out for a couple of miles, so they had fresh water right there where they were. But they had no idea. In the same way, we're surrounded with joy, with happiness, with love. Most people have no idea of this whatsoever. The reason: They're brainwashed. The reason: They're hypnotized; they're asleep."*
> *– Anthony De Mello*

How can we know what we want in life and how to end our own suffering if we have no idea who and what we are? Doesn't that make sense? Shouldn't finding out who and what we are be the primary step to any journey, any life? Yet that's the last thing we teach our children, if ever. We were not taught who we are. Society teaches us who it thinks we are and who it would like us to be and we continue to buy it. We have forgotten what we are and we can't see the solution to our suffering because from the time we were born, society, has conditioned us to be a much smaller and more limited version of our Self. There is no meanness in this action; people teach what they know and experience themselves. Until we know better, we can't do or share better. There was a time that kids were taught that the universe revolved around the earth or that the earth was flat and ended at the horizon, or that diseases were caused by evil spirits, and on and on it goes. With all the ongoing progress, science is discovering what sages for thousands of years have been saying about the reality life and about who we truly are. If history is any guide, many of the things we take to be absolutely true today are not, and time will reveal how misinformed we actually are.

Dropping Our Baggage

As discussed earlier, the shedding of our false self is primary to any true change and transformation. Most of us, for most of our lives, try creating a new happier more peaceful life by improving and bettering ourselves. We work on gratitude, on kindness, on patience, on generosity. We visualize, meditate, journal, exercise, build vision boards, and practice the law of attraction, all the while carrying our baggage with us. Trying to create a different life, to be a different person, without letting go of all the stories, beliefs and positions that created the old life and the old self, is impossible. We try to make headway, we work hard at it, but we are so weighed down by our own illusory sense of who we are and our false opinions and positions, that we can never reach our destination. We are like runners trying to win a sprint marathon while carrying a 40lbs pack on our backs; we'll die of exhaustion first. This false self you believe you are, and all its illusory baggage that you have been carrying on your back all this time, is not meant to reach the finish line, just like the caterpillar is not meant to fly. You've got to be willing and have the courage to drop it, not just the heavy load, but also the false self who claims ownership of the baggage. You've got to be willing to see the illusory nature of the whole damn mess, to see who you are beyond it and to let the whole thing dismantle and disentangle itself, only then will you be able to journey to the finish line.

We come to recognize that all this suffering, the one we lay on ourselves, as well as the suffering we contribute to others, originates from believing in a number of illusions about our own essence and the essence of reality. These illusory assumptions and convictions seem to be at the foundation of our world and our understanding of it. All we have to do is turn on the news to see how well these beliefs have served us thus far. When we start to recognize that we might not be who we think we are and that what we believe to be true and real might be a very small portion of the totality of life, then we are ready to take a step back and start looking, start questioning our beliefs, our motives, our pain, our stories, our very sense of self.

As we step back, this aerial position offers us the space necessary to start uncoiling, unraveling and disentangling the false from the truth. From this spacious position free of labels and judgment, we can look at our baggage, our pain, our stories with clear and unclouded seeing, unharmed by them, seeing that they are not us and that we are prior to them. Our greatest choice and power as a human being comes in our ability to see the false as false and to shift our focus from what is dark, heavy and fabricated to what is light, Infinite and True. Our back is turned away from the sun, leading us to believe that there is no sun since we cannot see it, but in truth the sun is here shining brightly on us, around us and through us. It is our own illusion, our mistaken assumptions that lead us to focus away from the light. The only thing we have to do is shift our direction and turn around to what is real. As Kamal Ravikant tells us in his book *Live Your Truth*,

"Habits and goals and success are just details. The tip of a deep iceberg. What matters is the foundation, the stillness below the surface. The truth inside. Living it, the rest is a natural byproduct."

~Experiential Adventure: Meeting the Absolute Self~
The aim of this experiential adventure is to allow an initial connection to your Absolute Self. The Absolute Self is no other that an Aware Presence, the pure joy of simply Being without our attention being pulled by an object or the activity of the mind. Being is what happens behind the busy mind, when the mind is quiet, between thoughts and behind thoughts. Close your eyes, take a few deep breaths and bring your focus within. Allow your thoughts to pass by, without getting caught up by them. Shift your focus inside, find within you the sense that you exist, no matter what, however your life looks, you know beyond any doubt that you are alive. Get in touch with that sense of existence, this Presence that dwells deep inside you. Notice that it is this same Presence, this sense of aliveness that witnesses all your experiences. It is this Alive Presence within that hears through your ears, sees through your eyes, and senses through your skin, prior to any thoughts or judgments the mind has about your experience. As you keep your eyes closed, notice the colors and shapes at the back of your eyelids, just experience the screen of the closed eyelids, maybe some light filters in, maybe not, just notice the shapes and colors that are appearing there, and then shift your focus to the Presence that is watching and witnessing the shapes and colors behind your eyelids, that one is your Absolute Self. Let go of your focus on what you see and stay with the Aware Presence that sees. As you keep your eyes closed and shift your focus to that still and silent Presence within, notice how vast and open you are, without

judgment or resistance. While connected to your Absolute Self while simply being, prior and beyond thoughts, ask yourself the following questions. Take a couple seconds between each question to reconnect to your inner Aware Presence before you move on to the next question.

- *Does this vast Aware Presence, this existence that I am, have a gender?*
- *Does it have an age?*
- *Does this Knowing Space that I am have a shape, a form? Or is it spacious and formless?*
- *Do you, as your Absolute Self, as this Beingness, have a story? Do you have a past and a future? Or are you simply ever present and free of any definition and story?*
-

Dwell in this vast knowing space, feel its transparent substance, its peace and stillness.

~

3.
A Worthy Compass

*What is called peace by many is
Merely the absence of disturbance.
True peace cannot be disturbed;
It resides beyond the reach of disturbance.*
– Wu Hsin

The Unchanging Truth

If I ask you whether your friend John is successful, if you are like most people, your answer will be based on what he does for a living and how much money he makes. We live in a society that praises big houses, fast cars, slim bodies, large bank accounts, trophy wives, and just about anything shiny and ephemeral. Unfortunately, everything in this outer life changes, it comes and it goes, relationships, jobs, beauty, fame, and riches...they are all fleeting. One moment the stock market is shooting up, the next moment it is plummeting. One morning you look in the mirror and lines have suddenly appeared on your face or hair has mysteriously disappeared from your head. Our bodies change, our minds change, our valuables change, our entire lives change. All these things do not and cannot, withstand the test of time. They have no intrinsic and lasting value in and of themselves. A large part of our suffering exist in denying reality, in wanting things that are false to be true, in wanting the ephemeral to be lasting or in wanting life to always go our way.

You might not be able to always rely on others, your looks might change, and your bank account might fluctuate but the one thing you can always rely on is your deepest core, your essence, the peace that lives prior to your mind and any difficult emotion. This Aware Presence is your deep inner guide, your compass. When in doubt about what is right, what directions to take, which choice to make, always go back to it. You will find wisdom there, a deep calm, a knowing that all is as it should be and you will know what action or non-action to take. You will find what in this moment feels like an authentic and natural expression of the completeness of this moment. In the words of Ram Dass, "There are ways of knowing other than through the senses and through the thinking mind...Turn off your mind. There is a place in you beyond thought that already knows – trust in that."

Finding Our Way Home

Life is like a road trip, driving aimlessly can be fun for a time, but without a map, more than likely you will get lost or go in circles. Who you are at core, and only this deep Aware Presence is a worthy compass, guiding you toward your true north. It will not allow you to compromise yourself or to get lost; instead, it will remind you what is true and help you remember that you are prior to this life and all the things we believe are valuable in it. This Presence is the remembrance and the realization that all the while we have been digging and hunting for treasures out there, we have had the only treasure worth having, right here, inside of us. This Absolute Presence that you are knows which action, thought and choice will honor you and life, not just your life, but all of life.

I am not saying that becoming a person that lives life based on Truth is easy or instantaneous, but it is worthwhile. Until who and what you are is fully realized, coming back to Presence and living life from that position feels very much like effort, which we know from the beginning of this book, doesn't work. Unfortunately, we have gotten used to the false to such a degree, that the false feels natural to us, while Truth feels odd. Because of this, at first, coming back to our Aware Presence needs to be practiced so that we can once again be comfortable with it and remember that it is our True Nature. Just like opening our heart, we have been so used to closing our hearts to protect ourselves that we have forgotten that living with an open heart is our authentic expression, the way we are naturally. Children are open to life, enthusiastic about life, they trust and go with the flow, they are fearless and then society teaches them otherwise. We have to go back to our natural openness, and at first that can take a little work. It will require patience, willingness, self-compassion and courage. It will demand that you forgo the easy way, that you clench your impulses to go back to old ways of thinking and being and when you do get lost, that you slowly remind yourself who you are at core and get back on your path. It will require that you pick kindness over being right, because who you are doesn't care about right or wrong; what you are is beyond right or wrong. It will ask you to play the tape through and inquire as to how your deep Knowing, your Aware Presence feels and responds to this person or situation, never allowing the confusion, judgment and resistance of the imaginary self to lead the way. It will ask that you pass on short-term satisfactions to gain the Peace that exists beyond them. As you can see, it is not an easy journey. But what it asks of you, it will give back a thousandfold. Gone are the days of regret and shame. Gone are the days of saying yes when you mean no and betraying yourself so as to not betray another. Gone are the days of compromising your deepest longing. Gone are the days allowing your mind to drive you crazy with relentless worry and resentment, and gone are the days where volatile emotions rule the nest. It will lead to a deeply fulfilling and peaceful life. A life filled with confidence, laughter and harmony. Remembering and living your deepest Self is not a one-day makeover, it is a continuous magical journey down the rabbit hole that is your True Nature.

4.
Suffering

*All conflict
Between friends, lovers,
Family or States
Begins as conflict inside yourself.
Freeing yourself from conflict
Frees the world of conflict.*
– Wu Hsin

The Intimacy of Conflict

To eliminate conflict in your interpersonal relationships, you must first eliminate conflict inside yourself. The way to do that is to realize and remember that who and what you are is prior to your story, to your mind, to your problems and to any beliefs you imagine to be true. We are always in relationships, as life is made up of relationships. Life is nothing but an intimate relationship with everything that is. Life is intimacy itself. Of course, when we think of relationships, we think of our significant others, our family, and our friends, but we are also in relationships with our bosses, co-workers, employees, the cashier at the grocery store, the barista who serves you your morning coffee, the voice at the drive-thru or even the person on the road who did or did not let you pass and of course we are in a relationship with ourselves. Every exchange, as minute as it seems, is a relationship. Some relationships are a life-long affair and some are begun and done in a matter of seconds. Beyond all of this, even if you were a hermit at the top of the mountain, there is one relationship you can never escape, as you are in it for life and that's the relationship you have with Life itself, not as you would like it to be, but as it is. All of these relationships have one common denominator: You. It all starts with you. So how can we hope to reduce or end conflict in our lives, if we don't start with ourselves?

If conflict exists within, then rest assured, it will spread to the rest of our life. As we will explore in greater detail a little later, I have come to realize in my own life, beyond any doubt, that the world is our mirror, whatever conflicts reside inside us will, without a doubt, reflect itself in our outer reality, one way or the other. And it will keep reappearing over and over until it is worked through.

All about Nothing

Most of us are completely unaware of how much of our suffering is self-inflicted. We assume that the world out there, whether it be an event or a person, did something to us; we wouldn't be this angry, worried or sad without a good reason. But upon further exploration we realize that most of our pain is self-created. Let's take anxiety or worry as an example. Most people who worry tend to do so about an event, in some unknown future, that in fact will never come to fruition. Most people who worry experience some kind of neutral trigger event and out of this neutral experience they create meaning and judgment. What they fail to realize is that the entire inner experience is self-created. A neutral event takes place, and then the mind jumps in to make meaning out of it and categorize it as good or bad. Out of all these assumptions, it creates a story around it and a probable future.

Let's look at a more direct example. Jennifer just started a new job. She thinks she is doing pretty good and has received good feedback from her co-workers. One morning she sees her boss in the lobby, raises her hand in a wave and smiles at him, he seems to look right at her, but doesn't return her smile or her hello. Out of this event, Jennifer's mind starts spinning, wondering if she has been overconfident about her skills, wondering if someone said something negative about her to her boss, as the day progresses, Jennifer is in such a state that she is already looking at her finances to see how long she can survive on her savings while she looks for another job. This is actually a pretty common example of what our minds can do, as the saying goes "making a mountain out of a molehill." We have all been in a similar situation, where the mind just creates an entire story, a worst-case scenario out of a single misinterpreted event and turns a completely benign and/or neutral situation into a catastrophe. Another common area where that happens is in relationships, where one canceled date, one missed phone call or even being a half-hour late creates a chain reaction in the mind that translates to the end of that relationship. In the case of Jennifer, after driving herself crazy for close to a week, she approached her boss to ask him how she was doing and was very surprised when he announced that he was thrilled with her work. More than likely, her boss had been daydreaming that morning and not seen her. We allow our mind to make our life hell with regularity, even relatively normal concerns that we have, about health or finances or relationships tend to be for nothing. And even if our concern is founded, what we fear usually either does not happen or if it does happen, it is never in the way or at the time that we imagined, making the worry completely pointless and useless to us.

The same can be said about most other emotions. We assume or judge, usually incorrectly, another person or event and we hold unrealistic expectations about them, which creates a story of anger, resentment, jealousy, disappointment and so on. Notice, that the story and the emotion that colors it, is not based on reality, it is based on the assumptions and expectations we carry about life, which are created in our heads. Most of our life actually happens in our heads. In an effort to know, understand and control the world, we label and categorize everything. Rather than protecting ourselves, though, this only leads to being half alive. We actually end up missing life and Reality altogether.

A Living Inquiry

Suffering is simply our rejection of what is happening in this moment, it is an unwillingness to be open to and stay with whatever is occurring inside as well as outside of us. Suffering is never created in or caused by the world out there, it is caused by our judgment of our situation and by our projection in the past or future. The instant we leave this current moment, the now, and jump into a reality that only exists in our heads, we are in the process of creating suffering.

Scott Kiloby in his wonderful little book, *Doorway to Total Liberation*, describes this simple but potentially life-changing inquiry, which consists of asking ourselves two specific questions: "What do I want?" and "What happens when I don't get what I want?" Whenever any kind of frustration, sadness, anger or any type of emotional pain or resistance arises, he invites us to ask ourselves, "What do I want?" Most resistance and suffering arises when we don't get what we want in this moment. So when we ask "What do I want?" we look at what is it that we desire right now, that we are not getting, which creates our sense of lack or frustration that we call suffering. The answer will obviously vary depending on the situation. Once we have the answer, the next question is "what happens when I don't get what I want?" or we can word it in such a way to include the first questions' answer, such as, "What happens when I don't get what I want and my boss still doesn't appreciate me?" The answer is always "I suffer."

Let me give you a personal example, a couple days ago, I was walking my dog and witnessed this car blocking traffic. The driver was double-parked, chatting on his cell phone, completely oblivious to other cars trying to get around him, even the honking could not wake him out of his stupor. A feeling of anger deep in my chest and gut surprised me, I wanted to go knock on his window and tell him to stop being a selfish jerk. And so I stayed where I was, noticing the feeling and urge arising in me and asked myself, "What do I want?" – the answer was clear and immediate, "I want people to be more aware of others and to be courteous and respectful of each other." Then asked myself the second question, "What happens when I don't get what I want and people act in rude and thoughtless ways?" It is simple, I suffer, and since I want something that is unlikely to occur anytime soon, I set myself up for a lot of suffering. What is it that makes me suffer, exactly? Is it the behavior of this stranger, or is it my desire for it to be otherwise? The aim of the inquiry is to bring us back to the fact that our resistance to life, our want for things, people and circumstances to be other than they are, is actually what creates our suffering, not the situation itself. This simple yet potent inquiry, little by little, has the power to unravel the resisting habit and the wanting mechanism of the imaginary self and free us from all the related suffering it creates, leaving us open to enjoy life while allowing it to be as it is. It is only then that we are able to meet life directly and to be intimately and joyfully present to all our experiences. This is a very short synopsis of Scott Kiloby's simple inquiry and in no way makes up for reading his wonderful book, which I highly recommend.

Wake Up, Wake Up
All types of emotional pain and resistance are created when we either want life to look differently than it does or when we want to feel differently than the way we feel in this moment, and sometimes both; not only do we want to change our circumstance, but we also want to make this feeling go away. Either way, we want something that is not happening, which creates an inner conflict and we suffer. Through this process of resistance, we become disconnected from the authentic, playful and loving dance that is at the center of Life. We become disconnected from the beauty and aliveness that exists in every moment and end up living in a self-created hologram that is far removed from the reality of who we are and the Truth of Life. We hang on to false stories and beliefs and create our own version of life – well, really our own version of hell. Soon this becomes our automatic way of being, and we are lost and stuck in this nightmare, unable to wake up or realize that it is only a dream. But as all things in the dream world, this inner nightmare is not real.

In a dream, everything that is experienced – every thought, feeling, person and event is created by us and happens in us, it has no reality or power outside of the mind that gives it life. Throughout the whole nightmare experience, we are, in fact, safe and sound in our bed waiting to wake up. The same is true about our lived reality. By closing ourselves off to life, through our mental construction we find ourselves living in a tense, scary and difficult world, but this world is a construction of our thoughts, beliefs and judgments. It exists solely in our head and has no more reality than the dream we experienced last night, however real it may have felt. There is no way to change the story and circumstances of the nightmare from outside the mind that created the dream world in which the nightmare appears. The only way for things to change is for the dreamer to dream a different dream and thus create a different experience for himself, or for the dreamer to wake up from the dream altogether and see that he is safe always and cannot be touched by any illusion. The same is true of life, the way to transform yourself and transcend all the emotional and circumstantial nightmares of your life, is to change your beliefs, stop living through your mind, see the illusion for what it is and know that no matter what, who you are in essence cannot be harmed, you are always safe and always whole.

Shifting Your Focus

One main aspect of transformation is shifting your focus from others to yourself. The only way to end our suffering, and the suffering we bring to others, is to take full responsibility for our life and our state of mind, to become aware that the nightmare, the illusion, is in our head and not out there. Rather than noticing and paying attention to what is wrong with life and how people should change, look at what needs changing and exploring within you. Become curious as to who you are – I mean who are you truly, at core.

- Who is it that resists and is in conflict, and am I that one?
- How do I spend my time?
- What illusions am I holding on to?
- What in me is conflicted?
- What's going on within me, in my mind and heart?
- How do I treat others?
- How do I treat myself?
- What am I passionate about?
- What do I long for?
- What am I really afraid of?
- Am I happy? And if the answer is "no", then ask yourself:
- Who is it that is unhappy and am I that one?
- Does reality bother me or is it my perception of reality that bothers me?

Sometimes, concentrating on others is just a way out. It occupies our mind, keeping us from having to reassess our lives and make hard choices both within and without. It keeps us from finding the necessary time and space to grieve and heal whatever wounds we carry. If I am so busy looking at what's wrong with you and your life, then I might not have to face everything that needs to be looked at on my side of the fence. Maybe I hate my job, but I feel stuck. Maybe, somewhere deep down I want to write a book or open my own business, but fear paralyzes me. Maybe my marriage is falling apart, but I am more afraid of being alone than unhappy. Maybe I am bored and numb, I can't find excitement in anything, nothing moves me, but I don't know how to start over. Maybe I have never gotten over the abuse I suffered growing up, but thinking about it brings it all back. If I stay busy enough being pissed off at you and at life, with a little chance I might not have to deal with any of it.

Paradoxically, transformation – or ending suffering – is not just about being kinder and more patient with others but is also about being kinder and more patient with ourselves. If we take care of ourselves, reduce the stress in our life, listen to our inner longings and buried pain, only then can we hope to be available for others and have the energy to respond to life's challenges in calm, effective and kind ways that are in line with the higher values we aspire.

Our path to freedom requires that we are able and willing to pinpoint the roles we play in any situation in our life, even if our role rests solely in our perception of and the way we experience this situation, because that's the only real control we have. In some ways your accountability is your power, you can only change and transform what is yours to change and transform. If a situation, a state of mind, or an event is completely outside of your control, then how can you transform it? Without any accountability you are powerless, stuck in the role of victim, imprisoned in your illusion. Now I am sure you are thinking that life is filled with situations people can't see coming, like an illness or an accident, how can someone be accountable for those? There is no denying that life is how it is regardless of what we want, but it is not always about events as much as our response to them. We might not have much control over life itself, or other people, both will do what they please, but we can always choose how we live and experience life. In the end, what is important is whether we choose to create more suffering by resisting, fighting what is, by losing faith and becoming stuck in our problems or do we choose to respond out of love, out of trust, out of a desire to grow and create peace for ourselves and those around us?

As I heard the spiritual teacher and author Catherine Ingram say once, it is not so much about having responsibility, as it is about having "response-ability." We can't control life, we can't even control our own thoughts, but one thing we can control is our position, who we chose to be and what we chose to identify with in each moment, either the troubled imaginary self and its crazy thoughts or our Absolute Self and its spacious openness. The imaginary self is continually in conflict, with itself, with others or with life. It lives in a semi constant state of lack and fear and it responds from that position. On the other hand, our True Nature is open, at peace, free of judgment, undisturbed by life and the difficulties of imaginary selves. Whatever state of mind we are in, whatever situation life has dealt us, the one choice we always have, the one true responsibility we have is to choose to live and respond to life from the position of the Absolute Self. Only then can we be truly of service. Only then can we end our own suffering and the suffering we create for others.

- Are you living with your eyes and your heart wide open or with blinders on, denying and resisting reality?

There are plenty of times that our lack of awareness, our unwillingness to face what is difficult creates a more troubling situation, this can often be seen in relationships, where things that need to be addressed are not talked about. We live in fear of making waves only to end up washed away by a tsunami. Living beyond fear, moving beyond the storm starts with courage. The courage to constantly remind ourselves who we truly are at our core, until we no longer need a reminder, and the courage to live and make choices from that point of view. The courage to look at what's wrong in our lives, the courage to see that we are running when we should stay or the courage to see that we are staying when we should run. Take a look; our outer world is always a representation of us. If that's not power, than I don't know what is, but as you have heard before, with great power comes great responsibility.

I will end this chapter by the words of one of my favorite teacher, Jeff Foster: *"Seeing that nothing outside of ourselves really causes our suffering in the key to incredible freedom. Circumstances can never really cause our suffering; it is always in response to circumstances that we suffer. We suffer only...when we try to escape certain aspects of our present experience and, in doing so, separate ourselves from life and go to war with ourselves and with others – sometimes in obvious ways, sometimes in very subtle ways. Our suffering is rooted in our unwillingness to feel what we feel, to experience what we are experiencing now."*

~Experiential Adventure: Meeting the Conflicted Part~

The aim of this inquiry is to find within you, in your body, the aspects of you that feels constricted, afraid and trapped and to simply meet it. Whenever you feel any form of resistance, any kind of anxiety, fear, desire for something else, boredom, anger or any kind of nervousness or upset, inquire into the part of you that is in conflict with this moment.

- *What in me is in conflict?*

Sit silently, breathe deeply a few times and then slowly and silently ask the question. Then go look within you for the point of resistance. It might feel like a hard ball, or a hole or a burning sensation or an actual sense of tension, compression or restlessness. It could even appear as an image or a past memory. Find the part of you that is constricted, fighting or trying to escape? Go meet this part, welcome it and just stay with the feeling of resistance, with the discomfort or with the urge to run. Be with it without trying to change it, control it or fix it in any way, just meet it, receive it and stay open to it, as you breathe slowly. Stay with the sensation for as long as you can or until the constriction subsides.

~

5.
Our Greatest Longing

Happiness comes, happiness goes.
Stop chasing it.
Sorrow comes, sorrow goes.
Stop running from it.
Relax into what doesn't come and go,
What is present in every moment,
In every here and now.
– Wu Hsin

Our Common Desire

For all our differences, across generations, culture, gender, education, religion, status and whatever else we could think of, there is one thing we all have in common. At heart, in our core, we are all looking for the same thing. No matter who we are, how much money we have, what color our skin is, what religion we follow or what gender, age or culture, we all want peace, joy and fulfillment. In the end we all want happiness. Where we differ is how we go about trying to accomplish these illusive states. Part of the problem is that no one really knows what happiness truly is and how to get it. We are all experimenting, trying to find out what circumstances, in our environment, might cause us to feel fulfilled. If you were to ask anyone on the street what they would wish for if a genie appeared, most would tell you something like being a millionaire, being gorgeous, being healthy, having their dream career or mate...If you then asked them why that wish is so important to them and pressed a little you would discover that they believe that if this particular wish was granted, they would be lastingly happy, secure and at peace. We all want to feel happy, serene and safe, in the end that is our greatest wish of all. We just think that certain circumstances in our life can provide that. If the genie was to tell you, "I can grant you that wish, but I can see in the future, and it won't make you happy." Would you still want that wish granted? More than likely, no.

Another aspect of happiness that makes it difficult to pin point, is that there are as many definitions and descriptions of happiness as there are people. If you ask people to describe what it feels like to be happy, you will find that it is not as simple as asking someone to describe an object. Happiness, like every state is nebulous and amorphous, not only does it change from moment to moment, but it also changes from person to person. What made you happy once, no longer makes you happy and what makes one person happy, doesn't do the same for another. Some form of happiness feel more like contentment, subtle and steady and some form of happiness are more explosive, it all depends. We can't describe it, we can't pin it down, but when we feel it and experience it, we know it. The same could be said of our True Nature, we can't describe it and understand it, it is not of this world and cannot be talked about with words, or attained through things, achievements, planning, logics or effort, but when we remember and recognize the Aware Presence that we are, there is no doubting it, no denying it. As it turns out, it feels very much like happiness, fulfillment and peace, and thankfully it is not dependent on any circumstance. It is beyond any circumstance and it is always available to us. All we have to do is let go of our mind, let go of our story and just sense and explore this alive and tender Presence that lives within and around us. This recognition is what we have been searching for all along,

The only reason we have hopes and dreams is because we expect these hopes and dreams, once attained, to make us happy. If you are like most people you have a list of goals you would like to achieve, experiences you would like to enjoy and things you would like to acquire. My guess is that everything on your list is there because you think that achieving it or acquiring it or experiencing it would make you more fulfilled, at peace, happy and whole. Let's imagine that you developed this gift for seeing the future, and you could see which of these goals and experiences would bring you happiness and which would not; my bet is that you would cross off the list any goal that you could see would not deliver the joy and fulfillment you long for. You would do this without ever looking back, because, as I said, what you are really after is the feeling of being fulfilled, of being and feeling complete. What we are after, what we long for is happiness, not any particular experience, object or circumstance.

In the final analysis the hope of every person is simply peace of mind.
– The Dalai Lama

You probably already have some experiences with achieving goals and acquiring the things you desire, so let me ask you, have any of them brought you lasting happiness? If you are honest, you know the answer is "no." If something or someone outside of yourself had been able to bring you lasting fulfillment you probably wouldn't be reading this book. The fact that you are reading these words is an indication that you are still seeking, that you don't feel whole and fulfilled just as you are. Unfortunately what we expect to happen upon reaching our goal never seems to happen. Whatever joy it brings us, if any, is always short lived and soon we are searching or working on the next goal. Or if it does bring us momentary satisfaction, then we are clinging to, worried about and fighting to keep what we have just acquired, or soon enough it no longer satisfies us. We find that no matter what, there is no peace, we are always planning, resisting, fighting or chasing.

Michael A. Singer in *The Untethered Soul* writes, "What you will find is that the only thing you really want from life is to feel enthusiasm, joy and love. If you can feel that all the time, then who cares what happens outside?" Aware Presence, our Absolute Self is Peace and Happiness itself. Its nature is Peace and Happiness, it is whole and fulfilled in its own self, as it wants for nothing, needs nothing and is absolutely okay with every moment. We have mistaken our own longing to be for something outside ourselves, when all along we have been longing for our own Being.

The imaginary self is the one who feels a sense of lack and always desires something else or something more. As we know, imaginary means not real, when we explore into the nature of this illusory self we realize that it has no true existence and is simply made up of thoughts and feelings. When you stop your mind, as in deep mediation, deep sleep or when immersed in an activity, it ceases to exist. The imaginary self is not real in its own right, it feels so real to us because it keeps us from knowing and recognizing our True Nature which is present just beyond it. The imaginary self is a veil that hides the infinite and eternal Truth of our Being. The nature of the imaginary self is to always resist one or many aspects of reality and to seek for this happiness, which it can't seem to hold on to, out there somewhere. As Aware Presence we are at peace with, fulfilled in and okay with every passing experience, even the negative ones. The moment we veil our True Nature by identifying with our imaginary self, we find our self at war with the present, with others, with our own self and with the world, suddenly the okayness that lives deep within us is lost.

To be Free from Ourselves

As an imaginary self, we can never be lastingly happy. In the end, the imaginary self is nothing more than a collection of thoughts and feelings, which tells us that we are not okay as we are and that life is not okay as it is. And so the imaginary self is always trying to fight off and change life and look for something better in the future. It spends its life resisting and desiring. By definition, the imaginary self cannot see the peace and happiness that is already always present in this moment, just beneath its own surface, since the recognition of this already existing, ever present fulfillment is itself the dissolution of the illusory self and the dismantling of the illusion. Whenever you find yourself completely okay and intimately connected with this moment, you are, by definition, no longer identified to an imaginary self and its stories of the past and future. In that moment you are one with reality and living as Aware Presence. We mistakenly assume that the current circumstance brought us this peace we feel, when in fact it was the end of our resistance and desiring that brought us back to the Peace that is at the essence of our own Self. As Jeff Foster tells us, "It is crucial to understand this: our search for something abstract in the future – enlightenment, wealth, power, success, love – is always deeply rooted in present-moment resistance. Our search for future completeness is always rooted in an experience of present incompleteness...instead of facing that suffering head on, right now, and seeing the wholeness within it."

The imaginary self in its blindness to reality, in an effort to find relief, keeps its focus on the very thing it wishes to be free of. Rather than focusing on wholeness, on the beauty of this exact moment just as it is, the imaginary self focuses on what it is trying to escape from, its struggles, it's disappointments, and it's worries. In doing so it perpetuates the resisting habit and the search for something better in the future. The imaginary self, fails to realize that it is this very deficient habit of rehashing the past, keeping the mind on the negative and planning a hopefully better future that keeps it stuck in a cycle of distress and suffering. As we identify with this imaginary self, we fight with our perceived problems and miss the fact that suffering doesn't lie in the reality of our lives, but in the very movement and existence of the illusory self we identify with. In the end, the true culprit of our suffering is the imaginary self itself. All the issues and struggles the imaginary self has is, in fact, with itself and not with others or with life. All the resistance and the seeking is only a metaphor for what the illusory self truly wants, to be free of itself.

> *In the end, it is awareness of our actual dilemma that releases us from it...Our foremost wish is to witness what our false self is busy spinning out of thought so that we don't fall into its web...Higher self-awareness, through self-*

observation, puts us in direct contact with a new superior intelligence that already lives within us...This living Light sees the mindless self-serving antics of our false self...By this Light we see for ourselves what is real and what is not, which is the same as saying negative states no longer have the power to hold us down because we can no longer be deceived into mistaking their world for that of our own.
– Guy Finley

As an imaginary self, we are always on a mission, either running from the past or chasing some new thrill in the future. We are hardly ever in the present, where peace and joy reside and where our True Nature lives. Most of us do what we have been taught to do, we look for happiness in circumstances, in things and in people. As I have heard Rupert Spira say, "We look for peace in circumstances, for love in relationships and for joy or happiness in things or objects." All human stories always have some measure of success, some of us are somewhat more proficient than others, but no matter what we seem to accomplish, whichever dream of ours we reach, in the end it always leaves us wanting. Even our wildest dreams, like winning the lottery, landing our dream job, marrying the girl of our dreams, always fall short. It never satisfies for long. And so most of us are on this adventure for the Holy Grail, the elixir of life, trying to find where it could be hidden, and no matter what direction we turn, even when it looks like we found it, we soon realize we were mistaken, and back we go, on the search for this miraculous water that will finally quench our thirst.

Changing Direction

For many of us, after we have travelled the world, figuratively and sometimes literally, looking for this peace and happiness, we come home, exhausted and often disillusioned. We have looked everywhere we could think of, and nothing. We find ourselves at this junction in our life, where we realize that we are off the mark, mislead by our mind and by society. All this time, we have been looking in the wrong place, in the wrong direction. It is from this place of disillusionment that many of us shift our focus from the outside world to the inside world, going to church, finding a guru, mediating, learning yoga...This new approach seems promising, I mean with all their teachings and talk of love and liberation, this must be the correct direction. For a while this new approach seems to work, we are making progress, some of us even have blissed out experiences, our body feels great, we are more relaxed than we have been in years.

But this too has its limit, every moment of peace or bliss seems to come to an end, our mind can't seem to shut off long enough to meditate properly, we are at peace on retreat, then work, kids and obligations takes over and all our practice seems to fly out the window the moment we get home...And so we find ourselves at wits end, if changing our outer world did not land lasting happiness and working on our inner world doesn't seem to be much more effective, where else can we turn? We come home again, from this last adventure exhausted and disillusioned once again, every direction we have turned to so far has led in a different course then we were seeking, it seems that, after all, all roads do not lead to Rome.

Maybe as we come home, from this last journey, disheartened, we turn in the direction that has no direction, sometimes referred to as the Pathless Path or the Gateless Gate. Out of option, we might simply get curious about our suffering itself, about the part of us that wants to escape what is. Rather than focusing on what we want, we might turn to what we are and to who it is that wants things to be different than they are. This is the beginning of the end, the first echo of realization, the meeting of the self that is nothing more than a bundle of unsatisfied thoughts and feelings. Here begins the exploration that will lead us beyond this confused and conflicted self, into our True Nature. From this curious open position, we might investigate:

~Experiential Inquiry: Our Selves~

- *Who is it that is continuously unsatisfied?*
- *Who or what has been fueling this unending search?*
- *What has been with me all along, in all my adventures? Whatever happens, whatever comes and goes, what is always here, patiently waiting to be recognized?*
- *What looks trough my eyes and listens through my ears, always present to and in every experience?*
- *What remains when all thoughts stop?*

Look at the questions above and do one of the following:
- *Sit silently, breathe deeply a few times and then slowly and silently ask the question and then fall silent and just stay with the question, stay with the silent intuition of it, the energy of it. Do that a few times, staying silently with the question for a few breath each times. This is a more intuitive, meditative form of inquiry.*
- *Sit silently, breathe deeply a few times and then slowly and silently ask the question and then fall silent and just stay with the question, stay with the silent intuition of it, the energy of it and then go in your body and look for the answer, the felt sense of it in your body. Explore the question through your body, feel the part of you that is*

unsatisfied, meet it, see if it has any independent reality. Look for the one who has been seeking, can you find this self? Sense the Beingness that looks through your mind's eyes.
- If you like writing and exploring in a more cerebral way, pick up a pen and paper, sit quietly, calm your mind, slowly and silently ask the question and then fall silent and just stay with the question see what bubbles up. Every insight that comes up write it down, everything that arises from your core, that feels absolutely true in this moment, write down.

~

So simple and so quiet that it is easy to overlook. Just like your shadow, wherever you go, so it is, and whatever direction you turn to see it, you just missed it. We come to find that the peace and happiness we have been longing for and searching for all this time, was never in time, never out there, but in the ever Presence of our own Being. We come to realize that this happiness does not reside in the world, in people, things or circumstances and it also does not reside in a quiet mind or a particular state of mind, but in our Aware Presence. Jeff Foster in his book *The Deepest Acceptance*, says it beautifully, "You are not a separate person, not an individual self, but the open space in which all of the little waves of experience – thoughts, sensations, sounds, feelings – come and go. You are quite literally, what you seek. You are the consciousness that holds the dance of form."

It is the belief that peace and happiness are not present now that makes it so. It is our categorizing, judging and the constant thoughts that things need to be different than they are, that veil the contentment that is always already present in every single moment. The belief that peace and happiness are not present here and now and need to be found elsewhere, in some later time, also creates and reinforces the imaginary separate self, whose job it is to go in search of this future fulfillment. When your mind stops, when you suspend beliefs and the thinking process, two very important things happen, first, no matter what is going on, life suddenly becomes okay. For suffering to exist, a thought that says "I don't like this, this isn't okay'" is necessary. Without any thoughts of judgment or resistance, ease arises. Second, when thoughts are suspended, your sense of who you are as this separate 'me' also becomes suspended. Without thoughts you have no story, no history, no hopes and dreams, no age or gender and no boundaries, you are simply left with the direct and raw experience of this moment, where effortlessness, truth and wonder reside.

This is not to say that the goal of this path is to stop our thoughts. The mind thinks, that is part of its function, just like the body digests. Part of this exploration is to see beyond thoughts and to stop giving all our thoughts credence and care. When we withdraw our attention from the constant babble of our mind, two things happen. First, we realize that we exist prior to thoughts, that we are not our thoughts, we are in fact the listener of our thoughts rather than the thinker of our thoughts. Secondly, we realize that what our mind says is often, if not always, untrue. When these two things are known, that you are not your thoughts but prior to thoughts and that what the mind says is false, than you will slowly remove focus and trust in it. Out of this dis-identification, the mind will slowly, on its own accord, quiet down. It will start to relax naturally and easily, just like your car will slowly slow down and maybe even come to a stop when you stop pushing on the gas. To try to force the mind to be silent before it does it spontaneously, to get frustrated with it and with ourselves, is a form of violence. We do not have to do battle with our mind; there is enough violence in this world as it is. Just slowly start noticing that your emotions are often related to a thought, a judgment that is often inaccurate. When caught in a slew of thinking, slowly let the thoughts go by, coming back to the sensations of your body as you take a few deep breath. All you need is a little space to step away and notice that the one that you are is beyond any thoughts, spacious and aware. Your Aware Presence is the one hearing the thoughts, not speaking them. Notice that who you are in essence doesn't care and is not affected by your thoughts; it remains as itself peaceful, whole and still, no matter what story your mind is weaving. Come back to your body, to your breath, to this moment and notice the quality of who you are beyond thoughts, notice that your mind is only telling a story, not the Truth and that you are not defined by this story. Do this over and over until your identification with thoughts is loosened, until you know beyond doubt that this voice in your head is no more you than the voice coming out of the radio or of your neighbor's mouth. It is just a voice that your Absolute Self hears.

Now and then it's good to pause in our pursuit of happiness and just be happy.
– Guillaume Apollinaire

Behind the imaginary self and the thoughts and feelings that give it its reality hides the ever present and ever lasting peace and happiness that we have been longing and looking for all along. Jeff Foster makes that clear in *The Deepest Acceptance* when he writes, "We are so busy trying to move away from discomfort and pain and reach completeness in the future that we end up missing this present completeness...We are so busy trying to hold up an image of ourselves, trying to prove who we are to ourselves and the world, that we miss that what we are is simply the wide-open space in which all images come and go...*You are what you* seek." The act of seeking and resisting and the belief that peace and happiness cannot be found in the here and now, are in fact hiding the ever present and already existing joy that is here now. Seeking is no other than a bad habit of the imaginary self. Fulfillment exists in every moment, in every breath, behind our search and behind our thoughts. Once this is seen, it is so simple and so clear, that it is undeniable. The search for happiness and peace, by definition assumes that peace and happiness are not already present. It is this assumption that veils the already existing ever-present Truth of our Being. It is this assumption that projects us in the future, always chasing this ever elusive rabbit.

Beyond the Itch

There are two fundamental levels to our suffering. Life in many ways is like having the chicken pox. The first level of our suffering is that we actually got the chicken pox. As we know, the chicken pox itches like hell; in broader terms, life is uncontrollable, often uncomfortable, bad things happen, events, and people keep shifting on us. The second kind of suffering is that we want to scratch the itch, yet the scratching doesn't seem to alleviate our discomfort; on the contrary, the moment we stop scratching, the itch comes back even stronger and every time we scratch we create more long lasting suffering. In life, the second level to our suffering is that we have this urge to fix and control life. If only we could get circumstances and people to be the way we want them to be, we could be happy. The more we try to resolve our discontent by manipulating, by controlling, by resisting, by suppressing, by violence or even seeming kindness, the more trouble me make for ourselves. Screaming and banging our heads or other people's heads against the wall doesn't work. Chanting and meditating in the woods, doesn't seem to work either. Whether we explode or suppress our fears and discontent, we can't ever seem to be free of them. Whatever we do, we don't ever seem to find the lasting peace and happiness we long for; sooner or later the world out there affects and rattles our inner world. No matter what, there doesn't seem to be anything we can do about it. But there is a third solution that doesn't involve outer actions such as exploding, controlling or manipulating or any kind of inner actions such as mediating, chanting or suppressing. The third options is seeing rather than acting. The third solution is to step out of this entire insane cycle and to stop identifying with the imaginary self that itches and has the urge to scratch. When we become aware that we are prior to this imaginary self; that we are prior to the way life affects us and to any type of unsuccessful fix it strategy we employ, we can find our seat as this Aware Presence and live from that point of view.

Absolute and Undeniable Awareness

There is only one certainty in our experience, we exist, we are aware. Prior to being aware of this or that, we are aware or our own Beingness, of our own existence. We are aware that we are aware. If I were to put you in a state of sensory deprivation, with no light, no sounds, no movement, even without thoughts, you, the sense that you exist would remain, effortlessly. We know our existence deep within our core, we don't need the outside world, our body and its sensations, our mind and its story or our emotions to know and confirm that we exist. Our existence, our Essence, is beyond and prior to the outside world, to our thoughts, beliefs, feelings, sensations and to our stories. Even deprived of all of those things that we have assumed are us, we know, beyond the shadow of a doubt, that we are, we are alive and aware. Our existence, our sense of Beingness, is undeniable. Throughout our life, it is the only certainty we have, the only constant. Everything else, the world out there and our inner world, even our body, changes, comes and goes and wavers, but this unspeakable, indefinable and yet irrefutable sense of our own aliveness is here, always already present. David Bhodan, in *The Lazy Man's Way to Enlightenment,* writes, "Awareness is all there is, You are Awareness Itself, not somebody who is aware. Enlightenment is rather simple. It's really nothing more than remembering something forgotten. It is nothing more, or other than, the realization of the true nature of Realty." We are what sees and is aware of the world out there as well as the world in here; we are prior to either. Our location, our position, is such that we can be equally aware and equally undisturbed by the itch and by the urge to scratch it. We are the one that sees both and doesn't get involved with either. By the way, what happens to an itch if you just watch and wait without scratching? Undoubtedly, the itch disappears.

Freedom comes from being one thing, just seeing…The ego's complexity is exhausting, while Awareness is simple and ever replenishing. Our freedom is in this simplicity, which allows everything and is everything at the same time.
– Craig Holliday

~Experiential Adventure: The Ease and Eternal Nature of Awareness~

This experiential adventure's aim is to allow you to connect to the effortless and ever-present nature your Absolute Self. The Absolute Self is no other that an Aware Presence, the pure joy of simply Being without our attention being pulled by an object or activity of the mind. Being is what happens when the mind is quiet between thoughts and behind thoughts. Being is what happens when you come home from a busy and satisfying day and just sit in your favorite, most comfortable chair to rest for a few minutes, sipping a cup of tea or a beer. It is the ease and comfort of being present in this moment, without thought or effort.

You can close your eyes if you want, take a few deep breaths, and bring your focus within. Allow your thoughts to pass by, without getting caught up by them. Shift your focus inside and find that Aware Presence within that witnesses your experience, that which hears through your ears and sees through your eyes. As you shift your focus to that still and silent space within, notice how vast you are. Stay vast and open as you shift your focus and attention to all that seems to be happening within and around you, the light filtering through your eyelids, the sounds, the feelings and sensations happening in your body. Just quietly and effortlessly notice all of these happening. Ask yourself the following questions.

Take a couple seconds between each question to reconnect to your Aware Presence before you move on to the next question:

- *Do I, as this Aware Presence, make any effort to be aware of all these movements of light, sound and sensations or am I aware of them effortlessly and easily?*

- Is there anything I could do to make my Absolute Self more present, or is my Aware Presence naturally cognizant and conscious of all sensations and perceptions?

- Rub your thumb and index fingers lightly together. Are you not immediately aware of the subtle tactile sensation? Do you have to make any effort or focus your attention toward your fingers in any way to be aware of the sensation or does it just happen naturally?

- Now open your eyes and without thinking, notice your surroundings. Does it take any effort on your part to become aware of the colors, shapes and light around you? Of the contrast between these words and the page on which they are written? Is there anything that you could do to make that which looks through your eyes, more present, more easily and naturally aware?

- Whether you are lost in thought or otherwise lost in your imaginary individual "me," does your Aware Presence stop registering the sounds, sensations, light, shapes, colors, smells or feelings, or does it remain effortlessly aware and present, regardless of where your focus is, of who you believe yourself to be and regardless of what you are doing?

- Can you think of any situations or circumstances in life where your Aware Presence ceases or ceased to be aware and conscious of all experiences, perceptions and sensations? Or was it always here experiencing and being aware, eternally, regardless of your age or state of mind? Did Awareness hear and see out of your eyes as a baby? What about at 4 and 15 and now? (Some of you might say that Awareness disappears in deep sleep, but it is not Awareness that disappears but all objects. In deep sleep there are no stories, no dreams, no feelings, sensations or experiences of any kind to be aware of, so we assume there is no awareness, but that is incorrect. We will discuss deep sleep later on in the book)

- Has Awareness evolved or changed in any way, or has it always been this vast Presence, effortlessly aware?
- What about in the present or the future? Could you, as Your Absolute Self, ever not be present and aware of your perceptions, sensations and experiences? Could it ever require effort, or is it and always will be a natural aspect of your Self?

Dwell in this vast knowing space, feel its transparent and effortlessly aware Beingness, its peace and stillness. Experience the freedom and peace of being without a gender or an age, ever present, without a story, open to and genuinely okay with and present to all of life.

~

In *The Untethered Soul,* Michael Singer describes this natural and effortless awareness: "Notice that with a single glance at a room, or out a window, you instantaneously see the full detail of everything that's in front of you. You are effortlessly aware of all the objects that are within the scope of your vision, both near and far away...Notice that you take all this in at once, without having to think about it...When you just look without creating thoughts, your consciousness is effortlessly aware of, and fully comprehends, all that it sees." Every day, throughout the day, whenever you remember, check whether you are present and effortlessly aware of your experiences. Ask yourself, was I aware a minute ago, and 10 minutes ago, even when I didn't realize that I was aware? Become conscious, that whether you are actively mindful of it or not, your Absolute Self, your Aware Presence is always already here, still, steadfast and at peace, in the background of every experience; that it has the capacity to hold, welcome and be present to all and any experience. Even when you are raging or lost in a panic, your core, your spirit, your strength is here, quietly present, waiting to be recognized and remembered.

Notice that your Aware Presence also has two mode of awareness; it can equally be focused on something in particular or be a spacious and wide-knowing field. Your awareness can become very direct and intensely focus on anything that grabs your attention or needs direct concentration, like a project you are working on, a paper or letter you are writing, a book you are reading, a movie you are watching, a piece of music you are listening to, a scraped knee you are bandaging or a conversation you are having. Whenever something grabs you attention, whenever you are learning something new or whenever safety is at stake, your awareness has the ability to focus to such a degree that everything else is pushed aside, the world around you actually ceases to exist. Respectively, the opposite is equally true. Your Awareness also has the ability to go as wide as it wishes; to focus on nothing in particular, yet, with just a sweep of the senses gets a full and open experience of everything that is going on within as well as around you, from the sound of birds chirping in the background, the clouds passing by, the breeze in your air, the smell of rain in the air and the knot of worry or expansive joy in your belly, all can be received and held at the same time, without the need for thoughts to arise. You are that Aware Presence, both the wide, clear and open field that is prior to thought and the focused beam of attention that zeroes in on one particular aspect of your experience.

As you come back to this ever-present field of awareness, over and over, you come to see, beyond the shadow of a doubt, that this Awareness, this Presence is the most natural, effortless and essential part of your Being. It has always been with you as you, it never has and never will waver; it is always ever-present. It could never go away, be taken away, or abandon you in any way, as it is your very Self. There is nothing more constant and more primary to you than this Aware Presence; it is you. It is the only thing that is you, everything else is a projection, a temporary movement superimposed on top of who you are. This clearly shows us that we are not who we believe ourselves to be, we are not our thoughts however troubling or elevated they are; we are not our feelings however torturous or blissful they are; We are not our stories or any of our experiences, however tragic or successful they are; we are prior to and beyond all of that.

This realization, taking our seat as this Aware Presence, brings with it a deep sense of groundedness, belonging and wholeness. It carries a profound peace and a certainty in our worthiness, our competence and our boundlessness. The point of this realization is to be able to live as the Absolute Self, whether we operate as a wide field or a focused beam.

The point is to always remember that we are beyond the objects of our awareness and come back to ourselves. To know and live from the understanding that we are prior to our thoughts, emotions, sensations, perceptions, relationships, and all experiences, allows us to be fully present and fully open to the entirety of our life, even when it doesn't feel good. When we live this realization, we can be both, the field of Awareness as well as a human being who is struggling, experiencing, growing, without ever moving away from our center, our essence, the peace, wholeness and knowingness that is our nature.

The Futility of the Search

Our culture teaches us that happiness and peace can be found in the world out there, in a relationship, in changing our circumstance or in acquiring some kind of object or skill. And so the imaginary self goes on this journey always looking for his or her next happiness fix. When the relationship, circumstance or object is found, then for a short while we are fulfilled. Our anxiety falls away, we are content, all is right with the world. Unfortunately, that feeling of fulfillment never seems to last, and back we are on the treadmill looking for the next person, circumstance or thing that will once again give us this peace and happiness we seek. Of course, we are always hopeful that the next fix will be the "right" one, the one that will last. We assume that because the acquisition of what we desire brings us this initial fulfillment, even temporary as it is, that peace and happiness resides in the relationship, circumstance or object we obtained. What we fail to realize is that if peace and happiness truly existed within any kind of object or circumstance, than upon obtaining such thing, our fulfillment would last as long as the circumstance, relationship or object remained. As we know, that is not the case, as everything we have ever desired and attained loses its glimmer and whatever fulfillment we received turns out to be ephemeral.

Real happiness is causeless.
Happiness that is caused is not real;
It is transient.
Believing that the transient
Can take one to the intransient is

Self deception.
– Wu Hsin

We, as the imaginary self, can never really experience true love, peace or happiness since it views and experiences everything from the lenses of dissatisfaction. The imaginary self is continually created by the belief and assumption that peace and happiness are not present in this current experience and need to be found elsewhere. This ego self exists solely within the pursuit of this future fulfillment, without its resistance or searching, the separate self would run out of fuel. Once in a while we, as the imaginary self, get lucky and the object of our desire is acquired, we are in love, fulfilled, momentarily satisfied and gratified by our blessed circumstance, at which point, the search stops. For a while we are neither resisting anything nor seeking some other experience, we are intimately connected with this moment, we are happy. For once we are not living in the past or the future but deeply anchored in the present. We assume that it is the object of our desire that creates this sense of peace and okayness, but that is not so. By obtaining what we want we stop seeking or fighting and enter the present moment completely and openly. The moment that pursuing and running disappears, we are purely open to what is. By being completely open and present to the current moment, the imaginary self momentarily suspends and collapses, allowing the stillness and completeness of our being to shine through, the way the sun's warmth and light is experienced when the clouds dissolve. When the imaginary self achieves its goal of gaining the object, person or circumstance it believes will make it whole, at that moment the thoughts and acts of resisting and seeking drop and along with that dropping, the imaginary self is undone, releasing out of existence for a short while, allowing the Aware Presence that we are, in all its peace and wholeness, to be revealed.

As the imaginary self, our story, personality, past, hopes, dreams and worries for the future are dropped, the peace and happiness that is always already here, in and as our Absolute Nature, is revealed, no longer masked by the ego's constant dissatisfaction. We incorrectly assume that the attainment of our desire is responsible for our peace, when it is in fact the momentary collapse of the search for something better and of our usual resistance to this present moment, that actually uncovers and exposes the peace and happiness that is and always was at the core of our own being, present in every experience. The moment that the nagging feeling of dissatisfaction starts to rear its ugly head back up, by definition the imaginary self is back in command.

Soon enough we find ourselves right back where we started, searching for something better while resisting our current experience. When we see the futility of this unending cycle and become exhausted with the search itself, we come around and begin to question the reliability of our beliefs and the validity of the one who seems to be in command.

Peace and happiness only exist in the now, in the present moment. What one fails to realize is that the now is nothing more than the collapse of the imaginary self and of the search it is on. The past and future is nothing more than an illusion. Just like the imaginary self, time is made up of thoughts, thoughts of the past, which we call memories and thoughts about a possible future, which we call hopes, dreams or worries. The past and the future are the playground of the imaginary self, created by the imaginary self, to maintain its existence and to provide it with a place for its constant running, escaping, planning and searching.

Whenever you are in the now, by definition you are no longer an imaginary self running from the past or chasing the future, you are Awareness, without a past or a future, without a story, ever present, limitless and infinite. Peace and Happiness incarnated.

An Important Side Note

Before we move forward, I would like to clarify something about your imaginary self. At no point during this book, do I mean to imply that the imaginary self, the sense that we are a person, with our own individual story, needs to be destroyed for transformation to occur and for us to be able to live a peaceful and happy life. Even though it is illusory, it does serve a purpose. The illusory self helps us function in our day-to-day life, it is part of this great wholeness and completeness that is life. The imaginary self is a character in a play. It is here to play its part to the fullest. If an actor suddenly disappears or forgets the lines of his character, the play is incomplete, maybe even ruined. Our imaginary self simply plays its part, its many roles in this life. It is not unlike a puzzle, where every piece is important to the full picture. Each piece of a puzzle thinks itself independent, but in reality when all pieces come together, their seeming separation disappears into a seamless whole, a perfect picture. The illusion, the problem is in believing yourself to be that one particular piece, when in reality you are the whole picture.

What needs to be destroyed, or more accurately seen through is our identification to the imaginary self and all that it is made up of. The imaginary self does not actually constrict and enslave us. Our belief that this separate vulnerable self is real, our identification and attachment to it and our overall belief that we are it, is what keeps us bound. What I am talking about here is not an actual dropping of the separate "me" but a realization that it is not real, that it is not you, just a character in the play of life, just a small piece of a much larger reality. Let me give you an example. How can we stomach horror movies? How do we not get sick while watching them, run out of the theater screaming, or die right there in our seat of a heart attack? It is very simple, really – we know it is not true, and we know it is not happening to us or to the person on the screen. The same applies to our imaginary self. Once the lines and knots that bind us to it have been undone, and we know it to be an illusion, just part of this organism and this process called being human, and not who we are, then we can be free.

The imaginary self is still here with its preferences, it's weirdness, its affiliation, relationships, its personality, its talent, its likes and dislikes, but we no longer buy into it, we are no longer undone and affected by its neurosis, its fears and negativity. As I heard the great teacher Adyashanti say in an interview, "We lose the taste for it"; it is there in the background but we no longer reach for it, wallow in it, and get lost and stuck in it. Once we know who we are, we no longer desire to slip right back into our old persona, yet we are not in conflict with it. We go to work, enjoy our friends, love our family, deal with conflict and hard times, we feel all range of emotions deeply, and yet all of it is done and experienced with peace in our heart and a small knowing smile on our face. In some way seeing that we are beyond this small self and its limits, frees us to fully enjoy the ride and frees up the personality of the imaginary self to fully play its character. Life is no longer so damn serious. Our thoughts and emotions are no longer so damn important but instead are seen for what they are, a momentary movement in the timeless Aware Presence that we are. We can then live our lives from and as the Absolute Self, prior and beyond the imaginary self, watching this character do its thing and living life organically, at peace and happy with our self, with others and with the currents of life.

Once the illusory nature of your story is seen through and you have discovered the essence of your Being, this personality you have, this role you play can never sway you or define you. Your peace, your happiness, your freedom is beyond it and yet permeates it. In truth when you realize yourself to be the Awareness that is prior to your body, mind and story, you find yourself able to relax and enjoy your role much more than when you were completely identified with it. You now have the freedom to be entirely yourself, to play your role to its fullest, without ever getting completely lost in it.

~Experiential Adventure: An In-Depth Meeting with the Absolute Self ~

This experiential adventure's aim is to allow a more profound connection to your Absolute Self. The Absolute Self is no other that an Aware Presence, the pure joy of simply Being without our attention being pulled by an object or activity of the mind. Being is what happens when the mind is quiet, between thoughts and behind thoughts. Close your eyes, take a few deep breaths and bring your focus within. Allow your body and your mind to relax, as if dropping in your favorite chair after a long hard day. Feel that you belong and that you are safe here. Allow your thoughts to pass by, without getting caught up by them. Shift your focus inside and find that felt sense that you exist, that you are alive. Taste this alive Aware Presence within that witnesses your experience, hears through your ears and sees through your eyes. Notice the dark colors and shapes of the back of your eyelids, just experience the screen of the closed eyelids, maybe some light filters in, maybe not, just notice the shapes and colors that are appearing there, and then shift your focus to the Presence that is watching, that one is your Absolute Self. Let go of your focus on what you see and stay with the Aware Presence that sees, feels and experiences. Allow each exhale to loosen your body, melt the conceptual boundaries and expand your spirit. Allow the vastness that you are to come forth, your consciousness without an age or gender, without a story, a shape or a form, just a silent wholeness, feel and be it. As you shift your focus to that still and silent space within, which is outside of thoughts or any story, notice how vast you are. Ask yourself these questions but take a couple seconds between each to reconnect to your Aware Presence before you move on to the next question:

- When dwelling in this ever-present, infinite space, could I ever find something wrong or be bothered by life? Could this Absolute Self that I am ever be disturbed?

- When I enter this ever-present, limitless space that I am, is there anything I need to do to feel better or more complete or whole than I already am?

- Does my awareness have any boundaries? Does this Aware Space that I am have a beginning and an end? Can I find where I, as my Absolute Self, begin and where I end? Is there an edge to myself?

- Does this still knowing space have preferences, likes and dislikes? Or is it wide open to all of life?

Dwell in this infinite and limitless aware spaciousness, feel its transparent substance, its peace and stillness. Experience the freedom and ease of being without a gender or an age, ever present, without a story, open to and genuinely okay with all of life.

~

6.
The Unwavering Nature of Change

*Only the fool
Seeks to stop
The shaking of
The moon's reflection on the water.
The acceptance of what
Cannot be changed
Paves the way to
The changeless.
– Wu Hsin*

In our search for this happiness fix, we allow the outside world, our things, relationships, accomplishments to be the driving force of our lives. Has that not been true for you? Unfortunately, allowing things such as money, power, your job, your significant other or even your kids to be your compass is a sure way to end up exhausted, unfulfilled and lost.

Most, if not all things outside of us are limited and many are passing, sooner or later they either disappear or disappoint us. We can never fully rely on them, because if we do, our sense of self will be fragile and unstable, just like a house built on a sand dune, we will always be worried about the next bad storm or strong tide that might wipe us out.

Great Expectations

Human beings are imperfect and fallible. We can't help it, we make mistakes; we all make mistakes. Sometimes we can be fickle, false and emotionally driven, so if our sense of self and our life centers around another human being, the chance that we will end up hurt and disappointed, at some point or another, is basically 100 percent. Your mate will decide he or she doesn't love you anymore. Your child will decide that college is not for him but that tattoos are cool and you're not. Your best friend will tell you, at the last minute, he can't help you move because something else came up. Your boss will give the new position you have worked so hard for to her nephew. We need to accept that people cannot always be depended on and that in the end they will do what they think is right for them in that moment, regardless of what we think or of how great we have been to them. I would go as far as to suggest that behind every disappointment there is an unrealistic expectation. Expecting the fickle to be reliable and steadfast and the passing to be constant and eternal is senseless. This leads us back to Scott Kiloby's inquiry questions, "What do I want?" and "What happens when I don't get what I want?" The answer is simple: When our expectations are not in line with reality, we suffer. Take a look at your life, all your anger, disappointments or great sorrows, how much were you expecting and was it realistic to expect so much? How different would things have been if you had lived with the understanding and the recognition that sometimes people make poor and unkind choices and that life takes turns we wish it wouldn't? To live wide awake and wide open is not possible without accepting and permitting life to be what it is. To live from the position of our Absolute Nature is an agreement we joyfully make to allow life and people to move and evolve as they wish and as they need to. From the perspective of Awareness, we know that things change and move, just like water or the clouds in the sky, and that sometimes all this movement is not in the direction we would like it to go. We have to fall in love with this moment, whatever direction it takes, it is the juice of life, it is what pushes us to evolve and transform. Life moves, it is not meant to be frozen, its natural expression is to be in constant flux and flow. That is why we need to make our unwavering, ever-present and eternal essence our driving force, our compass, because it is the only thing in existence that is prior to the movement of life, everything else is transitory, impermanent and changing, as it should be. Our Absolute Self, our Aware Presence, is always right here, in the background, steadfast, pure and at peace. It does not come and go, it does not change its mind and it can never die or leave us in any way. It is, ever-present, infinite and eternal; that is the only thing we can truly rely on and trust. It is the only safe and worthwhile base for our sense of self to rely on. The rest we have to trust will change, sometimes in ways we wish it wouldn't.

What I find interesting is that rather than putting our peace in the hands of the unwavering Presence that we are, that is infinitely still and eternally with us, we put our peace in the hands of the precarious world around us, of complete strangers and in the hands of passing and ephemeral things. Let me give you some examples, you are in a relatively good mood, at peace with life and with yourself, enjoying your morning coffee, looking out the window and suddenly *BAM!* Some stranger allows his dog to poop on your front lawn and doesn't pick it up...or your day started great and suddenly your tire blows on the way to work...or someone doesn't say thank you after you hold the door for them, or your dog gets sick all over your bed and on it goes, life happening, doing what it does, people being people and you giving your serenity away. I am not saying that those circumstances are pleasant, but to me the worst injury is not the event itself, but how we respond to life, how much power we give to strangers and circumstances we have no control over. We allow our expectations of life and of people to rob us of our peace, we literally give away our birthright for no good reasons. Not only do we allow life's circumstances to disturb us, but oftentimes we continue to do violence to ourselves by thinking about the incident over and over, talking about it, focusing on it, getting more and more upset, sometimes for days on hand. For what? Really in the end, who injured you? Did life injure you, did this stranger injure you, did your mate or your boss injure you or did you injure yourself?

Ask yourself, what unrealistic expectations did you have that allowed you to be pulled off kilter and give away so much of your power, and so much of your inner peace? Look back at some of the great betrayals and disappointments of your life, with hindsight were your expectations realistic? How long, after the original incident, did you keep the betrayal or disappointment alive in your mind? How much of your suffering was self-inflicted?

~**Experiential Inquiry: Meeting our Expectations**~
Look back in your life to moments of sadness, disappointment and/or frustration. As you remember these circumstances and feel the pain of them in this present moment, be willing to explore:

- *Think back and come up with the expectation that was behind the disappointment, "What did I want"? Also feel the felt sense of this expectation in your body. Can you find the place in your body where this expectation was held? The part of you for whom this desire or need mattered?*

- Ask yourself, "What happened when I didn't get what I wanted?" Feel this hurt in your body and the part of you that was disappointed.

- Now relive the circumstance while dropping the expectation. How does that change your lived experience of the event? How is the disappointment, the hurt lived and handled, without the expectation?

- How is the suffering experienced in your body without the expectation?

Now do this inquiry with something that is going on in your life presently and that is creating pain and resistance.

- What is the expectation you have of this event or person?

- Is the expectation realistic, in line with reality?

- Can you feel the expectation in your body, the part of you that wants life to look and turn out a certain way? Can you meet, welcome and hold this part and the pain, fear, disappointment or frustration that lives there?

- Can you relive your current experience, while dropping all expectations, the constraint you put on life?

- Feel how that changes your situation? Feel the hurt, mixed in with the openness and resilience that you are.

Dwell in this vast knowing space, feel its transparent substance, its peace and stillness. Experience the freedom and peace of being without a gender or an age, ever present, without a story or any expectations, open to and genuinely okay with all of life.

~

In the end, we injure ourselves much more than any other person or circumstance ever could. We mistakenly choose to put our center, our happiness, and our faith in the ephemeral and undependable rather than in the Truth of our own Essence and we grasp unto unrealistic demands and expectations that cannot be met. When we realize that life and others cannot touch or offend who we truly are, we stop resisting and fighting what is, and allow space for life to be as it is and for people to be people, to change their mind, to evolve, to make mistakes and to have times of unkindness. When we live our lives from this realization, nothing can ever have the power to damage us, we still get disappointed or pissed off, after all we are still human, but it is only a momentary apparition, we don't get stuck in it. Everything is felt intimately and passes right through us and the stillness and wholeness of our Being is always right here with us. We can simply put our peace in our own hands, in our Absolute Self, in that which never changes, never has mood swings, never comes and goes. In resting in the peace that is our essence, we can never be pulled off kilter, and no one and no circumstance can or ever could rob us of our Serenity. This leads us to our next topic, our pesky mind, which happens to be the main culprit in our suffering.

7.
Mind - The Great Tormentor

What problems can there be that
The mind did not create?
The solution to problems begins with
The cessation in believing in
The content of one's thoughts.
– Wu Hsin

The main space where conflict resides and breeds within us is in our mind. If you are like most people, you have inside your head a major conflict-producing machine. Eight out of 10 thoughts is probably some kind of judgment, worry, blame or complaint. Talk about conflict! We get so used to these thoughts that they become a habit, an intrinsic part of our story. They happen all on their own, without even our recognition, like a soundtrack on replay.

The Voice

Let's talk briefly about what the mind is. Really it isn't even a place that can be located. It is just an accumulation, a repertoire of random thoughts, beliefs and attitudes that we carry along with us. The mind is a program, similar to a computer program, created by our early experiences of the world around us and our responses to them. Actual events, people, as well as information we were fed, crafted this program. As we experienced the world, we were taught "good" from "bad." We were taught what labels and names to call things, what things should mean, what is real and true compared to what is false. We were even told appropriate ways to act and feel. This programming is continuous. The experiences of our lives continue to shape and shift this program and the more detailed our mind program becomes, the narrower our life experiences become. One of the main issues is our identification with this program and as such the more constricted and detailed the program is, the narrower and more restricted we become as well. The more the program is used, confirmed and repeated, the denser and stronger it becomes. When it is fully in place and no longer being disputed, we seem to lose our self in it and not be able to differentiate between the program and who we are. At that point our mind program is us, it is our sense of self, our personality, it is our likes and dislikes, our beliefs and judgments, and our hopes and dreams. We forget that we existed prior to this program. We forget that we were born without this program, that during the first few years of our lives we were free, aware, joyful and experiencing life fully without this program running our lives. So who were we without these thoughts, beliefs and judgments? We have lost our self in the mind, as Descartes said, "I think therefore I am." As it turns out, that's not quite accurate, as there is so much more to us than what goes on in our heads. It might be more accurate to say "I am therefore I think". We have to remember that we are, we exist, prior to and beyond all and any thoughts.

Most of us have a voice in our head, that we assume is who we are, our inner self. We make that assumption without ever checking to see if we truly agree and believe what is happening inside our head. Have you ever stopped long enough to question your association to this voice and assess the validity of what it is saying? Is what it says a fair representation of who you are and of your life? Is what it says deep and important or mostly nonsense? How much of what it says is actually based on facts and ends up being true? If this voice in your head is you and these thoughts are yours, why don't they sound more like you and why don't you have more control over them? Most of us believe that we choose our thoughts, that we can make them stop when we want to, but is that really true? How often do you know what you are about to think before you actually think it? Do you pick a thought or does it just come up, arising out of nowhere? My guess is it just kind of pops in your head without any real work on your part. We feel like we know these thoughts, like they are ours, because they tend to be related to our past, current and possible future experiences. They also are recurrent. If you pay attention, you'll notice the same type of thoughts over and over. This is our conditioning at work, the program that is running inside our head tells us what to feel, how to act and what to believe.

Suffering Revisited

What is suffering? Suffering is no other than the thoughts that tell you that you are not okay as you are and that life is not okay as it is, that's it. Thoughts such as, "I don't like this," "people shouldn't act like that," "I need something different to happen to be happy," or "I am not okay as I am, I need to do better and be better" delineate and limit our ability to enjoy and connect to life. What defines our suffering or the extent of our suffering are our thoughts of lack, our resistance, and the level to which we buy into them and identify with them. As Guy Finley tells us in *The Essential Laws of Fearless Living*, "The more we think, *the more we sink."* If we truly had control over our thoughts, wouldn't we just choose to replace all these negative thoughts with "I am okay with this," "this is great," "life is perfect as it is," or "I am perfect and whole just as I am" and be happy. Obviously if we could, we would. What about making thoughts stop altogether, can we do that? Any of us who have practiced meditation or have had insomnia know that quieting the mind on demand is basically impossible. If our mind was truly in our control, shouldn't we be able to just shut it up when we want to, just the way we can turn off the TV or the radio? So is this voice really us and is what it says truly in our control? It seems pretty clear, that your thoughts arise as part of this body/mind organism, the way twitching and burping arise, your mind is part of this instrument you have, but it is not who you are. Your thoughts are not really yours, nor can they define you. You do not think your thoughts, they think themselves into being, but they are seen, experienced and known by you.

We all have things inside of us we fear: haunting thoughts and dark feelings we sense are down there, but that we'd rather not face for fear they may drag us into their domain. So, instead of questioning the right of these negative states to homestead in our souls, they dwell in the dark of us – living there virtually unchallenged.
– Guy Finley

Pay attention to the thoughts in your head, step back so that you can objectively observe them and notice how crazy it sounds in there, see how they rarely stay with your present experience and usually relive the past or plan and worry about the future, and notice how they kind of say the same thing over and over. Pay attention to the process that happens when a particularly sticky thought grabs you and how you seem to become it and lose yourself in it. Notice how the moment you realize you've gotten caught in your inner drama, you are no longer trapped in it and you are, once again, able to step back and observe. When you realize this truth, that the voice in your head is not you, thoughts and what they say suddenly take on much less importance. Michael Singer said it best in his book *The Untethered Soul*, "No matter what the voice is saying, it's all the same. It doesn't matter if it's saying nice things or mean things, worldly things or spiritual things. It doesn't matter because it's still just a voice talking inside your head…Stop feeling that one thing it says is you and the other thing it says is not you. If you're hearing it talk, it's obviously not you." No, you are the one experiencing it.

The Veil of Reality

This voice in your head seems to comment and judge just about everything in life. It talks about everything and nothing. If you are like most people, you can't see a tree without the voice in your head commenting about it in some way. You might hear anything from "look, a tree" to "I wonder what kind of flowers it will have comes spring. Wow, it really is quite nice. I have to remember to ask Julie what kind of tree this is. Maybe it would be nice in the yard by the fence. Hmmm, I wonder if it might give us too much shade. I'll have to check how big it gets. If it gets big, maybe we can put a nice little tree house in there…" and on and on it goes. Your direct connection to the tree is instantaneously lost, veiled by the mind's babble. You were not able to enjoy the simple intimacy of the tree, really seeing it as it is, free of your labels and whatever stories you superimposed on it. The moment the mind made any kind of comment about the tree, you lost the tree and the intrinsic intimacy with it was broken. The moment the mind jumped in, you stopped seeing the tree, the collection of moving and ever changing textures, colors, shapes and smells. You stopped seeing reality and started seeing your program. In this example, your program is your idea, belief, story or attitude about the tree. Someone else could have a completely different response to that same tree, based on his or her program. Maybe they were told it is really a weed that grows into a tree, or that it has tons of pollens that contribute to yearly allergies, or that it attracts spiders or hummingbird, whatever they believe, whatever their program, will affect how they see and relate to the tree. And this, my friend, is what we do every day of our life, all day long. We don't see our spouse but we see our ideas, beliefs and attitudes about them, our program. We also see our current mood through them. If we are having a good day, they seem kinder, lovelier, but if we are tired or frustrated, they can't seem to say or do the right thing. In truth, when we look at our spouse or any other person, object or event, we don't connect to the truth of that experience, instead we see who we are in that instant and we see our conditioning, we see more our self in them than them.

The mind also takes us away from the present moment, from the ever unfolding now. By the time the mind catches up to our experience and comments on it, the experience itself is in the past. Thoughts are never fast enough to really capture reality. Thoughts are in fact always an afterthought and always late to the dinner party. In the words of Michael Singer, "What you end up experiencing is really a personal presentation of the world according to you, rather than the stark, unfiltered experience of what is really out there...Your consciousness is actually experiencing your mental model of reality, not reality itself."

Our mind program is a collection of our past experiences and our conditioning. It is also a collection of what we have been trained to believe are our hopes and dreams as well as our fears about the future. Every raw experience of sights, sound, touch, smell or taste, is interpreted by our program, through our past baggage and through the lenses of our hopes and fears for the future. The mind's focus is never on the now. In some way our mind cannot help but separate us from reality, from the mystery and movement that is life. As Michael Singer writes, "Reality is just too real for most of us, so we temper it with the mind."

The mind's role – its function – is to compartmentalize, control and understand. It will comment and label everyone and everything. It will think about thinking and even try to figure out the infinite and the unknowable. All this thinking only distances us from the Truth of our experience. We no longer see the reality of a person, object or event; we see our story of them as seen through our mind's program. And as stated, this story really is our story, not theirs. This story says much more about us than it does about them. We also don't see the reality and Truth of who we are; we only see a programed story of ourselves. We wonder why we feel lonely, alienated, misunderstood, yet how can we truly connect to another, to life or even to our true Self with this incessant noise in our head, this false program running and playing intermediary. Because don't be fooled, 99.9 percent of your thoughts are just noise, not only are they not true, but they are also hardly ever helpful or loving. As Ralph Waldo Emerson said, "Knowledge is knowing that we cannot know."

Finding a Piece of the Truth

One day Mara, the demon of illusion and delusion, was traveling through the villages of India with his attendants. He saw a man whose face was lit up in wonder, as the man had just discovered a piece of truth.

"Doesn't this bother you when someone finds a piece of truth?" his attendant asked. "No," Mara replied. "Right after this, they usually make a belief out of it.
– Zen Story

~Experiential Adventure: Experiencing Reality as it Is~
Pick five minutes to play around with this exploration. You can do this anytime and anywhere, you can do it for a few seconds or for hours. The description is deceptively easy. Just see, hear, touch, taste, feel and smell reality just as it is, without the narrative or imagining of the mind. That's it. Sounds easy right? I guarantee you it is not as easy as it seems; we are so used to our habitual commentary or visualizing from the mind that we have lost the ability to stay with the naked and raw experience of our senses.

Run your hand over the fabric of your couch, without any comment or judgment from the mind about it, without the mental image of your couch popping up in your head, just the pure sensory experience of it. Feel the feeling of the ground under your feet, feel of the breeze on your face, the sight of your partner's face, or of a tree, the sensations in your body, the smell of coffee, the rays of the sun...all without the buffer of the mind, without any commentary, *label, judgment, story or image, just the pure experience of it. Even the thought, "How beautiful" is a judgment, a label, albeit a nice one. If you are sensing a tightness or tingling in your chest, let go of the image and location of it in your body, let go of the definitions, to even define the sensation as tightness or as being in your chest is limiting it and boxing it in, just stay with the raw experiencing of it, with nothing else added. Allow your body, your senses, your heart, your intuition, to be wide open, but leave all thoughts behind, like someone cut off your head. Experience from your body, not from your head. As you play around with this exploration, you will notice how conditioned we are to experience and divide the world up in our head. This little exploration can be done in your living room, in your bedroom first thing in the morning, at work when you feel the pressure mounting or simply while hiking or swimming in the ocean. This can also be done with emotions and physical sensations, have you ever experienced a burn or stubbing your toe without the mind's commentary? Or the sensation of anger when the story around it is dropped?*

Start small, maybe for a few seconds, and then slowly increase your time, when the mind pops up, notice it, smile to yourself and come back to the naked experiencing of what is happening, without frustration, without violence to yourself or any resistance. Allow life to unfold as it does. When the mind pops back up, it is simply what is happening at this instant, just the mind doing what the mind does, what it has been conditioned to do. Notice the thought, let it pass, and come back to the raw experience of this moment. Over time, the mind will quiet down, and the programs will loosen up. When you withdraw your attention and energy from anything, it stops to flourish. Come back to this exploration over and over.

~

Our mind plays commentator and judge to everything we experience. It is the film that separates us from reality. It keeps us from seeing the completeness in all things and all people, including our self. It keeps us from seeing that, no matter what, all is well, just as it is. Our thoughts get in the way of our peace, just the way clouds block the sun on a cloudy day. The sun never disappears, it is just there, hidden by the clouds, waiting for the clouds to dissipate so that it may shine its warmth and light on everything.

The Function of Thoughts

Let discuss for a short while, how thoughts evolved and what the function of the mind is. This might give us some background to put the whole thinking process in perspective. Thoughts have a few functions, the first one is to think of solutions to problems and to plan ahead, without it we wouldn't be able to think ourselves out of a paper bag or give our lives any direction. This first aspect is a necessary function of thoughts. The other two aspects have to do with survival. These last two processes of thought were useful at some point in our evolution, but are no longer beneficial to us in this current society.

The second function of the mind is to protect us. Thoughts are inherently negative and tend to jump to worst-case scenario. The mind sees the world as a threat and believes its job is to announce, warn against, predict and protect us against such threats. This comes from a time where the smallest rustling in a tree might have been a predator. This comes from a time when going with worst-case scenario saved our lives. If our thoughts had said "There is a rustling, it could be a bird or a deer, let's not jump to conclusion just yet, let's wait and see," we might not be here as a species. So the mind did a good job and obviously was very effective at keeping us safe, but in most cases, that part of our thinking has now outgrown its usefulness. Fortunately, most of us now live in an environment where we can take the chance to not jump to conclusion and wait and see, but our thoughts are not wired that way. Most of us do not live in the jungle or in a war zone or in a gang infested ghetto, yet our mind keeps acting as if we do, creating conflict, distance and loneliness wherever we go. As Michael Singer states, "You will come to see that the mind talks all the time because you gave it a job to do. You use it as a protection mechanism, a form of defense."

The third aspect of thought is a stress relief. As the mind describes and reports our experience and perceptions, and plans possible outcomes, we tend to develop a false sense of security. We falsely feel more in control of our experience, we walk through life using the narrator in our head as a buffer from reality, we feel as if we can know and prepare for what's coming, when in fact, life is way beyond thought. Michael Singer, whose work is a major influence in my life, uses in *The Untethered Soul* a metaphor that I think is brilliant in its simplicity. He compares our mind to a teakettle. All the noise in our head seems to increase when we are stressed or under some kind of pressure, just the way a teakettle whistles when the pressure on the inside mounts to a boiling point. The whistling lets us know that the water is boiling, but it also releases some of the pressure inside so that the water does not over flow, the same is true with our thoughts. The more stress there is on the inside, the more steamed you are, the more noise the mind makes. If we feel ill at ease, stressed, angry or anxious, thoughts tend to get agitated as well, looking for people to blame, solutions to problem, looking to vent in some way, or to control the world around us, anything that will alleviate this pressure we feel on the inside. The whistling of the mind will usually continue until the pressure is alleviated. Its content will vary based on our conditioning and personality. Some of us will find someone or something to blame and rave and rant about unfairness and plot for revenge. Some of us will put the blame on us, put ourselves down and get depressed. Some of us will go in circle try to plan or think of solutions, growing more anxious and feeling more out of control, or maybe a mix of all of the above. The problem with these type of thinking is that it doesn't usually solve anything, it doesn't really release us of our stress, it keeps us stuck in the original problem and make us feel like the threat is constant rather than allowing the past to be left in the past, and living in the present. In the end, both the second and third function of the mind seem to create more stress than alleviate it.

Thoughts, especially when they come from a place of fear and confusion, have very little to no effect on the outside world. We can think, wish and pray that the weather stays nice for our party, that everyone on our list show up, that nobody makes a scene, but that will do very little to change the way things are. The weather will be what it is, people will or will not show up and those who show up will act as they see fit, regardless of our worry or planning, regardless of our minds' effort. We can think about how we want our mate or our kids or our boss or the stranger in the car next to us to act, but in the end, they will act as they wish, irrespective of what we think. Ultimately, we come to see that people and events do not cause our suffering, that life is not the perpetrator of our pain. Our suffering is caused by all the noise, all the upheaval our mind makes about the people and events in our life. So what can we do about it?

In the end, everyone has thoughts. Everyone has times when their thoughts are calmer and times when their thoughts seem to be on overdrive. The difference between those who are at peace and the rest of the world is not that one has thoughts and the other does not, or that one has nice thoughts while the other negative ones. No, the difference is that the one who is at peace knows that her thoughts have nothing to do with her. There is a recognition that thoughts come and go on their own, based on conditioning and survival mechanism. There is an understanding that they are not our thoughts per say and that we are not them, and that the less attention we give them, the better we are for it. The one who is at peace knows that she is prior to thoughts. She knows that thoughts are simply a mechanism of the body mind, just like digestion, and that outside of a few functional use, they are better left alone. The one who is at peace knows that his thoughts cannot be trusted to be accurate or fair. The one who is at peace doesn't try to control his thoughts, he just lets them happen in the background, just the way you might have the TV on low in the backdrop and go on with whatever business you are attending to.

> *The inherent nature of mind is*
> *To process thought.*
> *To attempt the cessation of thought*
> *Goes against what is natural.*
> *The goal, therefore, is not*
> *The cessation of thought.*
> *The goal is cessation of*
> *Identification with thought.*
> *– Wu Hsin*

Seeing our Blindness

The problem is that we believe our thoughts to be an accurate rendition of reality and of who we are. To be free from all our suffering, we have to see through the mind and call it on its nonsense. Only then, when we realize that we are not our thoughts and that they do not describe reality in an accurate and valid manner, can we dis-identify with them and actually come to intimately meet ourselves as well as life, as it is, one timeless moment at a time. As the French philosopher Proust said, "The real voyage of discovery consists not in seeking new landscapes but in having new eyes." The first step to having new eyes is to not buy into what the mind tells us about the landscape we are seeing. Only then, can we see it freshly, openly and intimately as it is meant to be experienced.

The Blind Men and the Elephant
Several citizens ran into a hot argument about God and different religions, and each one could not agree to a common answer. So they came to the Lord Buddha to find out what exactly God looks like.

The Buddha asked his disciples to get a large magnificent elephant and four blind men. He then brought the four blind to the elephant and told them to find out what the elephant would "look" like.

The first blind men touched the elephant leg and reported that it "looked" like a pillar. The second blind man touched the elephant tummy and said that an elephant was a wall. The third blind man touched the elephant ear and said that it was a piece of cloth. The fourth blind man hold on to the tail and described the elephant as a piece of rope. And all of them ran into a hot argument about the "appearance" of an elephant.

The Buddha asked the citizens: "Each blind man had touched the elephant, but each of them gives a different description of the animal. Which answer is right?"

The truth of our lives is that we are all blind men and the world is our elephant, we all see, feel and understand a different part of it. We are all wrong and all correct at the same time; there is never one way, all of it is the Divine. That is the paradox of life. In seeing this, a great freedom arises, we are no longer stuck in believing that we know the truth, we can be free of our beliefs and our program and just be intimately living life one moment at a time, without the need to know, control or be right. In this realization, the need to fight others, to be correct, to know what is true disappears and we are just left with the mystery of life, able to wonder, enjoy and go with the flow.

8.

Beliefs - The Lenses of Life

*The attachment to beliefs is
The greatest shackle.
To be free is
To know that
One does not know.
– Wu Hsin*

The Truth beyond Right and Wrong

People are often stuck on the concept of right or wrong. Clients will often ask me which belief, what view, which lens is accurate? The truth is, it doesn't matter since all we can ever know are relative truths, not Absolute Truth. Some things may seem very accurate in the relative form, such as, violence is not right or life is not fair. But that is a relative truth; it is based on this world, on our ideas and on our limited understanding and access to the Wholeness that is reality. Truth, the Absolute Truth, is unknowable by the mind; the mind never has complete understanding of all view points, all circumstances and all reasons, to decide what is right or wrong or what is true or false. One person's tragedy, like an illness, can become their greatest gift and life-enhancing lesson. Most people who are abandoned by their mate consider it a great heartbreak and an unfair circumstance in their life; yet ask them how they feel three years later, and it is not uncommon to hear, "it's the best thing that could have ever happened to me." We just don't know what is truly right or wrong, good or bad and fair and unfair, it all depends. The moment a judgment is made, we are back into the relative. Any judgment, wrong, false, right, fair or unfair...is a relative truth. The fact that all truths are relative is an Absolute Truth and a humbling important one to realize.

Awareness, our Absolute Self can be compared to the lenses of glasses before they get dirty and scratched up, like on the first day of wearing them, pure, clear and free of any residue. This clarity and transparency allows everything to be experienced directly, without resistance or judgment, nothing is blocked from being seen and felt as it is. This pristine seeing is pure freedom, a complete allowance for all of life to be as it is. Over time, our conditioning, our identification with the imaginary self and its limited and faulty habits seems to cover up the purity and clarity of our lenses, suddenly we are seeing and experiencing the world through scratched, smeared and cruddy lenses, and our world becomes distorted. The closest we can ever get to the Truth, at any given point, is an ever changing and partial understanding of it. All shades, both pink or black lenses, are inaccurate; they are aspects of the all-encompassing Truth, they are colored aspects of the purity and clarity of the uncolored lenses of pure Aware Presence. When living life through dirty or colored lenses, the truth changes constantly, based on each moment, based on each circumstance, based on who you are in this precise instant and of course based on whom you ask. As Ram Dass writes in his book *Polishing the Mirror*, "Part of the process of awakening is recognizing that the realities we thought were absolute are only relative." The great thing about the relative is that at any given point you can ask yourself, which world would I prefer to live in, dark brown or cotton candy pink? Granted, neither is accurate, only a distortion of the clarity and transparency of what is, but the fact is still that each lenses, brown, pink, black or red, come with a particular life experience. So as we are working on dropping our conditioning and coming back to the clarity of our True Self, we might still choose to wear the most appealing lenses.

Whether something is true or false is unimportant since we have very little knowledge of what is actually True. The lenses we wear – our beliefs – color our life experiences. This is important because what you see is what you get and what you see is directly dependent on your paradigm, your beliefs, the color of your lenses. So if your lenses are the color of cotton candy, what you see in the world is cotton candy, but if your lenses are dirty brown, then the world looks dirty brown to you, and as we know what we see becomes our lived reality. Our lived reality has very little to do with our circumstances, but everything to do with our lenses.

If what you believe is what you see and if what you see is what you get, then the accuracy of your beliefs has little importance, what matters in the end is whether or not you like your life? Do you enjoy your experiences in life? Do you have fulfilling friendships and intimate relationships? Are you happy with the successes in your life? Are you fulfilled by the direction your life is taking? If the answer is yes, then congratulation, you are way ahead of the game. If your answer is "no" or "not always" or "not completely", then you might want to take a look at your lenses.

So the important question is never "am I right?" The question is always "Is this belief, are my thoughts useful?"

Over and over you have to inquire whether or not your views are helping you achieve a life that is successful, kind and peaceful? Are they in line with the life you want to build and do they support the transformation you wish to make? Do they honor the point of view of the still, wise and loving Self that you are or do they promote the illusion and lack of the imaginary self? As we change our mind, we change ourselves and our lives.

If your heart's desire is for freedom and liberation, then you will realize that all beliefs, all lenses, are only partial truths, and in the end you will drop all beliefs and choose to live in the open and pure space of not knowing and respond to life from that nameless place, where right action spontaneously arises in each moment, free of past conditioning and half-truths. When we live from the position of and on behalf of our Essential Self, we are in deep intimacy with the moment and the flow of life. Our actions emerge out of that intimacy. If true freedom is your aim, then all beliefs need to be dropped, so that you might experience reality as it truly is, not a colored version of it, however beautiful it might be. But if your aim is simply to find more peace and fulfillment in your life, then there are practical steps you can take to change your paradigm, to switch the lenses you look through to a more pleasant and harmonious color. Changing our lenses to more peaceful and harmonious ones can also be a stepping stone to dropping them altogether. It can be a way to get closer to who we truly are and in alignment with the Truth of our being.

Our beliefs create mental and emotional state that is peaceful or unpeaceful, content or discontent, accepting or angry, happy or unhappy, loving or unloving, fearless or fearful. Our beliefs are very powerful – if we believe them,

They create an internal reality, or internal emotional climate. They also influence external reality – what we do, how we behave, how others respond to us, what opportunities we take advantage of. Those who grow up with beliefs that cause them to fear and distrust life live with an internal state that not only is uncomfortable, but also blocks them from experiencing love, abundance happiness and peace.
– Gina Lake

Challenging Beliefs

There are many ways to challenge our beliefs. One way is to surround ourselves with people who believe differently than we do and make an effort to view things from their perspective. This will show us that we have more in common with them than we originally believed. It also will allow us to challenge ourselves and widen our narrow mindset. This little exploration works with people we admire, with historical figures or even with people we are in conflict with or that we fear. Our goal in this exploration is to connect, listen and understand, so that we may see life through their eyes.

- How would you and your life be different if you had their beliefs and saw things through their eyes?

This will help your mind shift and adapt to different paradigms; it also will help you realize that all paradigms are superimposed on the pure open Awareness that we are, like clothes, they are not intrinsic to us, they do not define us and can be seen through. The dropping, changing and adopting of new beliefs is described in Neuroscience as plasticity. Neuro or brain plasticity is the ability the brain, or more specifically the neural pathways, have to evolve and change structurally in response to changes in our environment. So as you challenge yourself, put yourself in different situations and surround yourself with different people and points of view, your brain becomes more malleable and adaptable, and it changes right along with your beliefs.

Another practice to challenge our beliefs revolves around not jumping to conclusion. Before you judge someone or react to a situation ask yourself if you are absolutely sure that you have all the facts necessary to you know, without any doubt, the Truth about what is happening. I am sure you realize that I just tricked you, since there is no way for us to ever know the Absolute Truth of any circumstance or person, including our own self. If you follow this adage, then you will never judge another person, including your own self, or react to any situation for the rest of your life. Obviously, I don't expect you to be Jesus Christ or Buddha (at least not right away), but not jumping to conclusion and giving others the benefit of the doubt is a worthwhile lifelong practice. It puts you back in the open, humble and wise space of not knowing, in the peace that is at the center of the mystery of life. Every time you remember that more could be going on than meets the eye, that your view is just one view among infinite views, that you don't have all the facts and can't have all the answers, and you refrain from jumping to conclusions, your brain evolves and your consciousness expands. You become kinder, more loving, more patient, more understanding, more empathetic and lighthearted. You become peace and love incarnated.

I always ask clients, "Why do people cheat, lie, act rudely, talk behind other's backs and entertain all sorts of nasty behaviors?" All types of creative answers come up: "because they are unhappy"; "because they were abused as children"; "because they didn't have parents to teach them right from wrong"; "because they don't go to church" and so on. But the answer is much simpler, much closer to home, to all of us. People behave badly sometimes, not because they are damaged, or bad but because they are human and human beings are imperfect and fallible. Until we wake up to and live from the vastness and peace of our Absolute Self, we cannot help but respond to life from our conditioning, from the limited and faulty program running through us. Until we remember the truth of who we are, then we can only live from the point of view of this illusory self and from its ignorance. As imaginary selves we are always stuck in a position of lack, defense and illusion and so we make mistakes. WE all make mistakes; we all act in lesser ways than we could at some point or another, some of us more often than others. We all forget who we are at our core and let the imaginary self and its worries, sense of deficiency, resistance and even paranoia direct and rule us. As a human being, life is a lesson in humility, kindness, patience, generosity and forgiveness. When we remember our True Self and see clearly that all beings in their essence are so much more than what they seem or how they act, then life becomes easy and humility, kindness, patience, generosity and forgiveness become natural and spontaneous ways of being and responding.

When people behave in ways that you perceive as "bad," before you retaliate or act rudely yourself, allow them the space to be human, to make mistakes, to be stuck where they are. That doesn't mean you allow everyone to step all over you, hurt others and wreak havoc, but as you approach their behaviors allow a deep sense of your own past mistakes, imperfections and illusions to permeate your Judgment. Respond from a humble, wide-open and loving space and you will find yourself to be much more compassionate than you could have ever believed and your response much wiser and productive than before.

The bottom line is we never know what is going on with people, in their life and their head, we don't know how deeply in the grasp of the imaginary self they are, and we don't know what plans life has in store for them or for us, so all we can do is buckle up, stay open, stay in the space of our Aware Presence that is at peace with everything and enjoy the ride. As beliefs and absolute truths are dropped, we grow wiser and come to the great realization of not knowing. We recognize that we actually know very little about right and wrong, true and false, about ourselves and about life as a whole. What is most surprising of all is that not knowing, living, and being in this mystery feels wondrous and freeing, like a heavy weight as been lifted. We no longer need to know everything, to figure things out, to judge or plan ad nauseam. As always, life works in great paradoxes; as we drop the need to know and the illusory certainty of the mind, we gain the wisdom and certainty of the heart. There is great insights, great peace, great openness and guidance in this alive mystery, in allowing ourselves to rest in not knowing and trusting that a great loving intelligence is at work.

9.
Emotions – The Misunderstood Energy

Scared and sacred are spelled with the same letters. Awful proceeds from the same root word as awesome. Terrify and terrific. Every negative experience holds the seed of transformation.
– Alan Cohen

Our Emotional Climate

The mind is a program that has been refined over the years, similarly your body/mind has an emotional program running through you as well, which gets stronger and more difficult to change as time goes by, creating an emotional groove in our being. Over the years, our emotional program has become very defined, creating a life with narrow emotional range and a relatively constant emotional climate. This leads to not only a limited range of emotions but also constricts our life experience and our sense of who we are. Emotions are so powerful that we can feel like hostages of whatever recurring emotions we experience in our program. Guy Finley writes in *The Essential Laws of Fearless Living*, "We know that negative states limit our freedom because, in their dark presence, even our natural power of making proper choices is put to the test." Suddenly we are not only identified with a dense and narrow mind program, but we are also identified with its corresponding constricting and intense emotional charge. And so we seem to get stuck in the energy of particular emotions. Both mental and emotional programs together create an inner reality that we identify with. These programs become who we are, our personality, our sense of self, our story, and our lived experience. Some people are prone to the emotional energy of sadness and depression, some are prone to the emotional energy of loneliness or anger or anxiety. We find our self always repeating the same emotions, sometimes out of nowhere, for no particular reason, the energy just shows up in our body, in our mind and we feel stuck, unable to prevent them or escape them. My recurrent emotional patterns were anger (and the resentment that came with it) and anxiety in the form of worry and excessive planning. Sometimes I would find myself walking the dog, perfectly okay, only to be hit by an internal energy movement that I labeled as anxiety. Out of nowhere I would feel worried, ball in the stomach, clammy hands, rushing thoughts, the urge to bolt. Those of you who have felt anxious know what I mean. The same might happen with Anger, out of nowhere, for no particular reason I would be angry and start replaying in my mind a situation that upset me. I have had clients tell me of feeling lonely in the most unlikely situation, just hit by a wave of loneliness while out with friends or at a concert. Where do these emotions come from, why do they keep coming back, and why can't we seem to shake them? Our mind/body instrument is conditioned to a certain emotional vibration, anger, sadness, worry, depression, joy, gratitude and as the program is replayed continuously, over the years, we begin to identify with the emotion. It is that identification that keeps us stuck to that particular emotional signature. At some point, we begin to think "I am an angry person," "I am an anxious person," "I am lonely," "I am depressed," and it becomes us, part of a continually more defined and narrow identity, part of our life story and our experience. But what you are, your Absolute Self, that vast open space of Aware Presence, is not any particular emotion. It is unaffected by all and any of them. What you are is the pristine, still, space in which, through which and out of which the emotional energy comes into being, moves and dissolves. An emotion appears, it lives its life, and then it disappears, yet you remain. You are the one who witnesses and experiences the emotion's life cycle and when unidentified, remains unscathed by it. You are the background of the emotion, just like the paper or screen is the background of these words. Any emotional energy comes up in you, through you and is witnessed by you, but never truly defines or affects you.

~Experiential Adventure: The Absolute Self and emotions~

This experiential adventure's aim is to allow a more profound connection to your Absolute Self and its connection to emotional energy. Close your eyes, take a few deep breaths, and bring your focus within. Allow your thoughts to pass by, without getting caught up by them. Shift your focus inside and find that Aware Presence within that witnesses your experience. Allow each exhale to loosen your body and expand your spirit. Focus on the vastness that you are, your consciousness without a beginning or an end, without boundaries, without a shape, age or gender, ever present, ever free. As you shift your focus to that still and silent space within, notice how vast and open you are. Now think back to an emotionally charged time, try to feel the emotion inside you and then move back to that Aware Space that you are and ask yourself these questions? Take a couple seconds between each question to reconnect to the emotion you are working with and to your Aware Presence before you move on to the next question.

- *Is this vast Aware Presence that I am affected by my emotion or does it just witness it?*

- *Does it have a preference as to what it wishes to experience or is it completely open and unaffected by whatever experience presents itself?*

- *Do I, as my Absolute Self, want this emotional charge to go away, or am I okay with and unscathed by it?*

- *Does this still knowing Spaciousness that I am judges this emotional charge as good or bad, positive or negative? Or is it wide open to all of life, without judgments, labels or preferences?*

Dwell in this vast knowing Awareness, feel its transparent nature, its underlying peace and stillness, regardless of what shows up in it. Experience the freedom and peace of being without a gender or an age, ever present, without a story, open to and genuinely okay with all of life, including all emotions. Allow yourself to feel the peace of your True Nature and the charge of the emotion simultaneously and know that no matter what you remain pure, unchanged and undamaged.

~

The Benevolent Alive Core of Emotions

Our emotions are not a problem; at core all feelings are neutral. Have you ever heard the saying, emotion stands for energy (E) in motion? A Feeling is nothing but an alive energy that passes through us. We are the ones who with our labels, judgments, grasping and resistance have given our emotions a positive or negative charge. All emotions are neutral in nature; they are never bad, even the ones we consider negative are not bad. Emotions – our feelings – hold aliveness, they are energy and we need their energy to bring depth and vibrancy to our lives, without them we would be numb and live in a constant boredom, although even boredom is a type of energy. Emotions color and spice our every experience, without them everything would be bland. The problem is not our emotions but taking them personally, allowing them to define who we are and our life in each moment. We forget that emotions are simply passing movements; just like thoughts, neither are they ours to claim nor do they define us. When we forget this, we lose ourselves in them and become identified to our labels and judgment of them. As a personal imaginary self, you can't help but be identified to them, but as Aware Presence, you know yourself to be prior to any feeling that is arising.

The other mistake we make is to label and judge our emotions. It is our very judgments – bad, painful and negative – that make feelings seem that way. Through our labels and the beliefs that certain emotions are right while others are wrong, we freeze our experience. The moment that we put a particular emotion in a specific category we have limited ourselves as well as life. What is worse, the moment a feeling enters a category, we tend to keep it stuck there rather than allow it to change and evolve. If we decide that a specific movement of energy we feel in our body is called sadness or fear and that sadness and fear is bad, then we automatically jump to the conclusion that it is always so. We have then frozen and limited life's infinite expression, which is what the imaginary self does. Through its belief that it knows the truth of reality, the illusory self actually freezes it. The imaginary self takes a very alive emotional flow and sucks the life out of it by giving it a name or label, by defining that label as good or bad, and lastly by believing that it is always so. Have you ever stopped to see if what you label as joy or sadness or anger actually feels the same from one circumstance to the other? If you lived your life unrestricted, free of labels and judgments and other conceptual prisons, you would see that no two emotions are ever the same. That what you call anger today is completely different that the sensation that you experienced and called anger three days ago. You would know that the sadness you felt at your dog's death is completely different than the sadness you felt when your partner left, so why is it that we give them the same name. Life cannot be named or boxed in, it is fresh and new moment to moment, emotions are no different. Life is fluid, evolving and continually changing, the same is true of emotions. What feels like sadness in this instant could subtlety transform into loneliness or missing someone in the next moment and then to gratefulness for having known them in the next moment, tears of grief can turn into tears of love and gratitude, but if we stick to our label and judgment, we will miss the spontaneous movement that life always takes toward wholeness and healing.

Throughout life, if we look, we see that emotions can't be judged or boxed in. Without fear, a known 'negative' emotion, and the alertness it brings, we would not be here as a specie. If fear is always bad then no one would ever go see horror movies. People watch horror movies because they enjoy being scared, and since it is not personal, it is okay. Why do people enjoy drama? Because it makes for good entertainment, as long as it is not our drama. Even grief is an expression of our love.

As you can see, emotions are not the enemy; they are part of the perfection that is life, an intrinsic part of it and of us. Think of your favorite novels and the ones that have been acclaimed. Are they stale and flat or are they alive with movements and filled with different emotions? When a novel is good, you can't help but connect to the sorrows as well as the joys. You want to experience the full depth of it. You cry with the characters, you mourn with them and for them, you fear for them and with them, you laugh and you fall in love along with them. You don't run from any emotions, you are outraged right alongside them, as well as ecstatic. You don't close the book, the minute something bad is about to happen, no you get even more into it. If everything went absolutely perfectly and the characters had no heartaches or struggles whatsoever, it would be the most boring book ever, you probably couldn't stomach it till the end. The more a novel moves its audience, the deeper it touches them, on both side of the emotional scale, the more meaningful, rich and successful the story is. These are the books that we acclaim, label as masterpieces and read over and over. Why is it different with our own lives? Would you really want a life where you always felt the same thing or nothing at all, or a life where you only experienced a narrow range of emotions? Would you consider that a meaningful and rich life? Where would the juice come from? Your life would be flat, without meaning, excitement, vitality or depth.

Unfortunately, in an effort to protect ourselves from what we judged as bad or painful, we have in fact done the exact opposite. Through our resistance, we have created exactly what we were trying to prevent. We find ourselves stuck and repeating the exact emotions we meant to escape. We find that our life has become predictable, uncomfortable and too small for us. We find that the juice of it, the radiance of it has been muted. I am here to tell you that the antidote to your problem is in the poison itself. Open yourself up to all your emotions, stop fighting them, stop running from them and allow them to move and flow as they were meant to and you will find that you and your life will come back to life.

For us to feel alive and honor life, we need to be willing to feel it, with openness and gratitude. Without emotions, especially the ones that we label as hard and painful our life is dead. Life is energy, it is movement, it is experience and it needs to radiate with the depth of all our emotions, no restriction. There is no such thing as a negative emotion. The problem is not emotions, but the way we take ownership of them and make them personal. Emotions are not ours; they are an expression of life. They are just something we experience, a movement of energy that appears, lives and disappears in us and through us.

True happiness is not about experiencing a limited number of emotions. It's about Experiencing the full range of emotional movements and frequencies in all their glory.
– Robert A. Scheinfeld

The Prison of Definitions

As we explored, emotions one of the infinite expression and form that life takes. In and of themselves, emotions are nothing more than a movement of energy created by a particular bio-chemical signature in the brain. As specific feelings arise more and more often, our emotional program becomes set and more ingrained. As that happens, the brain will start to produce a relatively constant biochemistry creating a persistent emotional climate within us that can seem to be part of who we are. In itself, that is not the issue; the issue is our labeling, judging and then identifying to the emotions that flow through us. As the labels and identification to our emotions dismantle so does our emotional program, allowing us to feel deeper, broader and with more awareness, rather than being stuck and lost in our usual default setting. If we can stay open to the sensations, to the energy of the feeling, without resisting or grasping, without naming or judging and with the full understanding that we do not own it and that it does not define us, then we can be free of any suffering associated with the emotion itself. Emotions don't make us suffer, it is our conceptualization of them, our labels, stories and judgments of them that make us suffer. When we can drop the mind chatter and just stay with the pure and raw experience of whatever is traversing us, we are then free to live in the moment and know the aliveness that resides in every experience. Since identification to our emotions is what creates the program in the first place, without associating to the feelings that move through us, the program is slowly undone. Do you think a small child has any idea that anger is anger or that happiness is happiness or that one is good and the other is bad? The child is free to experience whatever emotion directly, free of label and judgments. A rush of a particular energy flows through your young daughter, it is experienced with openness and maybe some curiosity, maybe it feels good or not, maybe a reaction follows such as laughter or a scream of rage or tears, but whatever it feels like or whatever reaction erupts, the energy and its sensation is accepted and experienced without being shoved in a category, given a name or judged, and then it passes. If your brain was producing the chemicals that you associate with feeling happy, joyful or peaceful, you wouldn't be complaining about it, but after years of rehearsing, our mind program has a name, label and judgment for every energy pattern that comes through us, and suddenly we find ourselves imprisoned by these patterns and the labels we have given them.

> *The most important thing is this: To be able at any moment to sacrifice*
> *what we are for what we could become.*
> *– Charles Dubois*

Emotions usually include thoughts, anywhere from a label and judgment to an entire story around that particular feeling. This story, these thoughts are what stimulate and maintain the emotion. Pay attention to how the intensity of your felt emotion is in direct relation to the intensity of your thoughts about it. If you believe an event is not so important to your safety, way of life or happiness, just a part of life, then your emotional charge will be much milder and accepting. On the other hand, if you believe that a circumstance is a terrible injustice or tragedy, then the strength of your emotion will be in direct relation to those thoughts. As expected, thoughts, whether they are labels, judgments or an associated story, are the problem. They are what maintain the feeling in place in this moment and what propels it in the future. Keep in mind what was discussed in the previous chapters, we don't have access to Absolute Truths. Any thought, judgment or story we tell ourselves is just that a story. Always question the validity of your thoughts, especially the ones that are emotionally charged. The more you believe your thoughts, the more charge they have. If you know a thought to be unfounded, then how can you get worked up about it. Also question, "Do I and can I know, for sure, that this is true?" You will come to realize that you can't know anything with any certainty, whether it is a worrying circumstance about the future, a person's motivation for their action, a situation being ultimately good or bad. We simply don't know, all we have is our current lived experience.

Imagine that you are at the grocery store looking for a parking spot, you see someone leaving, so you stop and put your blinker on, respectfully and patiently waiting for the spot. The car backs up and before you have the chance to park, someone coming from the opposite direction sneaks in and steals your spot. Right at that second, your entire system responds, a flow of sensations, of more or less strong raw energy seems to explode in your body. That's okay, it is a normal reaction; when treated in a perceived unfair or hurtful way, all human beings have a reaction, it is part of this body/mind system. The mind then will come in and name the energy flow – shock, outrage, anger or whatever else. This is the beginning of a slippery slope. The moment the mind gets involved, it tends to create more of a mess. Usually, the label is quickly followed by a judgment, about yourself and/or the other party involved, followed by a story of what they did, what you did or should have done, about Karma and what they deserve, about the world and how low things have fallen and on in on it goes...This is the time to stop and question the validity and identification we have to these stories. We just can't know what was going on in the other person' mind, whether or not they saw us, whether they are a good or bad person or that they deserve to be taught a lesson, or that their behavior has anything to do with the world and human nature at large. This is the time to question what we are saying to ourselves and realize that these thoughts are just happening, that we don't have to believe them or attach ourselves to them. If we don't give them our attention, they will depart as easily as they arrived and so will the emotions associated to them. If we do believe them and identify to them, then the mind will often run these stories in loops, keeping us stuck in the past, recreating and reactivating the emotional energy in the body, imprisoning us in a vicious and helpless cycle. That example above is a personal one; within seconds I had another spot available to me, but that didn't stop me from thinking about it and feeling angry for hours. What for? Again I created my own suffering, expecting things that can't be controlled and allowing my mind to run havoc in my entire system through its judgment and continued retelling of my perceived injustice.

The key to emotional freedom is to stay with the raw emotional energy and keep the mind out of it. There is no problem, no suffering, and no confusion in the intimacy and immediacy of this present moment. Without mind involved, there is just life happening, all these movements of emotional energy arising and quickening in us, through us and around us, there might even be tears and painful sensations, but if we stay in the movement and simplicity of the Now, without defining it, judging it, grasping on to it, resisting it or needing to understand it, then we never truly suffer. When we are able to keep the mind out of it, we are able to put things in perspective and remind ourselves that it is the imaginary self that has stories, judgments and issues, not our True Self. When all stories and judgments are dropped, we are free and at peace, left with pure aliveness coursing through our body.

~Experiential Adventure: A Four-Step Process to Emotional Freedom~

The aim of this exploration is to allow you to intimately connect to any emotion without the intrusion of the mind. The next time you find yourself in the middle of a strong emotional reaction, follow the four steps bellow:

1.   Feel fully the raw sensation of the emotion in your body. Allow yourself to open completely and to connect deeply with the sensations you are feeling, the ache in your heart, the hole in your stomach, or the fire travelling through your core...

2.   Notice when the mind shows up to the victimhood party, with labels, judgments and stories. The moment you become conscious of the mind's involvement, drop all thoughts and come back to your body and the raw alive movement of energy. Acknowledge any form of resistance you might be feeling and with compassion toward yourself, come back to the sensation of the emotion.

3.   Once the mind stuff is dropped and you are back to the pure raw sensation, without any story or judgment, without any resistance or desire for it to go away. Simply welcome your feelings completely and open your body to the energy currents. You might have to do step two and three multiple times to break the nasty habit the mind has of always inviting itself where it doesn't belong.

4.   Once you are able to stay out of your head and simply remain open to the raw sensation, connect to the spacious open Presence that you are, to the vastness that looks out through your eyes and inquire whether it is the Absolute Self or the imaginary self that is distraught? Does that still

peaceful spaciousness that you are, feel angry or hurt or betrayed? Is it at all disturbed by the difficult circumstance, by the sensation coursing the body or by the story associated to it? Feel the freedom and carefree nature that lives within the depth of your own being regardless of any circumstance. Realize that it is only the illusory self that tells and holds on to a story of victimization, distress and lack.

Dwell in this vast knowing space, feel its transparent nature, its underlying peace and stillness, regardless of what shows up in it. Experience the freedom and peace of being without a gender or an age, ever present, without a story, open to and genuinely okay with all of life, including all emotions.

~

Just as our labels separate us from people and life and keep us from seeing the Truth and Reality of them, so do our labels and judgment of different emotional waves, separate us from our feelings and keep us from fully connecting with and enjoying this subtle and rich part of our self. Our labels, judgments and narrations are an unsuccessful attempt at shielding us and protecting us from life and the seeming onslaught of our emotional reactions to life. Unfortunately, these labels and narrations, in life or with our emotions, are ineffective at giving us any sense of control or protection. All they do is divide, freeze and defend the spontaneous and natural flow of experience. A truly successful and well-lived life is one that is undivided, undefended and in flow. The labels not only imprison us but also disconnect us from life and from our True Self. Rather than feeling whole and seeing life as the continuous stream that it is, we feel fragmented and our life feels fractured, which leads to this continued cycle of resisting and searching for wholeness, when in fact Wholeness was always here in us and in life all this time.

Direct Experience

As we have explored, disconnecting and resisting our emotional waves does nothing but freeze them. That freezing doesn't allow our feelings to pass through us effortlessly and naturally the way they would if we lived from an open and undefended position. This resistance, this immobilizing, builds a residue and tension in our body, which sometimes can take years to be loosened and released. Emotions without labels and judgments are nothing more than energy moving in slightly different ways, speed and frequency, each creating a slightly different sensation in the body. There was a time as a young child when we experienced all these emotional movements without having any actual words for them, it is only later that our culture gave us words for them and taught us which are good and which are bad. The truth is, what I call anger, sadness or excitement might very well feel completely different than what you call anger, sadness or excitement. For all we know, the energy movement and sensation in my body that I label "excitement" might feel very much like the energy movement that you have defined as "fear" we just can't ever know for sure since it is a totally subjective experience. So drop the story, drop the name, or the judgment and just feel the movement and the sensations; emotions without stories are not good or bad, pleasant or painful, they are just what is happening inside you in this present moment. Emotions are always moving, evolving and changing. They are just a momentary inner experience of the current flow and expression of life. This sensation that you feel right now will never return in exactly the same way, just like snowflakes, no two are ever the same. This is your one and only chance to experience it, to connect to it and know it directly, as it is in this moment, so drop all your assumed knowledge, all you think you know and just savor the movement of this moment. Don't just believe me, you don't need another belief fed to you by someone else. Explore what I telling you, find out for yourself whether sensations of anxiety or frustration when devoid of label, story and judgment are as uncomfortable or as bad as you believe. Next time you are experiencing an emotion, start with something easy and not too threatening, just drop everything that your mind is telling you about it and just experience it openly and intimately. This is life revealing itself to you, do you really want to turn your back to it? What happens to the emotion when our mind stuff is dropped? What happens to its intensity? To our experience of it? Start small and move on to stronger emotions, explore the reality of your experience, unveiled from the mind's garbage. Find out for yourself the reality of emotions and you will see that it is our resistance, our judgments of them as negative and painful, that make them so.

~Experiential Adventure: Emotions as another Movement of Life~

This experiential adventure's aim is to allow you to open to life undefended and experience that emotions are no other than a benevolent and neutral movement of life, no different than sounds, thoughts or passing sights. Close your eyes, take a few deep breaths and bring your focus within. Allow your thoughts to pass by, without getting caught up by them. Shift your focus inside and find that Aware Presence within that witnesses your experience.

Allow each exhale to loosen your body and expand your spirit. Focus on the vastness that you are, your consciousness without a beginning or an end, without boundaries, without a shape, age or gender, ever present, ever free. As you shift your focus to that still and silent space within, notice how spacious and open you are. Allow each breath to open you more and more and loosen any resistance that might be happening in this moment. Once you feel wide awake and wide open, allow your senses to open and see how effortlessly sounds and sensations come to you, flowing in and out naturally. If an emotional energy is present in your body, notice how it is no different than any other sensation or perception, albeit maybe a little more intense or intimate. Notice how it comes to you and flows and moves in and out of your awareness effortlessly. If no emotion is present, think back to an emotionally charged moment in your life. Once the emotional charge is present in your body, drop the story around it. Allow yourself to reconnect to your Aware Aliveness and notice how this feeling you feel in your body is no different than any other sensation or perception and how it comes to you and flows and moves in and out of your awareness effortlessly. If you want, you can even try this exercise with your eyes open, and notice that sights too, effortlessly appear to you and are taken in by your vast and open Aware Presence. Notice that, when we are not identified to them, our feelings are no closer to us, no more us, hold no more charge than any other sensation, than any thought, sight or sound, just an alive movement in consciousness.

Dwell in this vast knowing space, feel its transparent nature, its underlying peace and stillness, regardless of what shows up in it. Experience the freedom and peace of being without a gender or an age, ever present, without a story, open to and genuinely okay with all of life, including all emotions.

~

This is a great exercise to do when we feel consumed or completely taken over by an emotion. It is a great way to bring us back to our True Self and remember that feelings are just one movement among all other movements of life. When we look at an emotion from the perspective of our Aware Essential Self, we realize that who we are is not this emotion, that who we are is not and could never be disturbed by this energy flow that is travelling through us. It also reminds us that what we are is intimately close with all of life's movement, whether they are sensations, sights, sounds, smells thoughts or feelings, all of them flow in, to and through us and are seen and experienced by us, but none of them are us and none are closer to us than another. The sight of a glass on the table, the tree outside your window, the sound of traffic or of your neighbor's music, the smell of coffee, an ache in the belly, the grocery list floating in your head, or the energy sensation that might once have been labeled as frustration, all come and go in your awareness, you are the constant, the Aware recipient, open and awake.

Our Innate Freedom
All these movements of sound, sight, smell, sensation and taste are equally important and unimportant to who we are. They are equally real, equally close, and intimately experienced by our Aware Presence. There is no reason to allow our thoughts and feelings to be of greater importance to our experience than any other thing. The idea that our thoughts and feelings define us, define our experience and our Beingness, more so than a sight or a sound, is just that, an idea. It is a belief, mind

stuff that tells us that thoughts, feelings and sensations are closer to us, more us, while our experience of seeing, hearing, smelling or tasting is farther away, not us. But in fact, all these experiences are just that, experiences, no more or less us. They are all equally close, equally in our experience, equally seen and experienced by the vast open and knowing Awareness that we are. Our True Nature sees and experiences everything that enters our awareness effortlessly and equally, it is thought that chooses to focus on one aspect of our experience, such as an emotion, over another, giving us the impression that the sensation of anger is stronger, more real to us, more us, than the sound of the bird chirping outside your window. But in reality, our Aware Presence effortlessly experiences both the sensation and the sound simultaneously. It is our ignorance, our confusion, the imaginary self that choses to identify more closely with one over the other. We can choose to let go of that belief, of that confusion and we can choose to welcome all of our experience equally and as such understand that anger is no more or less real or defining, than the sound of the bird. All we need to do is dis-identify with the imaginary self and his obsession with particular sensations, feelings or thoughts and take our seat as the knowing Presence that is aware of them all. Again, don't believe me, just experience it for yourself.

The fact that the pure, raw experience of emotion is neutral isn't an idea or a concept. It's what you actually Experience when you Experience The Truth
– Robert A. Scheinfeld

10.
The Body – Our Intuitive Guide

I have been and still am a seeker, but I have ceased to question stars and books; I have begun to listen to the teachings my blood whispers to me.
– Herman Hesse

    Let me begin this chapter by saying that the body is alive. I don't mean alive in the way you might think. The body is literally a dance of alive movement. It is one of the ways that life moves and expresses itself. If you close your eyes and let go of any image, memory or thought of your body, what you will find is not a defined form or a particular shape, but a current of constantly moving and changing flow of sensations. The inner-feel of the body doesn't actually make or take the shape we think our body is. With your eyes closed and without involving the mind, your sense of your body might feel very vast, fluid, tender and even amorphous rather than this defined and dense mass of bones muscle and flesh. Our body is so much more than our looks, our shape, our height, weight, skin or hair color, most of the body actually resides in its inner aliveness, but unless we are sick or in pain, we often dismiss that inner world to focus solely on its outer shape. This vision is no different than looking at a cover of a book and thinking we know anything about the book itself. When I refer to the body, I don't ever mean its outer form, but its inner movement and the aliveness out of which it is made.

~Experiential Adventure: The Alive Body~

This experiential adventure is a simple exploration into the movement and flow of the inner energy of the body. The aim of this exploration is to help you feel the aliveness that moves through and in you. This exercise also should allow you to connect to your body in a curious, friendly and open way. Close your eyes, get comfortable, and take a few deep breaths allowing each breath to help you relax more and more deeply. Let whatever thoughts come up dissipate in the stillness and the movement of your breath. Let go of any image, thought, memory and beliefs about your body and simply stay with the soothing movement of the breath, feeling it come in and out, the way waves do. Breathe in and out through your nose, allowing each breath to not only relax you but open you to the flow of life that moves in and through you. Allow your awareness to lightly travel through your entire body, noticing subtle as well as less subtle sensations. Notice that with your eyes closed and with the mind free of thoughts and images, the body is not composed of flesh, muscles and bones, but simply of sensations, of movements of energy. Notice that without the mind, your body is freed of its shape and boundary, it is as vast, spacious and alive as awareness itself. Life can flow as it feels like, move in whatever direction it wants to.

Feel the vibration and subtle sensation that exist in your feet and in your hands. Notice how the aliveness moves and the different sensations and temperature it takes, sometimes cold, sometimes warm, sometimes sharp, sometimes smooth, sometimes hard, and sometimes soft and flowing.

Once you feel relaxed and connected to the alive current that is your body, come back to your head and slowly travel down your body, paying attention to how life manifests *itself in and through you. Don't hesitate to stop at any sensation that feels particularly good, loving it, swimming in it and if you encounter a point of tension, hold it gently, love it, kindly tell it that it is safe to relax for a while and breathe into it for a few breaths, before moving on. As you travel down your body drop any label or judgments of any body part and also drop any image or visualization of the body. By dropping the mind and leaving it out of it, you are freeing up the body to feel and take the shape it wishes to, not the one the mind gives it.*

Start at the top of your head and slowly move down:
- *Sensing your face (forehead, eye brows, eyes, cheek bones, ears, nose, lips, the inside of your mouth, chin and jaw)*
- *Sensing the back of your head and you neck*
- *Sensing your shoulders*
- *Sensing your upper arms*
- *Sensing your lower arms, wrists and hands*
- *Sensing your chest*
- *Sensing your upper back and down to your lower back*
- *Sensing you belly and down to your pelvis*
- *Sensing your buttocks*
- *Sensing your upper legs, both back and front*
- *Sensing your knees*
- *Sensing your lower legs, both front and back, and going down to your ankles*
- *Sensing your feet, both top and bottom*
- *Sensing your toes*
- *Dropping all labels and sensing the whole body from bottom to top and top to bottom; from front to back and back to front; from left to right and right to left, stopping to breathe in and through any point of tension, letting your*

body know that it is safe and loved in this moment
- *Sensing the whole body all at once, free of labels, images, judgments and being one with all the alive sensations*

~

The body plays a major role in helping us to not only connect to our Absolute Self but also in guiding us on our journey and in letting us know where we are stuck and whatever else needs attending to. As we saw when discussing emotions, feelings are not just a mental and emotional appearance, they are also very much sensorial. Emotions not only happen in our heads, they are felt and live in our body. If identified with, these beliefs, judgments and inner emotional movements create knots that not only bind us to our illusory state but also veil us from our True Nature. Not only is the body a guide, but it is also a mirror for the mind and emotions. Every trauma, every fear, every binding belief leaves an imprint, a hold in the body; they affect our cells, our nervous system, as well as our muscular structure. These knots show us what conditioning and what aspect of our illusory self, have yet to be explored and undone. This body, including organs like the brain and heart, has evolved in such a way to allow us to discover who we are. Most, if not all, other species on this planet are not able to realize, know and live their Essential Nature.

They don't have the ability to self-reflect, explore, transcend and transform. Whatever created us gave us this gift as our birthright, of which the body is a massive component.

Sometimes two hours of moving were as powerful as two years on the couch. I discovered that the body can't lie; put

it in motion and the truth kicks in.
– Gabrielle Roth

Our mind and emotions can lie to us, operating from a faulty program, they can trick us and keep us stuck in illusion and going in circles, but our body seems to stay true to its own knowledge. It is not quite as loud and direct as the mind and emotions, but it is a much truer compass. The body seems much more sensitive to truth and resonates with it in an intuitive way. It is also more sensitive to what is false and untrue. How many times have you known that something was off in a situation or relationship, that "this is going to end badly," yet your mind and emotions pulled you in that direction anyway, ignoring the subtle warning coming from your body? Exploring our body and the wisdom it has for us is a journey in self-love, trust and intuition, you have so much wisdom built right into you that goes unnoticed.

Our Greatest Ally
There are a few ways that your body will let you know you are heading in the right direction and shedding the false while letting in more light. In this way it is an invaluable guide and a wonderful tool. One of the sensations related to loosening knots and shedding what is false is a deep sense of relaxation in the body, sometimes it can even be described as a rush of energy or bliss. As you open yourself to truth, the heart and mind are slowly awakened and liberated, a sense of lightness, aliveness and spaciousness can be felt in the body. Another common sensation in the process of transformation is a soft and sweet feeling of tenderness or love in the chest area, which is usually concurrent with our heart opening slowly as the knots of conditioning are

loosened. When our identification starts to shift from the imaginary self to the Absolute Self, our nervous system relaxes, our muscles and the tension and trauma held there loosen and release, and our heart opens. As we take our seat as the Aware Presence that we are, we resist to life less, we hold on to positions and beliefs less, which leads us to experience less suffering and less stress. The reduction of suffering and stress is directly experienced in the body in the form of less colds, less headaches or stomach issues, an overall reduction of most aches and pain and finally a felt sense of trust, comfort and appreciation for this body that accompanies you on this journey, always supports you and never stops working and fighting for you during your entire life. Day and night, seven days a week, your body works for you and for your health, heart beating, breathing, digesting, cleaning itself, fighting viruses. It is one with life and without it, you could not have this beautiful experience of being alive, of growing, loving and transforming.

When we listen deeply and lovingly, when we slowly explore with our whole being the entirety and aliveness of our body, we find ourselves in contact and communication with the most powerful teacher, the most trusted confidant and the clearest guide on our journey to wholeness. There have been people whose entire transformation, whose entire recognition of their Absolute Nature has taken place solely through their body, through an illness or through dance or some other kind of movement, sport or somatic therapy. This was not my personal experience, but I say this to point out how important your body is in recognizing the Truth of who you are and living a life of freedom, peace and fearlessness. You can have a very clear philosophical understanding of your Absolute Nature, have experienced major changes in yourself and your life, but if you never go into the body where the knots that bind you reside, you will never be truly free. Without delving in the body and meeting directly, intimately and lovingly what binds you, there is only so far you can reach, and your journey is not complete. We are a thinking, feeling and sensing being and all transformation needs to happen on those three levels, the level of mind or thoughts and beliefs; the level of the heart and emotions and on the level of the body, the senses and all the knots of our conditioning. That is the holistic path to Truth and wholeness.

~Experiential Adventure: Recognizing the Voice of Truth~

The voice of truth, finding our inner compass, is not always easy. Our minds, our fears, our wounded parts, all have a voice and sometimes, to be met, heard and feel in control, they can speak very loudly. The voice of Truth, on the other hand, is subtle, sometimes even silent; it doesn't clamor or fight for attention, and it has no wish to control our lives. For so long, we have dismissed its quiet ways in favor of what is loud and commanding, that we have forgotten how to listen to it and how to recognize its sweet movement, as light as the breeze. Yet there is one place that this still knowing voice cannot be bullied out of, and that is the heart and gut. What a paradox that when looking for truth, when looking for wisdom and guidance, we must step out of our head and enter the body.

Every day, start meditating on the part of your body that extends from below your belly button to your collarbone. You can even put your right hand on your lower belly and your left hand at the center of your chest to direct your attention. Every day for a few minutes put your attention on this area, explore it silently, feel the breath move there, feel the sweet aliveness flowing there, stay with whatever knots you find coming up and, just hold this area in open curious tenderness, with a simple willingness to just meet it and receive it fully. Only then will you be able to remember the tender knowing voice that emanates from this area of your being. Once you meditate with, receive and connect with this area of your body a few times (notice that I didn't say "meditate on," but with, this is an intimate meeting, a communion and relationship), start going there during your inquiries about life. This can be done with spiritual questions and well as very ordinary questions, and see what it says. At first you might not hear or feel much, since we are used to boisterous answers from our mind, but the more you come back to yourself and your core (literally) the more refined your hearing will become and you will find there a peaceful, loving, tender Presence that is in harmony with all existence and its voice will never lead you astray. When you become connected to this inner Essence, you might feel that its guidance comes as a whisper that is different from the voice of the mind. Or you might sense an openness, expansion and easiness of breath when you are heading in the right direction and the answer is "yes" and a tightness, an inability to take a full breath, when the answer is "no" and you are going down an unnecessary path. Let your heart and core guide you. This is the seat of the soul, the seat of intuition.

~

The experience of one's own nature as subtle, unified consciousness – is revealed through deeply inhabiting one's body...(it) is not just an open intellect, but also an open heart, and an open body.
– Judith Blackstone

11.
Energy – The Fuel that Animates Us

I am somewhat exhausted; I wonder how a battery feels when it pours electricity into a non-conductor?
– Arthur Conan Doyle

The Vitality of an Open Heart

We have a body, but we also have a more subtle energy body. Our level of energy, in many ways, directs the kind of experience we will have. The most enjoyable experience is seriously dampened if we are exhausted and depleted. On the other hand, if we feel full of energy and enthusiasm for life, the dullest experience can seem exciting. Our energy level is affected by our health, our diet, the quality of our sleep and also by our openness and attitude to life. When we close our heart and resist an event, our energy level is automatically disturbed; just the way water flow is blocked when the hose has a knot. For example, let's say you are very enthusiastic about your new job, you feel alive and full of energy. In this enthusiasm, in this aliveness, you look forward to going to work, you feel like you could work 12-hour days without any problems. What happens to your energy level, to your enthusiasm when your boss comes in and dismisses your idea? My guess is that right away you feel a resistance to the comment, a disappointment, an embarrassment and your whole being closes in response to your resistance, lessening your energy, which is felt as a heaviness and tiredness in the body and a lack of enthusiasm toward your work. If we stay aware, we can feel this resistance, this shutting down happening throughout our body, like a punch in the stomach, an ache in the heart, a vulnerability and a need to protect and defend that was not there two minutes prior to the disappointment. From that point on, your energy level, your enthusiasm for your job is reduced, at least until you learn to reopen and become excited about work again.

People feel this heaviness and inner closing in response to any type of disappointment or grief. For example, the end of a relationship or the loss of a loved one always lead to feeling depleted, heavy, run down and closed off. Depression has been related to a persistent state of closing, a continued knot that blocks the flow of our inner energy and kills our enthusiasm for life. Our energy level can also be a guide, a form of intuition to what is in alignment with us and what is no longer healthy and beneficial for us. We can outgrow people, jobs, hobbies even geographical regions or belief systems. One of the first signs that an activity or relationship is no longer for us is a sense of depletion that we feel when we are involved with them.

Learning to listen to your energetic responses, learning to keep your energy level in check, learning not to close at life's disappointment and pain and learning to replenish your self is an important aspect of finding happiness and living life fully. We need to show kindness to ourselves by taking the time to notice when we are depleted and by taking the time to recharge our batteries. The way we respond to life's difficulties, our ability to find our way out of problems and find successful solutions, our ability to connect to others and build healthy relationships, and even our remembering of our Aware Presence and our ability to live from that spaciousness are all related to our energy level. Have you ever noticed how differently you react to a similar situation simply based on how tired or hungry you are? How do you handle a setback, a nasty comment or someone cutting you off on the road, at the end of a long rough day? Is your response and the way the circumstance affects you internally exactly the same than if you were rested and having a great day? If you are like most people, the answer is "no." When drained, we are more easily hurt, more reactive, less patient, less kind, less able to stay open and connected to the Aware Presence that we are.

Responding over Reacting

This has been a continuous theme when working with private clients. Over the years it has become very clear to me that when people are drained, their ability to answer gracefully to life's little annoyance is significantly decreased. Their ability to elevate themselves, recognize their innate wisdom and peace is muffled, the way music sounds when under water. As a matter of fact people's ability to handle any annoying or disappointing situation is directly related to their energy level. The more energy we have, the clearer, kinder and more effective our responses are, and the more enthusiasm we have for life. The more depleted our energy level is, the more reactive, nastier, louder, ineffective and miserable we are. Notice my word choice, when energy levels are up, we respond. When energy levels are low, we react.

Part of our job on this journey toward emotional freedom and fulfillment is to become aware of our energy level and help mediate it. The first effective way out of our funk, out of our depleted state, is to find the courage to relax and open to life and to our felt sense, no matter what circumstances we find ourselves in. For example, if we find ourselves depleted and depressed, to resist our depression only creates more depression. If we are willing and able to start connecting to and sensing our depletion and disillusionment, without mentally entertaining and encouraging it, but simply to authentically meet it, we find that our whole being starts to open and out of that openness emerges the energy we need to step out of our gloom and see life freshly. We must find the courage to stop closing, to stop resisting and embrace this moment, embrace this very breath, this sensation and perception we are experiencing right this second, and just stay here for a moment willing to be open, undivided and undefended because resistance always drains us further. Closing down creates a vicious cycle in which the more we resist, the more drained and vulnerable we feel, which leads us to close and defend even more, which continues to drain us and so forth. So having the courage to let our walls collapse, to open and feel deeply, even for one minute, is the first step and it can be as easy as taking a few deep breaths and asking our body to relax and let go of tension. Only then can we start to replenish ourselves. We are not unlike batteries, there is only so much vitality available to us in any given time. When our energy runs low, we start to breakdown, until we just shut down completely. Like a battery we need to be recharged regularly or we are completely ineffective and to some degree some of us can actually become malfunctioning.

The Scale - A Tool of Awareness
Everybody is different, you have to keep track of what depletes you in your life and the degree at which point you start to close down and become ineffective, no one

else can do it for you. An easy way to get to know yourself and your energy level is to keep track of it by using a simple scale between one to ten, 1 being you are empty, completely useless, maybe even nasty and 10 you are so full of energy you are high on life and nothing could get you down or affect your mood. At a 10, you could have the patience and kindness of The Buddha. Figure out around which number you start to become ineffective, tired, moody. Pay attention to the level where you start to lose track of your values and of your Absolute Peaceful Nature.

Keep a daily log of where your energy level is at and what you feel drains you or recharges you throughout the day. Become aware of chronically depleting circumstances or people and try to see how they can slowly be remediated and how you might try to accept them as they are and open your heart. By shifting your daily routine, by taking a few quick breaks here and there, by taking the time to breathe, by eating a snack, by choosing to avoid certain people or situations when you are already drained, by taking the time to connect to your Aware Presence and by choosing to stay open rather than close and resist, you regain influence and power over your inner energy source and by extension over your entire life.

In the end, apart from very specific cases, most of the time how we handle a situation and how happy or at peace we feel, has much more to do with how we are feeling energetically, how open we are to life and how connected we are the vast stillness that is our Essential Self, than to the events or circumstances of our life. You can handle a huge stressor very effectively if you are in the right frame of mind and have the right energy level. You can also handle the smallest of issues dreadfully if you are drained and completely identified with the anxiety, lack and confusion of the imaginary self. Without energy, there is no way to enjoy your life, and to find the peace and happiness that is your Essence. Outer circumstances are only a very small piece of the puzzle, even very blessed individuals can feel lost, afraid and depressed without the right energy level and a direct connection with their True Nature.

Making Aligned Choices
Once we have figured out what minimum energy level we need to maintain to stay effective, kind, peaceful and happy and to keep our connection to our Aware Presence, it is our responsibility, to ourselves as well as to the world to sustain and preserve it at all cost. This can be done in two ways, first by becoming aware of what drains us and finding ways to let go of those aspects of our life that are unhealthy or that we have outgrown, and secondly, by becoming aware of what recharges us and fills us with enthusiasm and following our bliss. It is important to keep in mind that life, even under the best of circumstances, is always a little bit draining. Working, taking care of children, commuting, doing chores, paying bills – just living – can be draining business. That is a normal part of life, but this kind of depletion, is easily remediated by resting, eating a good meal, taking a nice hot shower, or even going for a walk. On the other hand, the kind of depletion that arises from being out of alignment with our Self, with Truth and Love, such as being in an unhealthy relationship or in a job that no longer matches our values, cannot be fixed with a nap or a walk. These kinds of drains require some real honesty and the courage to make difficult choices for our sake and the sake of those around us. Every time we stay in a job, role, relationship or any type of situation we know to be

unhealthy, unloving or too small for us, we abandon ourselves a little more, we close a little more, and the voice of our Absolute Self and of our soulful longing gets a little weaker, and over time it becomes harder to do something about it. After a while, our body or mental health will start to show the wear and tear. They will start to abandon us just like we have abandoned them.

We need energy to live complete and fulfilling lives, our body and mind need energy to function optimally. This is something we all have in common, yet we are also different in what drains, maintains, refreshes and revitalizes us. Talking on the phone to a friend at the end of a long day can be draining for one person or a boost for another. Sometimes it is not what we do but who we do it with that can affect our energy level. To use the example of talking on the phone, talking on the phone with your best friend can be a boost of energy, but talking on the phone with your brother could be completely depleting. Get curious as to what drains and recharges your batteries. Find what helps you stay open and what makes you shut down, the healthy and successful functioning of your life depends on it. Your ability to transform yourself and live from the point of view of your Absolute Self depends on it. Being happy and at peace depends on it.

12.
Crazy Science - A World Inside Out

Nothing is as it seems.
The common view is that
There is a subjective observer
Observing an objective world;
The former separate from
The latter.
Nothing is as it seems.
– Wu Hsin

I have wondered where to place this chapter in the book. Should I have placed it at the beginning to give a theoretical and scientific framework for the book, but risk turning people off? Should it go at the end and be used as a conclusion and a scientific sidebar to the book, though maybe a dry one? Or should it go somewhere in the middle? This is probably the headiest of the chapters in this book, and it is not a necessary one to enjoy and get most out of the book, but it gives interesting credence to the message of this book, outside of my voice and the many quotes I use throughout. I decided to set this chapter somewhere in the middle, so that the scientific theory might color and further enliven the first half of the book, and also be an interesting scientific jumping board upon which the rest of the book is built. I have tried to make it as simple to understand as I could while keeping as close to the theories as possible. I am in no way a scientific mind; my degrees are in the social sciences, and my experience is in Spirit. This chapter is based on my understanding of the literature out there, with enough direct quotes from different physicist and other great minds to give credibility and support to what is written. All the books that are discussed in this chapter will be on the reading list at the end of this one, but if you have any further interest in the topic of quantum physics and the nature of Reality, Consciousness and spirituality, there are tons of great books out there that can be found in most retailers. A search on Amazon.com would be a great place to start. All right then, let's get started down this rabbit hole.

I think that science without religion is lame and, conversely, that religion without science is blind. Both are important and should work hand-in-hand...Everyone who is seriously involved in the pursuit of science becomes convinced that a spirit is manifest in the laws of the universe – a spirit vastly superior to that of man.
– Albert Einstein, physicist

Matter doesn't Matter
Reality is a tricky thing. If I asked you, "What is real?" you might say, "If I can touch it, feel it, see it, hear it, than it is real." Kind of like if it looks like a duck, it walks like a duck, it quacks like a duck than it is a duck. Makes sense, right? And for most of us, that is the way we live our lives. We never stop to consider, what is really real? What do we know for sure? Can we trust our mind, our senses? For most of us, what matters is matter, pun intended. But quantum mechanics has now shown that what we think is real is not made of "real stuff" and what we perceive as a certainty; only exist as a probability, a potentiality. When

we start to delve a little deeper, below the surface, in the nature of reality, we encounter problems, paradoxes, things, as it turns out, are not what they seem.

> *Everything we call real is made of things that cannot be regarded as real.*
> *– Niels Bohr, physicist*

The first problem we come across is that matter, which seems so real, so hard, so easy to measure and grab a hold of, literally and figuratively is actually not made of anything. Yes that is the end of the sentence. Matter, when broken down into smaller and smaller units, which are called particles, turn out to not be made of stuff at all, but mostly of an invisible substance, a sort of energy or field. The very thing that appears hard, material, easy to measure, weigh and see is actually made of a substance, if we can even call it that, that is invisible and cannot be touched or measured in anyway. The material turns out to be immaterial. The perceptible emanates out of the imperceptible. Everything emerges out of 'nothing' or what I like to call an empty fullness. Peter Russell, a physicist and psychologist, writes in his book, *From Science to God,* "As the early twentieth-century British physicist Sir Arthur Eddington put it, 'Matter is mostly ghostly empty space.' To be more precise, it is 99.9999999 percent empty space." For most of us, that's a difficult statement to wrap our mind around. We cannot comprehend exactly how this is possible and what it means to our lives.

Another problem we encounter while exploring consciousness and quantum physics is the issue of not having the language to explain it and talk about it properly. In the end, many of the greatest minds of our world agree that what seems so real to us, is not only made up of empty invisible space, but that space like energy is made up of mathematical forms or mathematical patterns of potentiality, which correspond to the infinite possibilities of material structures, all the shapes that this empty space could potentially take. Empty space is actually a field of potentiality that holds all probable and possible forms that matter could ever possibly take. This field holds and literally is infinite potential and can only be understood in mathematical terms. As the famous physicist Lothar Schafer writes in his wonderful book, *Infinite Potential: What Quantum Physics Reveals about How We Should Live*, "The most important part of the world is invisible...The virtual states are empty of matter but filled with potentiality. They represent the possibilities of the material world." Peter Russell defines it in this way, "They [subatomic particles] are nothing like matter as we know it. They cannot be pinned down and measured. Much of the time they seem more like waves than particles. They are like fuzzy clouds of potential existence." Even with my limited understanding and my personal dislike of math, there is one thing I can tell you without getting a PhD in quantum mechanics: Reality is significantly different than the way we perceive it or believe it to be. This seemingly empty space is not empty as we usually understand it, but actually full of possibilities, hence my reference of it as an empty fullness. Reality is not in fact made of matter but made of empty invisible space-like field that is empty of all things material but full of infinite potential and can only be grasped or understood through mathematical formulas.

There is no place in this new kind of physics both for the field and the matter,

for the field is the only reality.
– Albert Einstein, physicist

The Matter of Consciousness

The second issue we encounter with the reality of matter, involves consciousness itself. The same belief system and theoretical framework that puts matter as the center of reality, also believes that consciousness is something that arises out of matter, out of the developing outer material world. The theory is that as the universe developed, solar systems arose and then came planets, and with the right chemistry, life developed and with life, consciousness appeared. At first, the degree of consciousness was as simple as the life forms, but as life became more complex, as brains and nervous systems developed, consciousness evolved. At first glance, this concept seems to make reasonable sense. One problem scientists run into is explaining how consciousness, itself, developed. Science continues to explore how it is that consciousness developed out of matter, but has not been able to find an explanation that holds up thus far. As science tells us, there is nothing in our brain, nervous system or body or in that of any animal or plant life that explains an inner reference point. Animals, plants, and human beings all have an inner world. To some degree, all conscious life forms are aware of, interact with and respond to their experience and environment. For a long time science told us that matter itself, particles, all that creates the world, including conscious life forms, is insentient, inanimate; an electron, a molecule doesn't have feelings, thoughts, beliefs, it doesn't feel pain or pleasure, it doesn't evolve or learn new things. So how is it that a bunch of inanimate unconscious stuff can comes together and create a form that is itself a conscious being?

How is it that consciousness, an inner experience and reference point, evolves out of an unconscious fabric? As Peter Russell writes in *From Science to God*, "How can something as immaterial as consciousness ever arise from something as unconscious as matter?... the capacity for inner experience could not evolve or emerge out of entirely insentient, non-experiencing matter."

As we explored at the beginning of this chapter, at the core of matter is a field of energy, a substance that is itself immaterial, yet very much alive. This field is the substratum of life, it carries within it all potential forms that life could ever take. Peter Russell writes that the new theory is that "Experience can only come from that which already has experience. Therefore the faculty of consciousness must be present all the way down the evolutionary tree." Science is now exploring the idea that consciousness exists in the non-material aspect of matter, which means that consciousness is prior to matter. It is not that consciousness emerges out of a continuously evolving form of matter, but the other way around, it is matter that evolves out of an already existing consciousness. As matter evolved into more and more complex life forms, as organisms, brains and nervous systems developed so did the ability to channel, experience and understand the already existing consciousness. I would theorize that as we continue to evolve we become more and more able to know and experience the totality and wholeness that life is, that we are. One goal of evolution might be the continuous ever-expanding ability to recognize the completeness that already is. Max Planck, who is thought of as one of the fathers of quantum theory said, "I regard consciousness as fundamental. I regard matter as derivative from consciousness. We cannot get behind consciousness. Everything that we talk about, everything that we regard as existing, postulates consciousness."

> *Quantum Physics proved beyond a doubt, over three generations ago, that things didn't come first. First came the void...Actually, that space isn't totally empty; it isn't a vacuum, a void, or nothing: It is filled with potentiality.*
> *– Lothar Schafer, physicist*

The Primordial Nature of Awareness – You are That

What does that mean for us? Well it leads us back to our Absolute Nature, if the ground of all matter, of the entire material world, is a conscious field of potential, then the ground of your being is no other than it as well, an aware open field of potential. Everything that exists emanates, emerges out, is made of and is superimposed on top of this alive aware field. That is true of all of life, both sentient beings and objects. Everything that makes you who you are, your identity, your body, your personality, your thoughts, your beliefs, your emotions, your story, memories, hopes and dreams, your roles and your possessions, all are finite and changing. All of these things, properties and aspects of your being, emerge out of and are superimposed on top of an infinite, eternal and unwavering Beingness. Your true nature as Aware Presence is a vast conscious field of potential. You are that field. Prior to your story, personality and even prior to your body, age and gender, you are. As awareness, you eternally exist, prior to and after any of those other things that are overlaid on top of you. As David Bhodan states in his book *The Lazy Man's Way to Enlightenment,* "Overlooking the ever-present and necessary awareness prior to all content and deeming it insignificant, you don't see that without it, nothing is. Nothing can stand independent of the awareness that perceives it. And in this overlooking, you completely miss out on the discovery of what you really are." And what everyone and everything really is. He continues to guide us to recognize that this Aware Presence "is closer than breathing, nearer than hands and feet. You are prior to all mental constructions at the same time allowing all mental constructions...Emptied of all notions, consider that all along, you've been whole and complete, never lacking a thing."

Let's explore David Bhodan's words for a moment; if I was to remove everything that you think is you, your possessions, your roles, your feelings, if I was to leave your mind blank and empty of all beliefs, thoughts, memories and hopes and dreams for the future, even the concept and feel of your body, would you cease to exist? If I took everything that you assumes makes you who you are, your identity and all sensory stimuli, would you disappear, would you go unconscious? Imagine that you are in an accident and you wake up from a coma. All you see are white lights on the ceiling, you find yourself unable to move, your mind blank with no memories, no ideas of who you are, no concept even that you are a human being, a man or a woman, you have no knowledge of your age, culture or the color of your skin, or even that you have a body. Suddenly you hear a voice, and you find yourself understanding what it is asking, "Who are you?" It says, "What can you tell me about yourself?" Given your current state and situation, without a story, a past or a future, or a concept of self, what can you answer? What is the only thing you can know about yourself at that very moment? Obviously you know that you exist, that even without the idea that you are human or that you have a body, a name, a history, even without any beliefs or concepts, without all these "things," you remain, aware and alive. If I remove all of your inner as well as your outer experiences, you might not be aware of this or that, but you would be aware that you are aware, aware of your own existence; that is undeniable. That is who you are, the unmanifested formless Aware Presence, which is timeless and prior to all objects. You exist outside of time and regardless of the appearance or disappearance of any object, thing, circumstance or form.

Even the material world around us, the chairs, the tables, the rooms, the carpet, time included, all of these are nothing but possible movements of Consciousness... Quantum physics has been so clear. Heisenberg himself said "Atoms are not things, they're only tendencies". They're all possibilities of Consciousness.
– Amit Goswam, quantum physicist

It's All Inside your Head

The next issue we have with the nature of reality shows up in the disparity between our inner perception of the world and the reality of the world outside of us. All alive beings, whether human, animal, insect or even vegetal have awareness, but each experiences the outer world in a different way. Even within the same species, experiences and perception can vary. For example, there is no way to know if all or most human beings experience and interpret the outer world in the same way. Obviously how experiences are lived is an inner relative movement based on the person and their state of mind. But what about what is perceived with the senses? We assume that the world out there exist as it is, independently of us and we also assume that our senses – our sights, smells, hearing, tastes and tactile sensations –are stable from one person to the other and even from one specie to the other, but can we be sure of that?

Our experience of the world says a lot more about the development of our brain, nervous systems and other function of our body/mind than of the actual world out there. What you perceive to be reality, a world outside is only an image and sensory interpretation of your brain. Light hits the retina of your eyes, sound vibrations hit minuscule hairs in your ears, molecules in the air hit your nostrils and receptors, and sensations come to your skin cells and nerve endings...They all transfer electrochemical impulses as messages that travel to different centers in your brain. Your brain then creates an inner interpretation of all your senses and constructs a full image and experience of what you believe to be the outside world. Everything that we take for granted as existing out there, such as colors, sounds or smells, only exists on the inside. Your mind is an extraordinary rendering machine. Michael Singer explains, "When you take in the world through your senses, it is actually energy that is coming into your being. Form itself does not come into your mind and heart. Form stays outside, it is processed by your senses into energy patterns that your mind and heart can receive and experience. Your senses are, indeed, electronic sensing devices. But if the patterns that are coming into your psyche create a disturbance, you will resist them and not allow them to pass through you." It is not reality itself that we struggle with, but it is the impression our mind creates about reality that with struggle with and resist.

Reality is merely an illusion, albeit very persistent one.
– Albert Einstein, physicist

Coming back to our rendering of reality, we find that the light that hits our eyes and the electrochemical impulses that travel through our optic nerves to the brain is colorless. It is only in the brain, once the data is processed and constructed into an image that a color appears. Peter Russell in his book *From Science to God*, asks us to "consider our experience of the color green...In the physical world there is light of various frequencies, but the light itself is not green...No color exists there. The green we see is a quality created in consciousness. It exists only as a subjective experience in the mind." Can we even know for sure that we all see the same green? Maybe your green looks like my blue? Or your green is dark, while mine is light. There are indigenous cultures that don't experience colors in the same way as we do in the western world. Animals see colors in completely different ways and variations than we do, so what is real? What we experience is not out there, only an interpretation, a creation constructed in our mind and body. The same is true of sound, as Peter Russell explains; "There is no sound in the physical reality, simply pressure waves in the air. Sound exists only as an experience in the mind of a perceiver – whether that perceiver is a human being, a deer, a bird, or an ant." Mind blowing, isn't it? Now add beliefs to the mix, and the world we perceive is completely constructed in our mind and probably has little to do with what is actually out there. All we ever know of a world out there is our experience and perception of it, and both experience and perception occur in our awareness. Experience and perception are inner happenings, part of us, and never independent of us. Look at a tree or any object in the distance, can you tell me where seeing, your inner sense and experience of sight ends and the object begins? Or does the object appear within the awareness and experience of seeing? It is impossible to say where we and our inner experience ends and a supposedly outer world begins. There is no such thing as an objective real outer world; there is only a subjective inner experience, an extension of self. The world doesn't exist out there; it emanates and lives within, inside awareness. As the physicist Lothar Schafer wrote, "You might say that you have no experience of things, but only of your experience of things. Thus, watching the world can tell you nothing about what the world is like." There is no telling how much of us transfers in what we see, hear, feel, sense and experience out there. We can't ever say where we end and where the world begins, both are One, each extending out of the other. Just like beauty, perception is in the eye of the beholder.

> *Our perceiving self is nowhere to be found*
> *within the world-picture, because*
> *it itself is the world-picture.*
> *– Erwin Schrodinger, quantum physicist*

Peter Russell writes, "In short, all that I perceive – everything I see, hear, touch, and smell – has been reconstructed from sensory data...Our perception of the world has the very convincing appearance of being 'out there' around us, but it is no more 'out there' than are our nightly dreams... The truth is, our waking reality is as much a creation of our minds as our dreams...all experience is an image of reality created in the mind...We suffer a delusion when we believe the images in our minds are the external world. We deceive ourselves when we think that the tree we see is the tree itself." We can't know reality directly, our understanding and experience of it is always filtered through our body, our nervous system, our brain and our beliefs. In reality the world exists in consciousness; we live in an inner world and know very little, if anything, about the outer world. And since everyone does the same thing, we are all trying to communicate and relate to each other through our inner interpretations and filters, rather than through reality itself. Since we can never remove ourselves out of the equation, even in scientific studies, we always have an observer bias. Physics might be the study of matter, of reality, of the objective, but in the end, it can only be experienced, explored and understood from our subjective stance, from the observer, from our consciousness. We can assume or theorize how your neighbor, your dog, a bat, or a dolphin experiences the world, but we can never experience it and know it directly.

As Many Worlds as there are Beings

We all know that animals experience the world differently than us. They experience a different aspect of reality than us. Take your good friend the dog, his auditory system as well as his sense of smell is much more developed than yours. It is said that a dog can remember someone's scent for years after they have last seen him or her. As it turns out, we all have a very specific personal smell. The dog doesn't recognize an old family friend he hasn't seen in years through vision, but through his highly developed sense of smell. Not only is the way your dog experiences the world completely different than you, but I would guess that his entire world is a completely different world than yours. What about other species, how do they experience the world? Think of cats, bats and certain birds and insects that possess a visual system so developed that they can see at night or experience many more colors and visual details than us, sometimes seeing different frequencies of light such as ultraviolet. What of certain types of fish or aquatic mammals that seem to have a sonar-like sense – what does their world look like and feel like to them? These differences are also true of time and space. Not only do different species experience time and space in different ways, but people also experience time and space differently. Even something as fundamental to reality as the concept of time and space is a mental construction. Two people can be experiencing the same activity and have a completely different experience of time. Why does time fly some of the time and seems to stand still at other times? So which is the true reality? The one we experience, or the one the dog or the whale experiences? Or the one the bat experiences? Or even the one your neighbor experiences? Obviously there is no true reality out there, only aspects and interpretation of potentially infinite realities.

We can conclude that the visible reality emanates out of a realm of potentiality that is underlying all things...The visible world is an actualization – an emanation – out of a domain of transmaterial and transempirical potentiality forms...
Physical reality is driven by inner images.
– Lothar Schafer, physicist

From Waves to Particles – From Particles to Waves
There is a theory in the world of quantum physics that asserts that everything in the universe, including maybe the universe itself, exists only as a form of potentiality

wave, as an aware field of infinite possibilities, until a seeming observer interacts with it. It is only when the wavelike aware field of potentiality encounters an aware subject, a mind of some type, that the waves turn into particles – matter, measurable, visible stuff. It is the observer's expectations and assumptions when interacting with the field of possibilities that create a stable and coherent image and experience that is put together and interpreted in and by the observer's inner world. Most of the law of attraction theories are based from this understanding of physics.

What that means for us is that at night, when you go to sleep, your body, your bedroom, your story, all that makes you who you think you are and what you think your life is, all matter, goes back to invisible waves of potentiality, and when you wake up, the aware field that you are recreates your mind, your body, everything that is you, and a world for this body/mind to interact with. When our mind emerges out of the Aware Presence that we are, our stories about ourselves and the world also reappear in this mind. Through these emerging stories and beliefs, all the invisible waves of potentiality are transformed into the material particle state, which takes the form of our body, our bedroom and the world we supposedly live in. What that would mean is that the moment you leave your bedroom to go to work, it ceases to be in particle form – real, visible – and goes back to an invisible wave like field of potentiality; that is until an observer, yourself, your daughter or roommate, comes into contact with it, at which point it reappears to match the observer's expectation and is experienced in their mind through their senses. This is a working theory at this point, but it sure would explain why we all notice or see different things. Have you ever sent your mate or child in the other room to grab something you know is there, like your purse or keys, only to have them come back and say they didn't see it? Sure enough as you go back in the room it is right where you thought it was, and they are confused that they failed to see it. How often do we look for something for an hour that someone else finds in two minutes? Is it possible that the object you were looking for wasn't actually there when you were looking for it, but materialized for the next person based on their expectation? We can't ever know for sure since we can't really be in two places or two minds at once, but it is a theory that is worth considering. In the end, there are as many worlds as there are subjective minds. As the physicist Lothar Schafer writes, "When electrons, atoms, and molecules [what the material world consists of] are left alone, they become waves!...In interactions with objects in their environment, these fields can contract abruptly to a point, which then appears to us as a material particle." We all see the world through our own lenses, our own beliefs, and expectations. There is not one world inhabited by seven billion people, but seven billion worlds that are continually interacting with each other, and significantly more than that if you account for other sentient life forms, which also create their own reality, their own version of planet earth. It is unclear how scientifically accurate this theory is; it can't quite be proven or disproved, needless to say when you encounter a theory as mind boggling as this one, there are going to be dissident views.

Science is clear about one thing. In scientific labs throughout the world, scientists have tried to see, measure, or experience the wavelike state of a particle but have been unable to. The moment an observer – a subjective mind – enters the picture, the wave/particle goes from potentiality wave state to material particle form. We, as observers, never can see or experience a particle in its invisible wave like field, the moment we interact with it, it takes the shape of a particle or a physical form, which is experienced in and through our awareness. Let's go back for a second and revisit what this theory means for us.

All forms, all objects, all things that can be seen and experienced, such as the world, your body, your thoughts, stories or your identity only exist within you and from the point of view of an aware observer. In deep sleep or if you are knocked unconscious, all those objects, the world, your body, your thoughts, beliefs and your identity disappear, only the aware field of infinite potential remains. It is not that all objects cease to exist per say, but they (including mind stuff, thoughts, feelings, beliefs) return to a sort of wave like potential limbo, waiting to be once again, resurrected and rematerialized by a subjective aware observer. In deep sleep, when your mind is not active, only pure Aware Presence, without any object to be aware of, remains. You are that Awareness, that field. Out of you, the aware field of infinite possibilities, a subjective mind appears and with it an identity and a world, this is experienced when you enter dream sleep or when you wake up. So out of Aware Presence, a mind comes into being, out of that mind arises a story in time created of the past, present and possible future. This mind also has beliefs, expectations and assumptions, which create a body and a world. You as the Absolute Self, are prior to the mind, to its story and beliefs and to the body and the world. You are prior and beyond all of those 'things', they emerge out of you, not the other way around. Both your inner world and your outer world arise in, through and out of the vast, open field of Awareness that you are. Both your inner and outer world are an extension of you, one Wholeness.

If reality is an 'undivided wholeness", as David Bohm, one of the pioneers of quantum physics, believed, everything that comes out of wholeness belongs to it, including our consciousness.
– Lothar Schafer, Physicist

I speak of an infinite and limitless Awareness prior to any object, some of my clients have asked me, "How do I know that I am still aware in deep sleep? I don't have an awareness of my Absolute Self in deep sleep, I have no awareness of myself at all?" That is a fair question since most human beings who are identified with their imaginary self don't have a sense of being "here", of their exitense, when they are in deep sleep. It is not that you don't have an awareness of yourself in deep sleep, but simply that since your mind is no longer active, you don't have a sense of time or space and without time and space there is no memory, no story, no sense of a personal self. In deep sleep, your imaginary self and its world fall away, there isn't any sense of past or future, no thoughts, objects, shapes or sensations, there aren't any dreams present either, and of course without thoughts and a story, there are no problems, no suffering, so there is no reference point for us to grab unto. In waking life, we know our own sense of self by separating or relating to a supposed other or outer object of some type, like a tree or another person, or by identifying to some type of personal or inner object like our body, a sensation, a thought or an emotion, but in deep sleep there are no objects whatsoever to compare ourselves to, grab unto or delineate ourselves from, there is no mind, no world, no sensations, so we assume that we are not there. The truth is, you as Awareness, are present, but you just don't have an awareness of who you think you are, you no longer have a definite shape, a beginning and an end, a story, a body, a personality, problems or goals, so you believe we are not there, when in fact it is the imaginary self that is absent. The imaginary self is gone, but life, the Absolute Self, the potential field, doesn't cease to exist, the one you are prior to your story, doesn't cease to exist. You remain as a clear aware field. How do we know that? It is simple, you wake up and an Aware Presence notices the change, the transition from state to state – deep sleep, dream state or waking state. This awareness of a transition from deep sleep to waking state is proof that something was there aware in both state, or the transition would not be noticed. To notice that movement from one state to the other you had to be present in both state. A mother can awaken from the deepest sleep at the first sound her child makes next door, defying what we would even think we are capable of hearing, making it clear that even though she has no memory of it, she was present and conscious in deep sleep. You are never without awareness, you can be without a body, a mind, a story, a past or a future, you can even be without a world, but you can never not Be. In deep sleep, we are simply resting in our own Beingness, in Awareness without any objects, any problems, any past betrayals or worry about the future, without anyone to become or anything to change. This is why we love deep sleep and the deeper we sleep, the less of ourselves and our life trickles into our sleep, and the more we enjoy it. When someone says they slept wonderfully or that they had the best night sleep they've had in a long time or they slept like the dead, all it means is they, as the imaginary self with all its thoughts, beliefs, issues and confines, disappeared and they rediscovered the subtle peace and happiness that is their essence, free of form, concepts and limitations. Beingness always is, with or without a material world. It is the substratum of all life; the background of all existence, and everything emerges out of it. As Roy Melvyn tells us in *Disillusionment: The Doorway to Present Moment Clarity*, "There is no experience of deep sleep because there are no objects of experience. However, the absence of objects must no be taken to suggest the absence of consciousness."

Upon the realization that matter is nothing but space and potential energy, that consciousness is what we are and that it is the primary substance of everything that exists, and that the reality we perceive, experience and interact with is never out there but in here, in us, and made of that same conscious field that we are; we come to understand that the whole world we know and live in, not only arises inside of us, but is made out of us, of our Aware Presence, not unlike the way a dream arises in us and is made of us, out of our consciousness. Nothing really exists out there, nothing that we could ever really know, independently of us. To say that life is on earth is a misunderstanding; a more accurate statement might be that earth is in life. Life doesn't arise out of the earth, but the other way around, it is earth and all its components that arise out of life, and we are that life. The physicist, mathematician and writer Peter Russell explains it this way: "The world we actually know is the world that takes form in our minds; this world is not made of matter, but of mindstuff. Everything we know, perceive, and imagine, every color, sound, sensation, thought, and feeling, is a form that consciousness has taken on. As far as the world is concerned, everything is structured in consciousness. (Even) space and time are not fundamental dimensions of the underlying reality. They are fundamental dimensions of consciousness."

So we come to this point, probably with a blank look on our faces and a hell of a headache, unable to quite fathom what has just happened to our neat little view of the world – of Reality, really – and incapable of formulating what this means for us and our daily lives. If you can remember one thing, understand that something that varies, wavers and changes from person to person, from species to species, from time to time, cannot be the Absolute Truth or the Absolute Reality. What this new understanding of Reality does is that it forces us to put everything we experience, everything we think we know, believe and perceive to be true, under scrutiny. We must doubt everything we have ever believed and thought about Reality and Truth. In the end, we must reach the conclusion that we know nothing and cannot ever know anything outside of the fact that we exist, that we are conscious and that everything arises and is experienced in that consciousness. We also cannot know anything outside of our immediate present experience, not the idea, definition or our story of our present experience, but the direct intimate felt sense of it, before and beyond thoughts. We cannot even say what it is that we are conscious of or ever prove that anything actually exists outside of the Awareness that we are, all we can say is that we are conscious and different sensations, perceptions and movements are happening.

Everything that all beings know and could ever know or experience is always within their awareness. That is true of us, of every human being and of every other sentient life form. If there is no Awareness, no Consciousness nothing can ever be known or perceived. As science now shows, the underlying, fundamental substance of all that exists, has ever existed, or could ever exist is a conscious field, Awareness itself. Nothing exists outside of it and everything is made of it, just this immaterial alive field taking on different shapes and forms that seem to be solid. What science has referred to as the unified field is no other than the Pure Consciousness that all great spiritual masters have been alluding to. In the end everything comes full circle. As Roy Melvyn writes, "What has not changed is this ever-present energetic consciousness. It is the unchanging background against which a changing world appears, disappears and reappears." Awareness is primary to any experience. Consciousness, Existence, Awareness, Presence is the one and only constant, the only Truth, the only Reality. And you are That! It is your essence and your core, everything else is a superimposition.

Everything we experience is a construct within consciousness...The faculty of consciousness is, as we have seen, the only absolute, unquestionable truth. Whatever is taking place in my mind, whatever I may be thinking, believing, feeling, or sensing, the one thing I cannot doubt is consciousness...We place this image of self at the center of our perceived world, giving us the sense of being in the world. But the truth is just the opposite: it is all within us.
– Peter Russell

13.
Mirror Mirror – Our Vision of the World

Each person we encounter in our daily life holds up a mirror either reflecting the clarity of our essential Beingness or the drudge of our mistaken perception.
– Prajna Ana

Our Misguided Focus

The world is a mirror in more ways than one. It does not exist outside of us, just like a reflection does not exist outside of the mirror. Whatever we see and experience in the world is either a reflection of our imaginary self, of its beliefs, conditioning and fears or a reflection of our Absolute Self and its peace, love and freedom. When you find yourself resisting, realize that everything you see or perceive is deceptive and only a reflection of your false beliefs and misunderstanding about who you are and the nature of reality. Truly there is no real distinction between the inside world and the outside world, they are one seamless reality.

When you look in the mirror and you smile, what does your reflection do? It smiles back at you, right? Now what if you pull your tongue out, frown or give it the middle finger, what does your reflection do then? Well, as can be expected, you find yourself looking at a frown, a tongue or a middle finger. Life operates in the same way; whatever you put out, reflects back at you. Now I am not saying that, if you are a Jerk, the only thing life sends your way are terrible circumstances. Life is neutral, it is everything, endless possibilities, as we just saw in the chapter on science, Life is no other than a field of potentiality. We are the ones who, among all options and possibilities, choose, see and create a reality that reflects our state of mind. So to live from the point of view of an imaginary self, with all its beliefs in lack and inadequacies, as well as its distrust and bias toward life, can only perpetuate the cycle of lack and suffering in our outer life. It is not so much that life sends us what we expect, it is more that everything exists here and now and we can only see and experience what we expect. As long as our focus and identification is on the image, we will struggle, struggle to keep the image pretty, to fix it, to control it and to make it better. We have to change the direction of our seeing and notice what is prior to any image, what is the essence of the image. We look at the mirror and focus on the image it reflects, while failing to recognize that the mirror, the glass, is primary to any image, that any image that shows up on the mirror is no other than the mirror itself taking that shape in this moment. There is in fact no image, only mirror. Our focus is misguided, once we see that we are not the image, but the mirror, suffering ends because it becomes clear that as the mirror, we are unaffected by and at peace with all and any image. It is really very simple, so simple it is beyond our grasp.

To Believe is to See is to Experience

Now let's look at what I mean in a little more detail. Albert Einstein is known to have said something along the lines of "The most important question we can ever ask ourselves is whether we live in a friendly or hostile universe. The way one answers this fundamental question defines one's destiny." That's a pretty strong statement from a pretty smart guy. What do you think Einstein meant? From a relative, very human point of view, he was probably referring to what modern scientist call "confirmation bias." Confirmation bias refers to the mind's ability to notice and give meaning to information and sensory input that confirms our beliefs while filtering out what does not. We are only conscious of a minuscule amount of reality; the brain automatically filters out information that does not line up with our beliefs and paradigms, hence human beings are masters at proving themselves right. The way we view our world, others and life will decide the kind of experience we have. The shade of our lenses colors everything we look at, and as we discussed earlier, the imaginary self cannot help but have not only colored lenses, but also dirty lenses, which provides a distorted view of reality. When we wear dark sunglasses does that mean that everything is really dark? Obviously not, the lenses color our view of reality. If our lenses are dark brown, the world has a taint of brown and if we wear pink lenses, everything looks a little pink. Both are inaccurate and incomplete perceptions of reality, but both seem real to us while we wear the glasses. Our emotions, our beliefs, our views and opinions of life are nothing more than particular lenses we wear, maybe that is why we say that when we are angry, we see red. Our belief system, which can also be referred to as our paradigm, colors everything we see and experience. In the end, what we believe is what we see and what we see is what we experience. Guy Finley reminds us of this fact in his book *The Essential Laws of Fearless Living*, "Things are not as they seem. No event of itself has power...The only power any unwanted moment holds over us is the power we give to it." This change of paradigm is the end of victimhood and the beginning of true power and freedom.

Suffering, Our Greatest Ally

Our entire life, our sense of self and all of our relationships are tainted by our beliefs and expectations. These are nothing more than a heavy baggage we drag through life. The problems in our lives, our overall suffering and resistance are a great guiding light. Like a teacher, they show us where we are still stuck, where we are still seeing through the lenses of illusion and what inner knots need to be untangled. They show us what kind of erroneous and shackling belief (lenses) we have on and what baggage we are still hauling around, sometimes completely unbeknown to us. Our conflict is like a map of our evolution. It is well known that human beings, without some motivation, tend to be very happy coasting through life. If you get a room full of people and ask them to name their greatest life lessons thus far, many if not most would tell you of something they learned through some kind of conflict or tragedy, whether their own or that of someone close to them. What can I tell you other than it seems to be how we learn, grow and evolve? Without this inner and outer conflict, this suffering, you would not be reading this book and trying to elevate yourself. Your problems, what you resist and where you feel stuck are an exact map of where you are yet to be liberated. They let you know what you need to work on, what illusions and obstructive beliefs you need to let go off, and what inner part of you needs to be met, heard and healed. Your resistance shows you the depth or lack thereof of your understanding; it shows you the depth of your illusion or the depth of your connection to Truth. If a person is deeply immersed and pervaded by Truth, their inner and outer life will reflect that Light. Just like daylight illuminates and pervades everything it touches, so will the Light of Being shine on every aspect of yourself and your life.

> *Life will give you whatever experience is most helpful for the evolution of your consciousness. How do you know this is the experience you need? Because this is the experience you are having at this moment.*
> *– Eckhart Tolle*

The Inside Out World Revisited

Another aspect of this inside out world was introduced in the chapter on science. It is not only that the way we view the world affects the way the world seems and the way we interact with it, but literally the outside world is an inner creation and construction that happens inside of us. The materialist mindset tells us that the real world is out there and that consciousness, awareness arises out of it, but science now theorizes that consciousness is primary and that it is matter that emerges out of it. So who we are, what in us experiences and constructs our reality, is our primary reality and the world out there doesn't actually exist the way we perceive it. The supposed world and our interaction with it, is always experienced within us. The materialist point of view makes us victims of our environment. If the world out there is real, or at the very least, more real than our own inner Beingness, than, our peace, our happiness and our potential for fulfillment is always at the mercy of this external world that has nothing to do with us, doesn't care anything for us and is much greater than us. On the other hand, if we let go of the materialist view and turn it around, we then live in a world where we are at the center of our life, technically we are the center of our world, rather than the world being the center of our world. When our Aware Presence, consciousness is more real than the world out there, when we realize that we are prior to everything else, then our peace, our happiness and our fulfillment seats at the essence of our being and emerges out of the depth of our being, and not out of unstable outer circumstances. From this non-material position, we find that everything, no matter what it looks like or feel like, is an extension of the clarity and purity of our being. We find that peace, happiness and fulfillment is always already present, regardless of what seems to be going on both inside of us, in our minds, body and emotions, as well as outside of us in situations and circumstances. Suddenly we are empowered, we realize that the victim we believed ourselves to be was nothing but another arising mental construction, a shape the imaginary self takes in the Aware Presence that we are. We realize that we were never at the mercy of the world out there but simply at the mercy of our own illusion.

14.
Reality – Our Own Creation

We don't necessarily see things as they are. We see them as we are... In that sense, you can say our reality is a projection of how we identify ourselves.
– Ram Dass

Our Unconscious Invitations

We have been given this great gift of awareness. What we are – our Aware Presence – shines through our eyes, our ears, our taste buds, our nose, our touch and even our mind. Through our senses, it openly experiences the world, without judgment or resistance, and through our minds it gives us the potential to inquire, explore and realize our own Essence. Whatever the mind focuses on with our directed attention, awareness sees, experiences and welcomes. Think of awareness as the space of a room; everything in that room is equally welcomed. The space doesn't resist one person and embrace another; the space doesn't favor one piece of furniture or art over another. The space has no concept of likes and dislike, good or bad, everything that could ever enter that space is welcomed; it is all embraced.

If you focus on something, Awareness, having no concept of exclusion, embraces it. What is embraced, Life brings more of. If you resist something, that resistance is a form of focus, which Awareness embraces as well. Life having no concept of exclusion will continue to bring you the very thing you resist. Whatever you deny, exclude and resist you actually invite in and include into your reality. If you hate someone, your energy, your emotions, your focus is directed towards them. From the perspective of Reality, which does not know hate and has no concept of exclusion or resistance, the hate you feel, which is no other than a form of energy, is an embrace and call to life. The universe has no concept of love and hate; for Life, it is all love, all welcomed and all invited. By resisting, by hating, you are doing nothing else but calling for and welcoming that person or someone like them into your life. Whatever Awareness sees or experiences, it wants more of. Everything you focus on and act on is an invitation for that to come to you, even the things you wish to exclude. Anything you focus on, whether it is perceived as negative or positive, sends a "yes" to the universe. This is why the direction of your focus is primordial and unfolding your life.

    This Aware Presence that we are is equally enthralled with anger, anxiety or depression as it is with peace and happiness. All emotions are just energy in motion, just different aspect of the same thing, vibrating in different ways. It is the imaginary self, in its limited understanding and relative experience, who prefers one reality to another. Life itself has no preference, it is not affected by either, it does not have a problem with anything, just the way a screen is unaffected by the movie being played on it. Our main and possibly only choice in this life is our perspective, so we have to choose our reality very carefully. Anger breeds anger, always has and always will. That is clearly seen in day-to-day life; if you are having a bad day and being somewhat of a jerk, people tend to respond to you in kind, making your day even worse. Unfortunately, it does not stop there; the ripple keeps going out in more subtle ways and suddenly years later your life looks like a bad dream where you find yourself surrounded by rude and selfish human beings. We tend to blame the people around us, but they are only playing the role we assigned them. Guy Finley writes in *The Essential Laws of Fearless Living*, "In this world of ours, response is request...The way you respond to life is also a request you make of it... Our refusal to let go of some negative state amounts to a request for its continuity." The way you respond or react to life, to people, to circumstances, to your own state of mind, is in fact an invitation for more of the same. You want to be happy, at peace and fulfilled, then you only have to look upon yourself, others and life from that perspective, and you will see the fullness and completeness that has been here all along. Wholeness resides in all emotions, all states, all circumstances and all beings. If you can find the wholeness in the places you least expected, then the wholeness that you are will shine through and your life will mirror that understanding. You want folks to be kind then respond with kindness and patience. You want life to be generous to you, be generous, to yourself, to others and to life. You want to feel good about yourself, feel good and be open, nothing is stopping you but your mistaken point of view.

This is not a new concept, as Gandhi said, "Be the change you wish to see." So pay attention to what you are focusing on and what you are trying to exclude from your life, because in reality there is no such thing as exclusion. Whatever you focus on, whether it is as a resistance, a grasping or a longing, becomes who and what you are, and is reflected back in your life. Whatever you resist is actually being included. Become an "includer" of Life, rather than an excluder; fo-cus on, act on, and become what you wish to experience, not what you wish to run away from.

> *We become the very negative state we don't want by identifying with our resistance to it.*
> – *Guy Finley*

The Limitations behind Beliefs

As we discussed earlier, the imaginary self survives by being in some kind of conflict with life. All experiences, including emotions, are maintained by the energy or attention we give them. The way we feed, build and maintain our imaginary self and its mental and emotional programing is by indulging in the feelings, judgments and stories we tell ourselves or by resisting them and struggling against them, both in a way confirm our belief in their reality. You would not indulge or resist a mirage; we only indulge or fight what we believe to be real and as long as we believe something is real we give it life. You cannot identify with and believe that you are lacking, limited and finite and expect to feel and create a life that is abundant, infinite and limitless. Our beliefs, the story we weave around them, the energy we give them, the choices we make based on them construct our reality. If we like this particular experience, we don't mind giving it life, we don't mind believing it is real and continually creating its reality. The problem comes when we indulge in feelings and stories of victimization, resentment, disappointments, lack, violence, worry and worst case scenarios, because these, too, we feed and give life to; we make them just as real as any of our favorite experiences. The reality of it is that there is no more truth in the positive beliefs than there is in the negative ones; both are stories, projections, imagining or memories. All stories are a form of conclusion, and they constrict life.

Any belief, whether seemingly positive or negative, keeps us from fully experiencing the raw aliveness that is expressing itself in this very moment, beyond any concepts. By raw I mean pure, authentic, spontaneous, free of labels, free of models, free of judgments and free of any type of lenses.

As we explored in the chapter eight, all beliefs – the hateful ones and the loving ones, the mundane ones as well as the spiritually elevated ones – are created by the illusory separate self in an effort to understand, box in and control life. By definition, something that is not real, such as the self-referencing personal "me," cannot conceive of and birth an Absolute Truth. All truths that come out of the imaginary self cannot ever be more than partial truths. That is not to deny that certain beliefs are more loving and peaceful than others; that certain beliefs are not more useful to a constructive life, but in the end they are still partial truths. All beliefs, even the seemingly positive ones are a form of judgment, sometimes you judge things, circumstances or people to be bad, negative or painful and sometimes you judge them to be good, positive or pleasurable, it is the same thing. The mind, the imaginary self doesn't have the necessary wisdom and knowledge to discern one way or the other. This life, this infinite ever-present flowing Awareness is a mystery that cannot be known, comprehended or grasped with our minds. Any judgments on our part, even positive ones are a form of arrogance. Only when we live from and as the Absolute Self can we live life in a natural, organic and peaceful way that does not necessitate beliefs, rules or labels to guide our choices, views and reactions to life. From the position of Aware Presence, we no longer need to have beliefs and judgments about others and life, we are intimately connected to it all. We cannot live in any other way than in harmony with others, with ourselves and with life, and living in harmony doesn't always feel good. In some ways when we are willing to give up *our* life, our stories, our positions and beliefs, what we gain is Life itself, free of all limited and limiting views, labels and concepts. From the point of view of Aware Presence, all beliefs, preferences and positions are obsolete.

The Law of Attraction
This understanding is where the law of attraction comes from, and to some degree it has merit, but please understand that only an imaginary self who believes in lack and limitations would try to escape its life by manifesting endless blessings and possessions through vision boards and affirmations. The law of attraction taken to its deepest core is about transcending the false and seeing, knowing and living the Truth of your own Being. Only then can you truly be infinite and limitless and live as such; only then can you be whole, fulfilled and at peace despite the fluctuating and unpredictable nature of the outer world of forms. The law of attraction uses will to provide an idea of peace and fulfillment, while truly living and knowing our limitlessness is about trust and flow.

Even if we were able to create and manifest endless objects and happy circumstances for ourselves, we would be trapped under the weight and worry of maintaining and keeping them all. All circumstances that have their foundation in and are initiated out of illusion come with their own kind of suffering. Our blessing does not lie in what we can manifest outside of us, but in the discovery, recognition and living of our Essential Nature. Knowing the infinity and limitlessness that delves and lives in the depth of our being is the only thing that will ever fully satisfy our desires and calm our fears. Having no limits, being free of fears and living effortlessly is directly related to knowing who we are.

What is limitless in life – that which is without end within us – is our God-given potential to transcend limitations.
  – Guy Finley

A Movement of Love

When we operate from the point of view of our Absolute Self, there are no longer any problems. Let me explain what I mean by that. I don't mean to imply that life suddenly gets easy and that we no longer have any difficulties or that we never experience pain. Life itself doesn't change, we don't suddenly become cured of cancer or lose the 45 lbs. we have been trying to drop for three years. Our boss doesn't suddenly become friendly and give us that promotion we've been hoping for. Our loved ones don't become immune to sickness or death. No, whether we live from the point of view of our imaginary self or Aware Presence, life remains as it is, with its ups and downs, sometimes it is sunny and sometimes it pours. So what's the point you may ask? Well the point is that no matter what happens, when living life from an absolute, united, point of view, you are always at your best, unwavering in your knowing that you are beyond this – whatever this is – you know yourself to have the inner wisdom necessary to effectively respond and rise above anything that comes your way. You glow with an inner light, a strength, a stillness, a conviction and confidence that life, however tough it gets, whatever it throws your way, can never shake. When you know your Essential Self and live from that perspective, you are at peace, touched but unharmed by life's events and in harmony with all the movements of life. You don't suddenly, upon realizing your True Nature, get the job your have been seeking, the mate of your dreams or the body of an athlete. What does change, though, is that the one who was unhappy with his current job, the one who thought he needed a different job to be whole, no longer feels that way. From the place of Aware Presence, the new job can or cannot happen. You might still pursue a different career, but not out of need, fear or feelings of lack, but out of pure openness, pure natural enjoyment, just because it feels good, it feels right. Suddenly the one who wanted a new mate, to feel better, be less lonely or more complete, is whole. The feelings of loneliness and inadequacy are a distant memory. As the Absolute Self, relationships happen organically, out of joy, not need. Similarly, weight loss and healthy life habits may happen, not because of feeling ugly or less than, but because you are moved to do it, it is a natural exploration and evolution of your life. The Essential Self, what you are beyond this "me," is free of conditioning, it has no issues with weight or aloneness or different types of jobs. Remember that what you are is at peace and okay with all of life, it cannot say "no" or resist any of it, whatever it does, it does out of love. When you let go of the false, you gain the freedom to feel fully and be who you are, free of fears, free of shame and free of the baggage of the imaginary self. You, as the infinite, eternal, wide-open spaciousness that you are, become limitless in your potential within the realm of possibilities. As you lose your finite self, you gain infinite possibilities.

~Experiential Adventure: Releasing Beliefs and Judgments~

This experiential adventure's aim is to allow a more profound connection to your Absolute Self and to help you slowly unwind the imaginary self by letting go of all beliefs and judgments. Close your eyes, take a few deep breaths, and bring your focus within. Allow your thoughts to pass by, without getting caught up by them. Shift your focus inside and find that Aware Presence that witnesses your experience. Allow each exhale to loosen your body and expand your spirit. Focus on the vastness that you are, your consciousness without a beginning or an end, without boundaries, without a form, age, gender, concepts or any defining stories, ever present, ever free, vast like space itself. As you shift your focus to that still and silent spaciousness within, notice how boundless and open you are. Now, from that place, take a belief or judgment you believe to be true, whether positive or negative, feel and experience the energy of that belief and or judgment in your body and the effect it has had in your life. Stay open, without judgment of it, and as you reconnect to your Absolute Self, ask yourself these few questions:

- Is this belief True? Can I know with absolute certainty, beyond any doubt that this is always True? For something to be True, with a capital T, it must always be so under all circumstances. It must also be True to all and from all perspectives, and to truly know for certain, it must be your direct experience, not someone else's.

This is not about hearsay and what books, teachers or others say is true. It is about your direct experience, not what you believe, hope or wish to be true, but what you absolutely know to be True.

- Does this belief/Judgment, whether positive or negative, make me feel more spacious or more constricted? If I dropped this belief/Judgment and replaced it with nothing but space, would I feel more open, more vast or smaller, more closed?

- Is this vast Aware Presence that I am, affected by this belief/Judgment and its energy? Or does it just stay open, untouched and free?

- Do I, as my Absolute Self, care whether or not I hold unto this belief/Judgment or am I okay without it?

- Does my Aware Presence judge this belief/Judgment as negative or positive? Does it believe it? Or is it wide open to all of life, without judgments, labels or preferences and without beliefs?

Find the peace and freedom that you are beyond concepts, beliefs and Judgments. Allow the energy of this belief/ Judgment to flow through you, let it go, and dwell in the vast spaciousness that is your true nature, feel its transparency, its underlying peace and joy, regardless of what shows up in it. Experience the freedom and peace of being ever present, without a gender or an age, without a story, believing nothing and having no judgments, open to the mystery and genuinely okay with all of life.

~

The Natural Flow of Life

The issues in our lives start when we either resist an uncomfortable experience or when we hold on to and indulge in a positive one we don't want to let go of. Unfortunately, life is in a constant flow; things come and go, whether we want them to or not. By resisting or holding on, we go against our nature and the nature of life. We ask reality to not be real, to not be itself, which doesn't make much sense. This is one of the ways that the imaginary self keeps itself into business, by saying "No" to life. By indulging, holding on or resisting, we keep emotions, sensations, perceptions and events static. Life, our true Self, is a vast fluid openness. Whatever we try to indulge in or resist, we tend to freeze, this freezing of time and of our experience goes directly against the nature of our Absolute Self and of Life. It is through this freezing that the imaginary self is born and maintained. The way Life lets us know that we are going against our true nature is through suffering. Suffering is a direct consequence of freezing reality, of believing that we are this small imaginary self. An imaginary self can be harmed by the world, it needs to fight and protect itself from both the perceived inner and outer demons. This self-referential personal self feels a sense of lack and inadequacy, it believes that it could lose something, become less than it is and damaged without this or that and so it needs to struggle and fight for what it believe it needs to make it whole. It is our imaginary self, in its ignorance, and in its great struggle to maintain its sovereignty, that not only creates our suffering but also perpetuates it. Through its faulty beliefs and its misguided attempts to control life, the 'me' reinforces and generates more of the same in our outer reality. The All, as we know, is pure openness and it cannot say anything but "Yes," so even the imaginary self, with its mistaken perceptions and the havoc they create, is embraced by our Essence. The story of an imaginary self with all its faults and tribulations, is simply the experience that is unfolding in the flow of this moment. Awareness will neither resist it nor indulge in it. It will allow that movement to pass naturally until we wake up to see that our true nature was never lost and that which seemed so real was nothing more than a story, a dream without any reality.

The Gift of our Pain

We were given a gift to help us navigate this illusory world and find our way home. Unfortunately, it is rarely seen as the blessing that it is. Just as physical pain is a message that something is wrong in our body, so is suffering a message that something is not quite right with our perception. Pain and suffering are really an ingrained defense in the body mind, set up, to let us know when we are on the wrong track. Suffering lets us know that we are caught in the grip of illusion, either resisting or grasping. It lets us know when we are going against our nature and taking ourselves to be a powerless imaginary self, rather than the still effortless Aware Presence that we are. Suffering is there to warn us that we are feeding an illusion and to remind us to redirect our focus and position to something that is more in line with our own growth and evolution. Whenever you suffer – whether it is through worry, anger, desiring, seeking, sadness, shame, loneliness or disappointment – it is a direct consequence of forgetting who and what you are. What we are at core, our essence, needs nothing and is damaged by nothing. It is infinite, limitless and everlasting peace that embraces and is open to all movements in life.

15.
Awareness – The Ultimate Subject

The arising of any thought,
Feeling or emotion, is
Independent of the person.
It is only when involvement
By a person occurs, that
The thought, feeling, or emotion
Becomes Personal.
– Wu Hsin

Know Yourself as That

If you ask your friend to describe a beautiful spot he saw on his travel, he will describe objects; the buildings, the trees, the animals, the people, maybe the hotel room, but he will fail to mention the most present aspect of anything he experienced on his travel, the space. We look around us and all we see and notice are things, but what about the space that allows, holds and connects all things? There is so much more space than there are things, just like there is so much more sky than there are clouds or stars, and yet we focus on the objects and miss the bigger reality, or at the very least a major aspect of reality. Our inner world is the same. We have all these things that arise, such as thoughts, feelings, sensations, beliefs, dreams, memories, and just like the objects of the world appear in this continuous, unchanging, ever present and infinite space, so do all these internal movements appear in a similar ever-present, unchanging, limitless spaciousness. Behind each thought, allowing and holding each thought is space. When a thought ends, before the next one begins, there is space, a palpable consciousness that exists without objects. Between the in breath and the out breath, there is space, a gap that is empty of activity, of objects and movement but is full of a silent peaceful vastness. And there is space in the background as well, while a thought, an emotion, a sensation or perception is taking place. In fact all inner movements, such as thoughts and sensations, occur in a background of empty still conscious space and are surrounded by that peaceful vastness, but our focus is on the objects, the thing we are experiencing and not on the spaciousness that holds it and permeates it. All forms of our inner world appear and disappear in this still unaffected formless space. This Spaciousness that is the background of all experiences is no other than Awareness itself, our own Essential Presence. This alive spaciousness is what makes every thought, every emotion, every perception and sensation possible, and it is what remains when all is quiet, at rest, but just like our outer world we only focus of the objects and miss the primordial aspect of experience. The moment we stop for a second, pull our focus away from objects, whether they are physical, mental or emotional, and take a second look with open curiosity, we can see and feel the peaceful vastness that is always already here and know that we are in it and it is in us, inseparable from ourselves. In this moment we know that without it nothing exist and we realize that this aware space has always been here, we were just blind to it. Once we change the direction of our seeing, it is undeniable that all along we have missed the primary aspect of all experiences, both inner and outer.

You are this spaciousness, this primordial aspect of experience, everything else is secondary, ornamental.

There is a spirit or a force that was here prior to your body/mind, it is here within and around this body and it will remain once this body/mind goes. It has been given many names, Spirit, God, Soul, Conscience, True Nature, Awareness, Self, Atman or Consciousness among others. This Aware Presence is the source and what animates the world. This wise and peaceful Aliveness makes the grass grow, the seasons come, the planets revolve, it is the light of the sun, the beat of your heart, the growing of your hair, it is the infinite movement of time and space. It is life itself and it dwells deep in you. It is you. You could never be disconnected from your source; it is your Essence and the Essence of the world.

You are it and at the same time live in it and interact with it. In other words, you are infin-ite, limitless, eternal, peaceful Presence living in itself and interacting with itself, nothing else exists but That. You lack nothing and no harm could ever come to you. As Ka-mal Ravikant shares with us in *Living Your Truth*, "I prom-ise you that the same stuff galaxies are made of, you are. The same energy that swings planets around stars makes electrons dance in your heart. It is in you, outside you, you are it. It is beautiful. Trust in this. And you and your life will be grand."

What you perceive yourself to be, this body and this mind is no other that a suit you put on for a short while in this everlasting dance. Do you ever think you are your clothes or your hair-do of the day? So why would you think you are this illusory self? You are so much more than you perceive yourself to be. This discovery or remembrance is your salvation, your liberation from all suffering. It is your path to peace and joy. To know the deepest, most intimate and eternal part of you, is to instantaneously know God and to know yourself as God.

Subject versus Object

In Absolute terms, everything is this Aware Field of potentiality, is one, made of the same stuff, your thoughts, emotions, your body, your car, your neighbor, it is all One aliveness taking the shape of many. From the relative point of view, things seem to be different and separate. We learn very early on that we are not what we can see, hear, touch or feel, and from a subjective aspect that is very true. Who we are is prior to and beyond any experience. You cannot be anything that you can perceive or observe. If you see a chair across the room, you know that it is not you. If you walk to it and touch it, you still know that it is not you, even though you can feel it. The chair is the object, the thing that you perceive and sense. You are the subject the one who sees and experiences it. What about the sound of a dog barking in the distance, do you ever mistake it for yourself? Or your friend talking, do you mistake his voice for yours? What about the warm breeze, which you cannot see but can feel, do you ever think it is you? Obviously, in everyday life, this is common knowledge, things that are outside of us, that we can feel, see or hear are not who we are. If you identified yourself to a piece of furniture or a tree or some other sentient life, you would be in a heap of trouble. But what about "things" or "objects" that seem to be so much closer to us, part of us, like our body or our thoughts, are those who we are? Many believe and feel that they are their body or their mind, but is that really true? Let's explore this belief from the perspective that if you can perceive it, experience it, then it is an object and cannot be who you are, you are the perceiver, the subject.

Let's start with a short introductory exploration. Can you see your body? Absolutely, you can see it by looking down or in a mirror. You can even touch and describe your body. So you can see, feel and experience your body, then, based on our premise, you cannot be your body; you are the experiencer of your body. The body is something you have not what you are. What about thoughts and feelings, can you notice and observe a thought or a feeling or even a sensation? Take a second and you will see that you can, you can sense and describe any of those, so they cannot be you either. You are not your body, thoughts, beliefs, feelings or sensations, you are the one in whom they occur and by whom they are seen and experienced. You are the subject, the witness of all these things. You are present before a thought, feeling or sensation appears, while it appears and you remain when it passes. If this seems a little confusing, don't worry, we will come back to this exploration in much more detail in a few paragraphs, which hopefully will make this quite clear to you.

All things that are observable by you, cannot be you, whether it is an object, your body, a sensation, a thought or an emotion. You perceive all of these. All perceptions, whether through sight, hearing, taste, smell or touch are finite, even emotions, thoughts and states of mind are finite. By finite I mean that they have a beginning and an end; that they change and evolve, and that they are limited and can be measured. You, Aware Presence, on the other hand, do not come and go, you do not have limits. Awareness doesn't have a beginning or an end; you, as that Aware Presence are changeless and ever present, infinite and eternal. You cannot be measured or observed the way any kind of form, object, state or phenomena can.

Who Are You?

You do not exist as you think you do. What you assume yourself to be is an illusory self, a mirage, a limited and momentary form that life takes. Your body and your mind are not who you are, they are an experiential instrument that you have. You are not this limited self who was born and will die, who seems to be a particular age, gender and has a specific story. You are the Aware, ever-present, still space in which this body/mind and its entire story appears.

When most of us think of who we are, we rarely, if ever, think of some kind of spiritual airy fairy, "still background of experience," "field of Awareness" type of crazy answer. No, as Michael Singer points out in *The Untethered Soul*, if I was to ask you, "Who are you?" more than likely you would start by giving me your name. But we clearly know that our name is not who we are. If it were, then that would mean that if you changed your name, you would no longer be you. I mean technically you existed and were you, before your parents even gave you a name and before you recognized the sound of your name. You would still be yourself if you decided to do away with your name entirely and choose a new one. So, one thing is clear, you are not your name. Your name is something you have, another instrument to operate successfully in this relative realm.

So if you are not your name, then who are you? Most people will then share their life story. So upon inquiring as to who you are, you might tell me how old you are, where you went to school, whether you had a nice childhood or not, what you do for a living, Whether you are married and have children or even grandchildren and so on…but that is not you either, that is just an image of a past and present story. You would still be you if your parents had suddenly decided to move to Boston and you had gone to a different university, married a different mate and gotten a different job. Granted you might have a different view of life, but the one you know yourself to be in the depth of your being, the one who experiences your life, would still be here, unchanged. If you hit your head and had amnesia, you would no longer have a story to attach to this body/mind, but yet you would remain. So your history and your present story is not you either, it is just an accumulation of experiences that you have, a reference point for this current you call your life.

When everything outside of us has been dismissed as not who we are, then usually we refocus the question closer to home. At which point, you might give me a list of your strengths and weaknesses or even your likes and dislikes, your values or hobbies, but are those really you either? Think of a weakness you have, would you not still be you if suddenly that weakness were transformed into strength? What about if you changed your mind about a particular value or political view you have, would you cease to be or become someone completely different? Or if you suddenly lost interest in one of your favorite hobbies, would you suddenly no longer be you? What you believed and liked to do as a child changed when you became a teenager and again shifted as you crossed into adulthood, but you are still yourself regardless of your hobbies, opinions, values and your likes and dislikes. What you are in essence remains unchanged. What about your choices, many people believe that we are the sum total of our choices. Is that true? Do you become more or less yourself when you make good or bad choices? Are you more you today, with a greater accumulation of choices than you were five years ago? Will you be more yourself five years from now, with even more choices under your belt? I think not. Your choices, how many choices you've make, how well or how badly they've turned out, have nothing to do with who you are, with the depth of your Being. You would still be you regardless of whether you ended up a convict or mayor. Your experiences would be different, your life would certainly look different, but the essence of who you are, what experiences this life, what sees through your eyes and hears to your ears, would not.

So far so good? Most people can understand relatively quickly that they are not their names, or their life story, or their habits, or preferences or even their choices. But where it gets tricky is when we come even closer to ourselves, into the realm of the body and the mind, into the realm of personality and selfhood. Many, if not most people would agree that they are their body, their mind, their personality and the voice that talks inside their head, so let's explore that further.

A Deeper Exploration of the Body

We struggle with the idea that we are not our body or at the very least in our body because so much of our identity, of the way we feel is linked to this form we seem to inhabit, so let's explore this belief in more depth. Look at your foot for moment, are you your foot? What about your knee, do you live in your knee? What about your hands, are they who you are? Your chest? What about something on your face, like your nose, your eyes or your mouth, are they who you are? It doesn't matter what body part I ask you to look at, not a single one of them is you. What about an organ, are you your liver, or your appendix, or your lungs, or even your heart? Granted your body might not be able to survive without some of those organs, but does that mean that they are you? You can lose a leg or an arm, or have your nose surgically altered and yet you remain, untouched and unchanged. You can have a number of organs taken out or partially taken out, or even go through a transplant and have a new organ, someone else's heart put in, yet you are not less you than you were.

Usually we are relatively comfortable admitting that no specific body part or organ defines us. We are quite clear that our ear lobe or intestine is not who we are, and yet we can't help but feel that the totality of our body parts and organs make up who we are, that our consciousness, our Beingness resides in them. How can it be that a bunch of "things" that, independently, are not who we are, can come together and suddenly make up who we are? It doesn't make any sense. It makes as little sense as the idea that a bunch of unconscious matter can come together and make a conscious sentient being. The reason it doesn't make any sense is because it is not true. The idea that you are your body or in your body is nothing more than a thought, a belief.

Is your body aware of you? Is your body aware of the world around it? Let's check. Can a finger hear or see, does a finger or a leg know you, does it know about you or care for you? Does it even know about itself? Could any body part or any organ have any independent consciousness? No, you are the only one who is conscious. You are the one aware of your body, the one who experiences your body. Whatever consciousness your body seems to have comes from you. You know, feel, experience your body and the parts of your body, but they do not know you or experience you.

What about the totality of the body? As you are well aware of, your body has changed somewhat over the years, so which of these bodies is you, the one you had at six, the one you had at sixteen or the one you had at twenty-six or the one you have now, or the one you will have in ten years? What about you – do you feel your age, do you feel like you have aged along with your body? Or do you feel like you have not moved, changeless, ever present, and ageless? Most of us never feel our age, that's because what we are doesn't shift, doesn't get older. We are the changeless, the one who sees our face in the mirror through our eyes, who sees our face change, the wrinkles slowly appear over time, yet this one that we are is faceless and timeless, no wrinkle appears on it. We are this changeless Presence that witnesses and holds all these changing movements, including our body. It is not that we are in our body, but the other way around, our body appears in us. You are the one who sees and experiences. It is the same Self that sees a fresh 16-year-old face looking back in the mirror and a grown up 40-year-old face and an aging 80-year-old face. The seer, who you are, never moved an inch, never aged, never evolved. It always was and always will be, it can never be other than it is. If that is so then you are not this changing body and maturing face that you seem to inhabit and carry along with you; you are the one who knows and experiences them, yet is untouched by time, infinitely ever-present. Your body doesn't and can't know and experience you, only you can know and experience it.

A Deeper Exploration of the Inner World

The same is true of your beliefs, thoughts and emotions. Could they ever be aware of you, or of themselves or of anything? Does the thought "I wonder what I'll have for dinner tonight" know that it is a thought, that it is arising in something called a mind and that it is experienced by you? What about an emotion? When you feel angry, does anger know itself? Does anger know that it is an emotion, made up of thoughts and sensations? Does it feel angry, painful to itself? Does it know that it arises in you, is experienced by you, and that through it you feel angry and suffer? Do any of your thoughts, beliefs or emotions, have any individual intelligence or knowledge or awareness independently of you? When viewed from that perspective, it becomes clear that we are not our inner movements, but the one who knows and experiences them. Beliefs, thoughts and emotions are movements of energy and stories we tell ourselves. They are words and sensations strung together, that some of the time carry wisdom or a message for us, but apart from that they have no intrinsic or individual consciousness. They are yours but you are not theirs. They have no awareness of you or that they come to and belong to you. Your existence is not connected to theirs, part of you doesn't disappear when a thought or a feeling disappears. You don't change when you change your mind. You are not your beliefs, thoughts or your feelings; they are known and experienced by you. Nothing that you can think of, perceive or observe is you, including your hopes and dreams, your fears and even your personality. All of those have no awareness or consciousness independent of you. You know and experience your hopes and dreams, your fears, your personality type, but they do not know you.

Just as your body has changed over time, so has your inner world. What you believed about yourself and the world as a child is not what you believe today. What was most important to you as a teenager is probably no longer important. Even your personality might have shifted to some degree, maybe you are more patient, kinder, less shy...My guess is your thinking, emotional climate, personality and views will keep shifting right alongside your body, that's growth, that's evolution, that's the movements of life and yet your Essence remains unchanged. You cannot be something that comes and goes and changes over time. If you are your thoughts, feelings and sensations, then who are you in between them? If you were your thoughts, feelings and sensations, you would have quite a case of multiple personality disorder since your inner state always changes from one moment to the next. Whatever you come into contact with, in your inner world, has no life independent of you. You exist with or without thoughts, feelings and sensations, but they do not exist without you. You are the only one with awareness. Your emotions, your feelings, your sensations, your beliefs and your thoughts have no awareness, they cannot experience you or the world, they cannot know or feel themselves either, only you can know and experience them. Even if they hold a message for you, they are not aware of this message, they are only the instrument used by life, which is no other than yourself, to communicate with you. Only you have the wisdom and Awareness to decode them and see discover their deeper meaning.

What about when your mind and body are quiet and at peace, when you are not thinking, reminiscing, imagining or projecting, when your feelings are still or in deep sleep, do you cease to exist? Obviously not; you exist prior to any movements of your mind and body, during those movements and you remain unchanged, when everything settles down. What about your memories, are those you? Well technically memories are no other than a story that is being told now. As we know, your story shifts, moves, is made up of thoughts, perceptions, emotions and sensations, all of which are not you. So no, even your memories are not you. The same is true for your hopes and dreams for the future; they are no other than a nice story made up of thoughts and emotions, all of which are not you. They do not have an independent life, they cannot switch place with you and experience you. Nothing you can think of or perceive is you, because what you are, cannot be claimed by a thought or experienced the way any kind of object or thing can be. You are prior to thoughts, emotions, sensations and perceptions; they are made of you, but you are not made of them. You cannot be experienced as an object because you are the experiencing itself, the ultimate subject, everything else is experienced through you, by you and in you. As Michael Singer, in *The Untethered Soul,* tells us, "It's actually pretty easy to see that you're not the objects you look at...It's you, the subject, that is looking at the objects. So we don't have to go through every object in the Universe and say that object is not you. We can easily generalize by saying that if you are the one who is looking at something, then that something is not you." I think at this point it is pretty clear that you are always the one who experiences everything, you are the experiencing itself. Your outer world, your body, your emotions, your feelings, your sensations, your thoughts, your beliefs, ideas, hopes and dreams and your memories, none of them are you; and yet, one cannot deny that they are part of you, that they define the life experience you have and the choices you seem to make. In some way we could say that they are made of you and appear in you, but you are not made of them. So really what are you?

> *Just as Physical objects are not One's Self ... neither are sensations, emotions and thoughts. They are what one seems to have; not what one is.*
> *– Peter Francis Dziuban*

The imaginary self and everything that creates its individuality, including the body and the mind, belongs to time. This limited human identity is fleeting and continually shifting with time. It is time-bound physically, mentally and emotionally, but there is a timelessness in us that permeates our life. That part of us is ever-present, and it never shifts and never disappears. Just like the world is made up of both space and object, so we are made up of both this time-bound being (the object) and a timeless Beingness (the space). Unfortunately, we spend our lives focused on the time-bound objects, our world, our body, our feelings and mind stuff and disregard the changeless and timeless. We have forgotten the most important primordial aspect of ourselves, and so we live fragmented confused lives. All we have to do is remember the entirety, the wholeness and the reality of who we are. Peace, fulfillment or wholeness is not something that can be achieved in time. They are not things or states we are lacking in this moment and can get to in the future trough accomplishments, acquisition or different practices. This great Stillness, this peace and wholeness that we are looking for, is already here, and it has always been here in the background of all our experiences; all we have to do is notice it. Stop looking for something you believe you don't have and need to get and just see what is right here, behind your eyes in the looking itself, in the space that holds all your thoughts, all your feelings and all your sensations, even the most painful and disturbing ones, that is your wholeness, your reality.

The Unchanging Nature of Reality
In the absolute sense, Reality is that which never changes. If something appears and disappears, it cannot be real. If something changes or wavers it cannot be real.

Your name might change, your looks might change, your beliefs might change, your story might change, your state of mind might change, but one thing that you cannot deny is that you exist, beyond all these things that you think make you; *you* are alive and aware, that is an unwavering fact. The path of knowing who you are revolves around looking for that which in you is always already present. The path to freedom is discovering that which never disappears and never changes, that which stays constant throughout your life, throughout all experiences. Things come and things go, that is the nature of life, look for what remains, prior to and beyond the movements of coming and going. Thoughts come and go, emotions come and go, even our body changes, we have a brand new set of cells every few years and in deep sleep as well as at the end of this life, the body goes as well. The one thing that is a constant in our life is this sense of "I" – I am here, I exist, child or adult, healthy or not, thinking or at rest, angry or at peace, I am, I never go away.

What is this "I"? Many would assume it is their personality, their sense of selfhood, their "me-ness" but that is also incorrect. This "I" is existence itself, the movements of life beyond and prior to selfhood, to this 'me' and to any personality it seems to have. This "I am me," the feeling that we are someone in particular, is in fact a movement of identification that comes and goes as well. Even this identity we hold on to and think so highly of, wavers throughout life. Can you think of times that you, as your story, your personality, your "me" drop away, even for a moment? Most people experience this when they are absorbed in an activity. For example when painting, rock climbing or even while reading a good book or watching a movie, you forget yourself and become one with the activity; your identity, your story and history and your plans, your me, your personality, who you think you are, all disappears for a moment, and you become the moment itself. You are so caught up in the now that you, as a separate individualized being, cease to exist. This also happens in sleep; as you fall asleep, you willingly and gratefully shed your sense of me, your story, your worries, and even your hopes and dreams. Maybe that is why sleep is such a common escape from the weight of the world. Sleeping too much is a common symptom of depression. Sleep allows us to shed this "me" that feels lacking and inadequate and finds issues with everything around it. In sleep there is no problem, no depression, precisely because there is no "me." It is not you who experiences depression or anxiety or stress, it is the 'me' you mistakenly believe yourself to be. Whenever we drop this "me" whether in sleep or consumed by a present activity, we come back to the natural ease that lives underneath and prior to this troublesome sense of personal self. In many ways to be at rest is a process of gladly letting go of the superfluous, of the false, so that we may come back to our underlying unwavering constant, to what is changeless and True, to the reality of our own Essence. This timeless thread is the Aware peaceful Presence that is your background and the background of all that is.

~Experiential Adventure: The Bliss of this Moment~
You can do this whenever you wish. Whenever you feel overwhelmed or disconnected, take a couple minutes for yourself. Wherever you are, if possible, close your eyes take a few deep breaths, quiet your mind and willingly drop all conceptual stuff, literally make your mind blank and silent, even for just a few seconds. Drop everything you think you know about yourself, life, this world, your beliefs, judgments

and preferences and just stay with your senses and the felt sense of being alive in this moment.

Wide open and aware, simply notice everything that comes up, the noise of traffic, the children screaming, the chair under your butt, the vibrating of your body, the taste in your mouth, the air on your face...Dismiss any comments your mind makes, don't entertain it or give it the time of day and just stay with the aliveness of this moment, intimately connecting to whatever arises, to the point where nothing else exist but this very moment, this sound, this sensation, this smell, this movement of light, if your eyes are open, these colors and shapes without a naming any of them. The the mind gets involved, that's okay, just drop it again and come back to your senses, to the spectacular mystery of Now. Feel your own aliveness coursing through your body, this Aware Presence that is experiencing all of these sensations and perceptions. Lose yourself and gain this moment. Just this, for a few seconds, reminds you that you are beyond and prior to any of your problems or stressors, changeless, constant and unaffected.

~

The Ultimate Subject

All of these things – your body, your emotions, your thoughts, beliefs, personality and all the experiences that correspond to your story – appear to you, are seen and experienced by you, but they don't affect, change or disturb the essence of your Being. Nothing that is observed and experienced by you is you and by that definition they cannot define you. They appear and are made of you, but are not who you are; they do not define you, in fact, you define them. Your Absolute Self sees them, knows them and experiences them, just the way you see, know and experience a piece of furniture in your living room or the sound of a symphony, regardless of the object or experience, it's not personal and you don't need to identify with it. Your Essential Self is no more affected by an appearance of anger or sadness, than it is by the appearance of a car. To your Absolute Self a feeling of fear, disappointment or gratitude is no more personal than the sight of a tree or the sound of a bird. It is all energy, life's many movements, not one better than the other, not one purer or more divine than the other, not one more intimate than the other. It is only a mind that would make those distinctions. Your Aware Presence does not identify with some things and not with others, it is intimate with all movements and all objects it experiences, yet this intimacy doesn't move or alter it. You are whole unto yourself and by yourself. You –your Awareness – need nothing to exist and be complete; nothing can be taken from you or added to you. Why identify with appearing and disappearing thoughts, emotions or sensations, with a changing body and this evolving story with its fluctuating beliefs, hopes and dream, when you, Aware Presence, do not change or evolve, you do not come and go; you are always whole and ever present. It is your light, your awareness, that shines indiscriminately through everything, every perception and experience and brings them to life. Without you, Aware Presence, nothing else exists to be seen, felt, heard, smelled or tasted. For you to observe and experience any "thing" or phenomena, such as a body, a world, a state of mind or an emotion, you must be prior to and independent from it. Without Awareness, all states, sensations and perceptions could not be known or experienced. It is you, ever-present limitless Awareness, which animates this body and this mind and that gives life to this story you call your life. You were here prior to this body, this mind and this story, during this body, this mind and this story and you will remain after this body, this mind and this story. You are the still, formless and peaceful light that shines deep within, illuminates and permeates all forms, yet has been forgotten even by yourself.

Clarifying your true nature, knowing who you really are will reveal the already-present-perfection that needs nothing to be whole and complete.
– Joshua BenAvides

16.
Lucid Living - The Way to Freedom

You are not a drop in the ocean. You are the entire ocean in a drop.
– Rumi

The Light of Discernment
   The first step to seeing the illusion is to step out of it. Most of our suffering is a case of misidentification and misdirection. We are so stuck inside our head and in the problems that are created in it, that we can't seem to see the forest through the tree. We have become our seeming problems, we have forgotten that we can witness our thoughts, we can see and feel our emotions, but we need not be governed and identified to them. Guy Finley writes in *The Essential Laws of Fearless Living*, "Most of us at least sense that whenever we fall into despair, lose our temper, or relive some past painful regret, we have lost possessions of ourselves." Rather than being lost in the abyss of our pain and struggles, if we can just remember that there is an Essential part of us that is Aware of them, but not them, if we can just step back and become the witness of whatever emotion, thought, sensation or perception we are experiencing, we can break the chains that tethers us to our pain and realize that we are so much greater than any pain we could imagine. The aim is to find that sweet spot between evading what we feel and being invaded by it. We don't want to step back to such a

degree that we become disconnected from our pain and yet we don't want to become so identified with it that we forget who we are prior to and beyond the pain. All we have to do is to become aware that we are aware and that awareness is our primary Essence.

At each stage of your life you have seen different thoughts, emotions, and objects pass before you. But you have always been the conscious receiver of all that was.
– Michael A. Singer

Part of our growth and of our journey to wholeness is to become aware that before we are aware of "this" or "that," we are simply aware. We are eternally and effortlessly aware of our whole life, both the inner and the outer, whether we realize it or not is beside the point. No matter what, we can never step away from Awareness, we can never not be aware. Could you ever turn off Awareness? What would happen if you did? Without Awareness, there is no you. There wouldn't even be a you to witness your own disappearance. Unawareness is the opposite of life. Awareness is the necessary precursory subject to the potential experiencing and appearing of any object. You don't need objects to experience your own existence and to be alive, but objects need you to be experienced and be alive. Without Awareness, there can be no experiencing, and as we saw in the chapter on scientific theory, matter arises out of Awareness, without it nothing else exist. It is the primary substance of creation. Awareness is not contingent on any object. It exists prior to any world, body or mind. It is its own, nothing can be added or taken away from it; it is Whole as it is.

Living Wide Awake

There are two positions, two different points of view from which we can live and experience life. Our first position is to become immersed and caught up in whatever we experience, a thought, an emotion, a sensation; forgetting who we are and becoming totally that which we experience. From this position, when angry we are anger, when afraid, we are fear itself, when anxious, we are consumed by worry, when in pain we are nothing else but in pain and when thinking, we become that stream of thoughts. When we identify to our inner world, we view the outside world as separate from us. From that point of view, life is independent from us and has no care for our well-being or desires. From this position, the outside world seems also more real and more powerful than our inner knowing and innate peace, and we find ourselves at its mercy.

It was we – who in ignorance of reality – carelessly attributed weight to events that were without substance, causing ourselves to suffer nothing less than the fervent magnitude of our own imagination.
– Guy Finley

In the second position, we are aware that we Are. We are, first and foremost, Aware Presence. Everything else, anything we could ever experience, feel or think about, is second to that. From that position, both the inner and outer world are equally seen and experienced by us, we are prior and beyond both. We see clearly that we are the subject and we never mistake ourselves for any object. Guy Finley in *The Essential Laws of Fearless Living* describes this higher point of view in this way, "the other way leads us to the gradual realization of an interior greatness that can neither be enslaved nor corrupted." The self-realized, awake person knows that she is Aware Presence. She experiences anger, sadness, joy, pain and all sorts of thoughts and sensations and yet never loses herself in any of those, she is awake to who she is. She knows that she is the one who experiences all of these, yet she is not them, they are not her and they do not define her. She knows that she is beyond everything and anything that can be experienced. She is touched by everything she experiences but as timeless and changeless Presence, she is never damaged or changed by them. She is awake to that Truth, she is awake to herself. As Michael Singer writes in *The Untethered Soul*, "As you pull back into the consciousness, this world ceases to be a problem. It is just something you are watching...The more you are willing to just let the world be something you are aware of, the more it will let you be who you are – the awareness, the Self, the Atman, the Soul."

You are home – even though you never left. The search for enlightenment is essentially a desire to be whole and complete, when all the while you've never been less than whole and complete.
– David Bhodan

This way of living, this realization has been compared to lucid dreaming in which the dreamer becomes aware, while asleep, that he is dreaming and that whatever he is experiencing in the dream is not independently real, just part of himself. The moment that you wake up in your dream, that you become aware that none of this is real, that the one you thought was you is not you, just a dream character and that whatever seems to be happening to him or her and everyone else is only make believe, you cease to be afraid, you cease to take the dream and everything that is happening within it too seriously. You are then free to openly experience and enjoy the dream, without worry, without heaviness, regardless of what is happening within it. The choices your dream character makes are permeated by that freedom and the light heartedness that comes with being awake in the dream. Your dream character can be sad or in love or angry, yet always remain aware that no matter what, his True Self is safely at home in bed. This is the experience of the awake person in real life. He knows that his true Self cannot be harmed, that everything is a gift, there for him to experience fully with an open heart. He loves, he laughs, he cries, yet he never loses himself, never forgets who he is. He remains at home within himself, safe and whole, prior to and beyond any experience and any state. All this time we have been seeking wholeness, feeling homesick, lost when all the while we have always been complete and always in the safety of our own home.

You are similar to a wave that is never separate or other than the ocean. The wave comes through and as part of the ocean. Out of the ocean's depth, stillness and power emerges a wave – sometime choppy, sometime soft and flowing, sometime raging and destructive – a seemingly independent form, that seems to come into being and crash on the beach to its dissolution, but where does the ocean end and the wave begin? Can there be a real distinction between the two? Is there any separation at all? Can they actually be said to be two separate things? The wave is no other than the formless ocean in a particular movement and is never separate from its inherent depth, stillness and power. This is the essence of transformation. As you refocus your identity from the illusory separate self to the Absolute Self, you reconnect and ignite the stillness and power within that was always already present, in the depth of your being. This still Presence is eternally and infinitely peaceful, resourceful and free. As Jesus Christ said in *The Book of Thomas*, "He who has not known himself does not know anything, but he who has known himself has known the depth of all."

Shedding the False, Embracing the Real

Our greatest and most important life's work is to prove the imaginary separate self and its fears groundless and illusory. As Guy Finley writes, "Whenever our present nature meets some barrier, a limit of any kind, all it's really run up against is itself. *The self that sees limitation... is the limitation it sees*." If we do not explore the reality of this imaginary self and of its beliefs, which we carry around with us, as us, we will never be free, whole and happy; instead we will find ourselves living for its sake and at its service, leading lives of confusion, frustration, anger and overall desperation. As long as we identify with, and live our life as a personal separate self, regardless of how well our life seems to be going, there will always be a sense of constriction, contraction, depression, anxiety and stress. Sometimes, especially if life is in one of its upturn phase, these feelings will be very subtle. At other times, especially when life is not going so well, these feelings will seem so overpowering that they become the totality of our own experience and of who we are. Even when times are good, the imaginary self is always afraid of what's coming next, and when times are bad, it is at war with the world. Being this separate self is directly connected to these sensations of contraction, worry and depression, it is inevitable. Living life from that stance is lonely, heavy and scary.

As we explored earlier, most of us grow up believing

that peace, love and fulfillment can be found out there, in a new job, a new pair of shoes, a new car, a new relationship, a new house, a new technique, a new practice, a vacation, a retreat and so on. Over time, we find different ways of testing that theory, getting more tuff, changing and enhancing our circumstances, jumping in and out of relationships, only to find out that no matter what we do, what we get, who we meet, what we change; the peace and joy we desire never sticks around for very long. Some of us stay in this insane cycle for our entire life, but others come to the understanding, sometimes through a book, sometimes through a friend or a teacher and sometimes on our own, through experience, that lasting happiness, peace and wholeness cannot be found by adding to and changing the "things" in our life, but by shedding what is no longer true and useful. We must come to see our beliefs, our desires, all the seeking and resisting movements of the imaginary self as the impostors that they are and moment by moment, be willing to see through them and let them go. As Guy Finley teaches us, "We must lose all interest in protecting the interest of this fearful self...In any moment that some fear appears in our mind, and we remember that what we're seeing here is simply the dark spawn of negative imagination, then where is its power to push us around?"

Eventually your will begin to realize that the outside world and the flow of inner emotions come and go. But you, the one who experiences these things, remain consciously aware of whatever passes before you.
– Michael A. Singer

Our great work as human beings is to work through everything that veils us from recognizing the depth and stillness of our Being. The way to freedom is to recognize that we are the witness of all the inner and outer movements of life. We are aware of whatever our body and mind is experiencing in each and every moment. Even when we seem to have gotten lost in identification, in the grip of an inner movement or of an outer circumstance, the deepest part of us, our Essence remains effortlessly aware. Our Aware Presence witnesses us angry, sad, disappointed as well as happy, joyful and at peace. If we can become aware of our feelings, emotions, thoughts, sensations and perceptions then we are obviously beyond them, prior to them. At the very least an important part of us is unaffected and simply witnessing them. Become aware, moment-by-moment, that you are experiencing existence, aliveness, move and unfold in all its infinite nuances and subtlety. Ask yourself:

- Who is it that experiences and witnesses life moving, am I this one?

- Who is it that sees that this body/mind, this person I believe I am, is losing its temper and growing angry?

- Is this witnessing Presence also growing angry and losing its temper or is that one pristine and unaffected?

- Can you see how you become aware of the hunger or thirst of your body, yet the one who is aware is not hungry or thirsty?

Awareness doesn't need any "thing" to exist, to be aware of itself. No thoughts, objects, emotions are needed for you to know yourself as this Aware Presence, but without awareness there is no way to have any knowledge or experience of anything else. Prior to all objects, a quieter, deeper part of us is aware and knows, without labels or judgments, simply a quiet steady knowing. Notice and connect to this One, your Aware Presence, it is your strength and your light. It is your guide in and through hard times, it is your anchor to peace.

17.
Staying Put - The Loving Undoing of the False

The Guest House

*This being human is a guest house
Every morning a new arrival.*

*A joy, a depression, a meanness,
some momentary awareness comes
as an unexpected visitor.*

Welcome and entertain them all!

*Even if they are a crowd of sorrows,
who violently sweep your house
empty of its furniture,
still treat each guest honorably.*

*He may be clearing you out for some new delight.
The dark thought, the shame, the malice,
meet them at the door laughing,
and invite them in.*

*Be grateful for whoever comes,
because each has been sent
as a guide from beyond.*
– Rumi

The Warmhearted Openness of Being

By connecting to this Aware peaceful part of us, we are better able to connect to the more human and alive part of us, to what flavors the very life we live. Our journey doesn't end by meeting our Essential Self. No, meeting and being the Absolute Self provides us with the fuel and stillness necessary for true healing and transformation to take place on this path to wholeness, fearlessness and freedom. Our unwavering Aware Presence provides us with the courage, the confidence, the peace and the faith we need to become intimately connected with the totality of our Being and the totality of our life. It enables us to meet and welcome all those things we tend to run away from and resist; only through this willing openness can we heal and become Whole. Through this process we are able to take back our lives and own our thoughts, emotions, sensations and experiences rather than they owning us. All these things that we resist and repress, negate, shy away from and reject, keep us bound. To be truly free and whole we must meet and open up to what has been denied and exiled, our fears, our shame, our guilt, our beliefs in lack, our resentments, our great sadness and disappointments, our boredom and numbness, our tension and anxiety must be intimately met and received. Emotions themselves do not enslave us; it is our very rejection and negation of them that keeps the light of our Being concealed. In denying these emotions and states, we, in fact, deny a piece of ourselves, a piece of life and keep ourselves trapped in this circle of lack, destined to always look elsewhere for Wholeness. Any part of ourselves and of life that is rejected, keeps us in a self-inflicted darkness, we have forgotten that we are the ones that closed the blinds and all we need to do is open up.

These denied pieces of us keep us in obscurity; they

reinforce the belief that life and who we are is limited, imperfect and filled with darkness. This seeming darkness acts like a dense cloud in front of the sun. It veils the joy, the brightness and the warmth that is always ever-present in life. We have two options, we can see that the cloud is not dense at all, it is made of nothing but transparent vapor and this knowing remind us of the ever shining sun that is always its very background. But for most of us this knowing only comes after an exploration, which is our second option. The other way to recognize the illusory nature of the cloud, illusory meaning not existing as we perceive, is to travel to and through it, realizing that it is in fact not solid, but made of empty fluffiness. Upon this exploration, we are able to know directly that it only seemed to be dense and hide the sun, but it, in fact, never did. In reality the cloud is penetrable, soft and spacious, it is space itself, it never clouded the sun; on the contrary, it is the light of the sun that actually made it visible at all. Sometimes the only way to the light is through the seeming darkness. We find the light by not running, by staying put and opening ourselves to everything that we feel and experience, by finding the light within the seeming darkness of our existence. When it comes to self-discovery, I have found that what we perceive to be in the way is actually The Way.

Any emotion fully felt, however 'dark' or 'negative' we have labeled it, leads directly to peace, for every emotion is a perfect expression of life, just as every wave is a perfect expression of the ocean. Taste the thrilling aliveness in fear, taste the sweet joy at the heart of sadness, taste the excitement in boredom, taste every expression of consciousness, and know that you are only tasting your own taste. Just remember, nothing is what is seems, and

nothing is against you.
– Jeff Foster

The extent of your freedom is the extent of your openness and willingness to become deeply intimate with all those subtle seemingly dark emotions, thoughts and sensations we experience. The first step to meeting, loosening and untangling these deeper emotions and blockages is to learn to stay put and openly notice what is arising in this moment. The following exploration is the ground upon which all deeper practices are built; you cannot work on something, embrace something or transform something that you are not completely aware of and intimate with. This constant feeling of unease or subtle tension that we hold deep in ourselves is innate to most, if not all human beings, we all have it, we just keep ourselves too busy to notice it, but deep down we know something is off.

~Experiential Adventure: Warmly and Openly Noticing what Is ~

Throughout your day, when you have a little quiet time, become aware and notice the constant, however subtle, constriction, tension, anxiety, depression or boredom that permeates you, both in your body, your mind and emotionally. Notice that no matter what, there is always a subtle sense of tension and resistance in you, especially during times when nothing much is happening and our attention is not being carried in one direction or another. During times of low stimulation, notice how much more you feel this underlying sense of unease and dissatisfaction that permeates your sense of self and your experience. Just become aware, without turning away, of that tension and deep restlessness. Stay with it, drop any and all agenda, like trying to make it go away or figuring it out or changing it; simply remain in a state of open and warmhearted curiosity, allowing all concepts and judgments to be put aside. Do this easy exploration for a few minutes, allowing yourself to become very intimate with whatever is closed inside you. The power of this exploration is not in how long you can stay with whatever resistance is coming up, but in the ongoing, day-to-day meeting and recognition of this resistance. At this juncture we are not trying to change anything, we are simply trying to become aware of what is actually taking place inside us and simply greet it at the door.

~

Becoming aware of all those subtle inner movements is a major step in recognizing everything that keeps you bound. Simply being open to and willing to meet and connect allows the light of Awareness to start dispersing the density of the many clouds that seem to block the warmth and light of the sun. For some, to simply and openly notice, without judgment, what is happening in this moment is enough to completely dissolve the cloud and let the light shine through; for others, it is the indispensable first step of a deeper exploration. Start here, work with just seeing what is here in a warm, open and nonjudgmental way. Notice the knots in your body, the resistance, the subtle density in your stomach, the ache in your heart, just notice.

To mistakenly identify with finite things instead of as infinite Consciousness, would be doing what? It would be needlessly subjecting oneself to all those finite limitation- when in fact as Consciousness, One is absolutely unlimited.
  – Peter Francis Dziuban

Knowing Who We Are

As we become still and stop reacting to every train of thought, sensation, emotion or perception that comes through us, we develop the ability to stay with whatever shows up, without running or resisting. In this quiet openness we are able to witness and inquire into the nature of all these things and states.

- Are they truly who I am?
- Do they define me?
- Can I find the One that witnesses all these states, yet is unaffected and unchanged by them?

We come to realize that our various mental and emotional states and all our perceptions, sensations and experiences are actually visitors in our body, mind and Awareness. We need not try to control them or identify with them any more than we would identify with the UPS delivery guy or any other guest that may enter our house. Just as easily as they arrived into our home, they will also depart, if we allow them to. That is one the great truths of my experience, life is constant flux, we can always trust that what we dislike will move on its way and that what we love will come back around. All we have to do is stay open, stay present and allow life to move as it moves and do its dance.

With a little clear seeing, examining and remembering, we are no longer at the mercy of our emotions, thoughts, sensations and perceptions. We have the choice and the courage to stay still and to watch, to not get involved any more than we choose to. Nothing can pull us away from our Self. We can stay open to the whole of life and to every experience, without getting lost or closing down. Guy Finley reminds us to "Practice this new understanding that starts with remembering the truth of yourself. Each effort will reward you with the growing realization that any time you start to feel miserable it's only because you have mistakenly identified with who and what you are not." I will leave you with a little poem I wrote a few years back:

The Pain and the Beauty of Life...

The pain: The fluidity of life makes it so that everything changes. Because everything changes, what we hate can never be kept at bay for very long, it always comes back around. Because everything changes, what we love, we cannot keep, it eludes us, slips right out of our fingers.

The beauty: The fluidity of life makes it so that everything changes. Because everything changes, what we hate never lasts for very long, "This too shall pass." Because everything changes, what we love always comes back around.
So relax and go fly a kite, will ya?

18.
Seeing the Wholeness in Everything

How can it be otherwise?
Perfection contains all
Imperfections;
The smaller within the larger.
Do not chastise your gods
For the aspects of life deemed
Unacceptable.
– Wu Hsin

Life through the Eyes of Awareness

As we have discussed, this still, infinite, ever-present Aware Presence is the background and the essence of everything. All experiences, all inner and outer states and circumstances are movements of Wholeness, the Absolute in its many shapes and forms. This wholeness that we are, this peaceful vastness is complete as it is, it is not a mistake and thus cannot make mistakes. Nothing can be, that is not meant to be. All that exist was meant to exist in the exact way it exists. All perceived flaws are no other than flaws in perception. All perceived flaws are Wholeness in disguise.

There are only two ways to live your life.
One is as though nothing is a miracle.
The other is as though everything is a miracle.
– Albert Einstein

We can live our lives from the point of view of the imaginary self, seeing flaws, mistakes, faults and blame everywhere and resisting everything, or from the point of view of the Absolute Self, seeing beauty, love and fulfillment in all experiences and saying "Yes" to all of life. Peter Russell, in *From Science to God*, writes, "In every moment I have a choice as to how I see a situation. I can see it through the eyes caught in the materialist mindset that worries...Alternatively, I can choose to see it through the eyes free from the dictates of this thought system. But it is not easy...Once I've been caught by a fearful perception, I'm seldom aware there could even be another way of seeing things. I think my reality is the only reality...The place for help is deep within, to that level of consciousness that lies beyond the materialistic mindset – to the God within." As we learn this new way of being and moving through life, we remind ourselves to breathe and relax. As Jeff foster said "Just remember, nothing is what is seems, and nothing is against you." When I catch myself worrying, angry, replaying a scenario, planning or trying to fix or control something or someone, I come back to myself, to the sensations in my body, to the part of me that is afraid, to the tension or ache or fear in my heart as well as the inner knowing that lies behind it and learn to relax, let go of my mind and stay with whatever is. It is not enough to believe that nothing is against me, that everything is a miracle and that all imperfections are in fact perfect, I have to live it; I have to be willing to let go of the tiller, relax and trust. Over time, slowly, I find that the imaginary self and its neurosis soften and being in flow, trusting and staying put becomes easier.

Regardless of which position we take, Life keeps flowing, keeps presenting us with new experiences, new sensations and new perceptions. The ones that are not denied, not resisted are allowed to flow right through us, they brighten and perfume our experience and they leave no residue. This is the way that life is meant to be lived. When we know ourselves to be the Absolute Self and live our lives from that aware perspective, life simply runs its course. It moves in and through us, moment by moment, allowing us to experience the world and ourselves in infinite ways and infinite flavors. We resist nothing and embrace everything; we see our own face in all experiences. We are touched yet not changed or tainted by any thought, emotion, sensation, perception or circumstance. We know, experience and feel a deep connection to all things. As Aware Presence, we are all movements of life, one with all shapes and forms, all people, all emotions, all states and all circumstances. Michael Singer, in *The Untethered Soul* describes that if we lived our lives this way we would be "a fully aware being":

An awake being lives in the 'now.' They are present, life is present, and the wholeness of life is passing through them. Imagine if you were so fully present during each experience of life that it was touching you to the depth of your being. Every moment would be a stimulating, moving experience because you would be completely open, and life would be flowing right through you.
– Michael A. Singer

The Knots of Resistance

On the other hand, the experiences we deny, avoid and resist tend to stay stuck within us, creating a residue, a soft spot in our psyche that lingers, binds us and hurts, especially when touched or stimulated. If the experience we deny and resist is especially painful or even traumatic, then the knot is denser and more constricting. These unconscious pockets of trapped energy unknowingly permeate, affect and haunt our lives and choices. Experiences and all perceptions are meant to flow right through us, by the time a seemingly negative or painful experience reaches our psyche; it is already in us, it has already entered our Beingness. If not, we would not be aware of it and experiencing it. So, if the experience, the perception of it, is already inside us, what is the point of denying it? It is not like the resistance pushes it back out, or keeps it from entering our experience; since we are already aware that we don't like it, we know it has already come in. On the contrary, with some exploration, we realize that resisting and denying our experience doesn't preserve us but actually keeps the disturbance stuck inside us, unable to leave. In effect, resisting does nothing but trap within us the very thing we were trying to escape from. How much sense does that make? It makes as much sense as closing all the doors and windows of your car, in an effort to get a trapped bee out, or locking all the doors and windows of your house with the robber still inside. The energies of the initial disturbance as well as the energies of our resistance are then trapped in our body and psyche, creating havoc, calling our attention constantly to be freed. Those wounded and trapped energies push all our buttons and pull all our strings in their plea to be released. All they wish is for us to open up, meet them and release them. Unfortunately, most of us resist their call because we are afraid and rather than allowing ourselves to feel them fully and help them move through, we end up stuffing them down deeper, denying them and ourselves the joy of freedom. As Michael Singer explains, when we reject our experience, we start a negative cycle in which "life must now compete with this blocked event" He then goes on to warn us that "Long term, the energy patterns that cannot make it through...stay inside and become a problem." The things we love, like or don't care much about, we embrace and feel fully, allowing them to come right through us, effortlessly in and out. Which is probably why time flies when you're having fun. The things we dislike or fear, we fight and resist, which does nothing for us, except that we end up trapped and haunted by those unwanted visitors, continually playing a game of hide a seek, alternating between evading them or feeling invaded by them, at least until we are willing to stop hiding, meet them and reopen the door.

When our longing to be truly free is stronger than our longing to distract ourselves from our suffering, we enter a deeper life, a life in which
everything - everything - is permitted to awaken us.
– Robert Augustus Masters, PhD

All of that resistance, these denied experiences stem from the imaginary self's belief in lack. The separate self, feeling inadequate and fragile, feels the need to constantly protect itself by being at war with the whole of life. This conflict creates knots, pockets of disturbed energy within us that reinforce the imaginary self's position. None of this would be a problem if we didn't mistakenly believe ourselves to be this imaginary self and its misguided beliefs. In some way, the imaginary self, feeling weak and unsafe, denies itself the space to be fully human and to experience intimately and completely what it means to be human, in all its glory and in all its anguish. Part of letting go of the habit of being an imaginary self is to stop acting like one and to relax in what it means to be divinely human, and see that all imperfections are the way to perfection.

These residues of denied experiences create our suffering, our inner struggles and they reinforce our misguided belief that life and things are not whole and complete just as they are. This imaginary self and its constrictive knots, is a heavy baggage we carry along on our journey, it slows us down, it robs us of our ease and of our spontaneous passion and joy for life. When we resist life, we feel tired, drained and weary; on the other hand, when we say yes to life, like when we are in love, looking forward to something or completely involved in a project, we feel light, enthusiastic, inspired, filled with an endless source of energy. Children are like that, their enthusiasm and amazing energy comes from their yes attitude to life, they do not hold any "no" in their body, they are yet to be weighed down by avoidance and resistance.

The more disturbed energy residues we hold inside of us, the more closed off we are to life and the more suffering we experience. These knots also affect our level of energy and vitality and they keep us bound to this false identification. A major aspect of this path is to release this energy and unravel the knots that bind us, freeing our vitality and recovering our natural enthusiasm. This release allows us to fully know ourselves as the peaceful Aware Presence that we are, as well as the perfectly imperfect human being, and it enables us to live life wide awake and wide open. One major aspect of this path is seeing all of life, including our pain, our shame, anger and fear as part of the great Wholeness that we are, a complete expression of life in this moment. This Wholeness is everything, it denies nothing and embraces everything.

Keep in mind that there is a difference between pain

and suffering. Pain is an inescapable aspect of life. Life sometimes is painful, both physically and emotionally. Being awake to who we are doesn't mean that we don't get sick or stub our toe or have car accidents, and it doesn't mean that we don't experience disappointments, setbacks and deep grief. Our loved ones still die, leave or hurt us, regardless of how awake we are. Life is filled with pain of all sorts, but suffering, on the other hand, is a choice. Pain is a raw and pure experience, it is a natural and spontaneous movement of life that is shared by all sentient beings. Suffering is conceptual; it arises in and is created by the mind as part of the imaginary self's false attempt to fix and control. Suffering is the movement of thought that judges, resists and denies this moment. Suffering is the movement of thought that rejects this current experience and projects in the past and the future: "What did I do to deserve this?"; "I should have seen it coming"; "Life shouldn't be this way"; "What's going to happen to me from now on"; "What am I going to do?"; "What if this feeling or situation never goes away?" Out of this projection forward or backward arises fear, worry, blame, anger, resentment, shame and guilt, the many faces of suffering.

> *From the point of view of*
> *The person*
> *Problems never cease.*
> *From the point of view of*
> *The Totality*
> *Problems never arise.*
> *Perfection is disturbed by*
> *The arrival of judgment.*
> – Wu Hsin

Wholeness Includes the Relative

That is not to negate the pain and suffering that is experienced by most sentient beings and to deny that truly tragic circumstances exist in the world. From the relative point of view, hurt and misery exist, we can never say that a mother's suffering at the death of her child or that world hunger or war or horrendous physical pain are illusions, and yet from the Absolute perspective, it is simply life unfolding as it does, raw and pure movements in open non-judgmental Wholeness. The relative and Absolute are both real in their own right, and they both exist simultaneously. Let's use the dream world as an example. In your dream, everything and everyone is made of you, of your mind, and appears in you. There are no multiple objects and multiple people, just you in many shapes and forms. You, the dreamer, are safely sleeping, regardless of what goes on in the dream, but for the characters in the dream whatever is going on is very real. For them, pain is real, problems are real, grief is real, lust is real and so is joy and love. In the dream world, everything is real and feels very real and yet in the Absolute sense none of it is actually existent and no one actually evolves, hurts, changes or loves.... It is just you the dreamer moving in different ways in your dream, taking on different shapes and experiencing different movements of dream life. Whatever the characters in the dream do is perfectly okay from the point of view of the dreamer, it is just the dream evolving as it does, nothing to fix, nothing to change, nothing and no one to blame or judge, simply the dream unfolding and the characters playing their parts. The same is true of life. The understanding and seeing that nothing ever happens outside of this One Aware Presence and that all of life is complete in every moment doesn't keep us from acting as we feel moved to in the relative world, whether that is feeding the hungry, rising in outrage and interrupting any violence, falling to our knees in prayer or in tears, because all of our responses, everything that we feel moved to do or be is also Wholeness, being as it is and moving as it moves in this moment.

> *Enlightenment sees whatever is arising as it is, without conceptualization or preference. It has no need or desire to improve upon or avoid anything. It is equally content with the mundane as much as the extraordinary.*
> *– David Bohdan*

Answering the Call

All our struggles are pointers, guides to our liberation. There are no mistakes in life; everything is as it should be. Every circumstance, every person, every perception and experience, however painful, is as it should be, complete and unbroken. It is in the image of the Wholeness that is its essence. Everything, that hooks and rattles you, is in fact an opportunity in disguise, it is Wholeness knocking on your door. All suffering is a message from your True Self, reminding you that you have forgotten who and what you are, and that you have identified yourself to the false. Guy Finley, in *The Essential Laws of Fearless Living*, tells his readers that "We are created to eternally transcend the limits of our present nature, to transform who and what we have been in the very moment it ceases to serve the good of us."

Whatever we resist and resent is a gift, a messenger sent from our Essential Self to guide us home. It shows us where we are stuck, where we are yet to be free and where the knots of illusion still bind us, and it gives us a direct way back to Wholeness. All suffering is there to remind us that we have yet again identified with what we are not.

Under your pain, your anger, your sadness, your jealousy, your loneliness, your shame, is the whisper of yourself to yourself, "Hey, wake up, you have forgotten who you are." While caught in our fears, in our thoughts, in painful emotions or memories, we become lost in that state, consumed by it and forget our Essential Nature. The suffering is a compass, there to remind us that we are looking in the wrong direction and we only need to shake ourselves out of our trance to realize that we are home, unharmed, unaffected and the rest is only illusion. All of our struggles and disappointments are a chance to cut the knot that holds us captive to the false, so that we may awaken more fully to the Real, to who we are. As Kamal Ravikant writes in *Living Your Truth*, "Our experiences are nothing but a series of gifts, and the less we resist them, the better things get. Through the joy, through the pain, through the growth, life is beautiful."

The first step is to notice what it is that we hold on to and what it is that we resist, since both are ways the imaginary self perpetuates itself. When you find yourself anxious, worried, angry, guilty, sad or disappointed, you know that there is something you are either holding on to that needs to be released or something that you are resisting that needs to be met and allowed to move through. Often, the way to let go and stop resisting is to become the witness, to open yourself up to the emotion that is your guide and follow it with curiosity and sincerity to its depth. The emotion, itself, carries the energy of the knot or blockage we wish to be free from. That which you are resisting or clinging to is imbedded within the form of resistance or emotion you are feeling. We discover that the messenger and the message are one and the same, undeniably connected. The difficult emotion itself and your resistance to it are the ways to peace and freedom. So during those difficult and uncomfortable times choose to connect to the raw energy that makes up the emotion and resistance itself. Drop the concepts and feel the flowing aliveness in the energy itself, just watch it, connect to it, open yourself up to it, sink or dive into it and follow it back to yourself.

See that you are not the emotion itself, it is happening in you, not to you. You, as Aware Presence, can experience and play with this pure raw energy and even enjoy it, while remaining completely unchanged by it. The more openness and freedom you allow yourself to find within the emotion, the faster any blockage will be able to flow, bringing you back to the Peace and Joy that is your Absolute nature.

> *To know that one is, is natural.*
> *To know what one is*
> *Requires a diving into the depths of*
> *One's own being.*
> *The pearl rests on the bottom.*
> *– Wu Hsin*

~Experiential Adventure: The Deep Dive - Releasing the Knots of Resistance~

This experiential adventure's aim is to allow a more profound connection to your Absolute Self and to help you slowly unwind the imaginary self by releasing any emotion or resistance you might be opposing or clinging to. The purpose of the first two steps is to help you release any resistance you might be holding. The third step guides you to fully connect to the emotion and through this intimate exploration untangle the knots that bind us. This exploration can also be very useful in releasing resistance to and seeing through physical pain, as well as emotional pain.

Close your eyes, take a few deep breaths and bring your focus within. Allow your thoughts to pass by, without getting caught up by them. Shift your focus inside and find that Aware Presence within that witnesses and knows your experience. Allow each exhale to loosen your body and expand your spirit. Focus on the vastness that you are, your consciousness without a beginning or an end, without boundaries, without a shape, age, gender or any defining stories, ever present, ever free. As you shift your focus to that still and silent space within, notice how vast and open you are. Now, from that place, watch and experience the energy of the emotion you are experiencing at the moment. Drop the label, judgment and story surrounding the emotion. Notice that whatever story and label you give this emotion and its corresponding physical sensation, whether it be anxiety, sadness, anger or whatever else, the label itself seems to freeze the emotion in place. Then proceed with the following steps:

1. Once you are connected the emotion, start the releasing process of the Deep Dive by inquiring into the emotion and its relationship to your Absolute Self. Ask yourself the following questions. Don't forget to take a few seconds in between each question and feel back in to the raw emotion and the Aware Presence that experiences it.

- Is this vast Aware Presence that I am, affected by this emotion and its energy? Or does it just stay open, untouched and free?
- Do I, as my Absolute Self, want this emotional charge to go away, or am I okay with it?

- Drop all concepts. Without the label, judgment and its story, is this raw movement of energy called an emotion negative? Or is it relatively neutral?
- Does my Aware Presence judge this raw energy, this emotional charge as negative or bad? Or is it wide open to all of life, without judgments, labels or preferences?
- Can I experience both at the same time? The raw energy of the emotion as well as the peace and stillness of my Absolute Nature, out of which the energy arises, through which it is experienced and known and into which it will dissolve?

Once you are fully anchored into your Absolute Nature and clear that you are not the emotion but the Aware Presence that knows and experiences it, and that you as Aware Presence could never be taken over or harmed by this emotional charge, then move on to the next step of the emotional release by letting go of any resistance.

2. If you sense a resistance to being with and fully feeling the emotional charge or to letting go of the story that surrounds it, then before you are able to release the emotion by diving or sinking into it, you must first release your resistance by feeling and inquiring into the physical sensation of the resistance itself. Notice the physical sensation of the resistance:

- Where do you feel the sense of resistance, the "no," in your body?
- Does it have a shape, temperature or texture? (Usually resistance will feel like a hard ball, constriction or wall or a dense energy.)
- Ask yourself whether your Aware Presence minds and judges the resistance or does it remain free and at peace regardless of any resistance?

- *Ask the resistance what it is trying to accomplish by resisting? (You will find that most resistance is a form of psychological guardian and only wants to protect you.)*

Stay with this blockage; open yourself to this energy and hold it with warmth, compassion and gratitude since its intention is only to protect you from the difficult emotion, knot or trauma that lies behind it. Thank it for its hard work thus far and ask it if it might be willing to step aside or soften just a bit so that you can experience what you need to truly heal and be free. Allow your breath to loosen any resistance and once you feel relaxed, open and safe enough to stay with the original emotion, then just experience the raw energy of the emotion without label or story; allow it to flow, to move, to express itself, stay open without judgment. At that point, you are ready to dive in.

3. Come back to the raw and pure charge of the emotion. Stay with it and relax into it. Feel it fully and allow it to move and express itself as it wishes. Slowly bring yourself closer to the emotion, see yourself as a miniature version of yourself and the emotion as a deep pool or dense cloud and dive in. If the concept of diving in seems too scary or maybe a little violent, than simply going in slowly and allow yourself to sink in. Breathe deeply into and through the emotion, allowing each breath to take you in deeper into it, the way a diver comes up for air and dives back in to reach deeper and deeper depth, as if searching for a treasure hidden at the bottom of the ocean. The in-breath allows you to reconnect to your source, your Aware Presence and the out-breath moves you deeper into the energy, sinking into it, meeting it and feeling it fully and seeing if its density and its charge changes at different depth.

Sometimes the beginning process of diving deeper into

the emotion can feel very intense, like feeling turbulence as a plane flies through a cloud. In the beginning of the Deep Dive, the emotional charge can intensify, stay at this level until you feel yourself opening and letting go of any resistance toward it and able to relax into it despite its intensity. Loosen any resistance, any impulse to close, with your breath, breathing in the Peace and Stillness that is your Essence and then diving back in to explore this tumultuous depth. Do that for a few breaths, until you are comfortable diving deeper. Keep diving and exploring each new depth; like Russian nesting dolls, each depth brings a different quality of emotional energy. You might sense the emotion changing, the sensation and movement of it might transform, maybe even turning into a different emotion. Just stay with it and keep diving. Throughout this exercise trust in your inner wisdom, if you find that you've done enough, than back off and stay just on your edge for as long as you can and then slowly bring yourself back out and do the exercise again at a different time, slowly going deeper over time.

At each new level, allow willingness, compassion and your breath to loosen and open up any resistance. Resist the urge to dive deeper if you have not undone your resistance first, only when you are relaxed and open to the current experience can you move on to the next level of emotion. Keep Diving Deeper until you feel that you have travelled to the essence of the emotion and are one with it, not resisting or clinging to it, but in perfect relationship with it. Take a few deep breaths at this level and then keep diving until you reach what is beyond, on the other side of the emotional charge. If you stay with this process to its completion, you will travel all the way through and out of the emotion, into the peace and freedom that resides beyond it and you will find yourself having come full circle, back to your Aware Presence, the knot of the emotion will have been fully released. This is true Alchemy, the turning of base matter into the universal elixir of life.

Sometimes knots are related to past imprints and memory, so it is not uncommon to have flashes of memory come back up, allow those images and senses to surface and flow through you, they are part of the disentangling and release of the emotion. Don't get caught up or cling to them, though, because they are nothing but a reflection, a conceptual story, stay out of any abstract imaging and simply dive back into the felt sense of it. Allow the stored up pain and fear to rise up, if tears come let them come, that's part of the release. If shaking arises, let your body shake, it is its way of helping loosen the knots and free up the trauma and its stuck energy.

Allow the energy to flow, without judgment, label or resistance until it comes to its natural end. Find the peace and freedom that you are, beyond the experience of the raw energy. Dwell in the vast knowing space that is your true nature, feel its transparency, its underlying peace and joy, regardless of what shows up in it. Experience the freedom and peace of being ever present, without a gender or an age, without a story, open to and genuinely okay with all of life, including all movements of energy, all resistance, all raw emotions and their sensations.

I often recommend that after finishing this exercise, clients drink lots of water and move their body in some way, whether that is going for a brisk walk, dancing, yoga or just actively shaking and jumping around in your living room. This exercises releases lot of toxins and pent up energy that need to find a way out of the body. After completing this exercise you might feel a little raw and vulnerable, so be mindful of your direct environment and of *the people, places and behaviors you engage in; be gentle with yourself.*

~

*Your task is not to seek for love but merely
to seek and find all the barriers within yourself
that you have built against it.*
– Rumi

This exercise can obviously be practiced with very charged and strong emotions, but it can also be very effective with more subtle forms of dissatisfaction such as boredom or numbness. We tend to forget emotions like these because they are not so bothersome and difficult to bear, but they often hide trauma and deep seated fears, like a frozen wall has been put up to shield us from what lies beyond it. Once you get passed the placid and desensitized façade, you will find an alive world, juicy with past pain that need to be released.

Deep Diving can be somewhat difficult and draining work. This is the part that people shy away from in transformation. Do you think that the caterpillar enjoys and looks forward to its metamorphosis? I'll spare you the grueling details; let's just say science has shown that becoming a butterfly isn't a fun process. Transcendence and transformation is that way, it has its cost like everything else and peace is the prize. Everything exists within you, negative as well as positive. All negative states seem to veil the peace, completeness and freedom that are at the core of your true nature, which is why they need to be seen trough. Notice my use of the word seem, all states exist, they arise out of your Essence and release back into it, but they could never conceal what you are, that is part of the illusion. Unfortunately, realizing who you are and knowing your Absolute Self doesn't always release the knots of our past suffering, we still have to do the work, but being awake to our Essential Self gives us the courage, stillness and compassion necessary to meet everything we have denied. It is only through the darkness that you can find the light. All these emotions that you run from and shun are the way to the peace, happiness and Wholeness you long for. Within anger exists peace, within hate, love; within fear, courage; within resentment, forgiveness and within worry, trust. This is the reason Awareness allows and embraces everything equally, because it knows that everything is only an extension of itself and always leads back to itself. This work is what freedom requires. It is what true and lasting peace and happiness requires. The more you explore your experience by diving deeply through it, to its source, the lighter and lighter you become, freed from all the knots that keep you bound.

Find the antidote in the venom. Come to the root of the root of yourself.
– Rumi

The Loving Expression of the All

Everything is flawless and seamless as it is and it evolves and moves, as it needs to bring us home to our Self. When fear, stories and illusions are released, all that is left is the effortless movement of life and the peace and wholeness of our True Nature, which is the ground and essence of everything that exists. Our perceived enemies and seeming bad luck are no other than us in disguise. Our seeming adversaries and unlucky circumstances are actually our best of friends and our greatest blessing as they offer us the greatest gifts possible, that to remember our True Nature, set ourselves free from our suffering and the ability to finally live life deeply and wide open. As we experienced in the deep dive exploration, if you travel deeply enough through any emotion, sensation or resistance, you find yourself immersed in pure stillness. Beyond, on the other side of, any experience, perception, sensation, emotion and belief, lies the openness, peace and love of our Aware Presence. That is true of all emotions. Even hate arises out of Awareness and when you find the courage to explore it and deeply dive in and through it, you find yourself right back where you started, in the love and peace that is your Essence. The opposites are really complimentary and belong to each other; all are aspects of the Whole. The only reason you can actually feel the full spectrum of emotions is because everything that is, ever was or could ever be already exists within the Absolute. The Absolute, which is no other than you, is everything; the beautiful, the ugly, the love, the rage, the masculine, the feminine, the ecstasy, the agony, the animal in us, the Divine in us, pleasure, pain, misery, bliss, and finally creation as well as destruction, nothing is ever left out.

There is nothing to fear; on the contrary, good luck, bad luck, it is all worth celebrating. So why resist, why seek something different? We can either stay angry, resentful and afraid, while living a miserable life, or we can use whatever event or circumstance upset us to set us free. If we can remember in, the grip of a difficult emotion, that this very feeling is our ticket home, no other than the Divine in disguise, then we can find the courage and willingness to put down our barriers, and to simply relax, meet, stay and explore what is arising. The way through our suffering and through our fear and resistance to it is in remembering that all experiences are grounded in love and with our liberation and freedom in mind. Everything, everyone and every experience is an invitation to come home, we have just forgotten the valuable art of deep listening. No matter what it might seem like, from our limited illusory position, this is a benevolent universe founded on and filled with nothing but love and goodness. As Guy Finley reminds us, "Always remember instead that real life is a secret and vital flux of possibilities rising up from the Ground of what seems improbable, much as a spring flower manages to bloom in a once-frozen field."

Based on this understanding what is there to fear? What is there to resist? What is there to seek other than this? When you understand and deeply know that nothing else exists but love and goodness, you cannot help but be open to life as it is, and to yourself as you are, fearlessly and gratefully, in awe and wonder. The entire universe conspires, all things in life work together toward one goal, your evolution. Everything that happens to you and in you is part of an intelligent design, with no other pursuit than to help you realize and remember what and who you have always been. The whole of life collaborates with you toward your liberation from illusion, your freedom from fear and your recognition that life and you are one unified Whole, peaceful and happy within yourself. When all this is understood, beyond any doubt, the only answer is trust. Trust that you are safe, even when it doesn't seem like it. Trust that this moment is as it should be, even when you want it to be completely different. Trust that you are loved and valued, even when you feel lonely and abandoned, and trust that everything that happens is part of a loving and intelligent plan that you devised for yourself so that you could remember that you are the light that give rise to and illuminate all things, beyond the seeming darkness. From this position, to all struggles and to all suffering we say "Welcome." The only way out is through and the only way to dissipate the darkness is to switch on the light. As the Buddha said, "Be a light unto yourself." You are the light.

~Experiential Inquiry: Seeing our Distress through the Light~

Whenever you are struggling, with someone, with some kind of difficult circumstance, ask yourself these few questions:

- *Where in this moment am I stuck in illusion?*
- *Where in my body does this resistance lie? Can I meet it, with warmth and openness?*
- *From whose point of view am I living this moment? Who am I right now? Am I identified to an imaginary personal self or to Awareness?*
- *Who is troubled about this person or situation? Is the vast peaceful Aware Space that I am, the one that sees through my eyes upset?*
- *Can I find the one, the part of me, which is upset? Does it inhabit my body? Is it a thought, a belief, an emotion or a sensation? Does it exist with any kind of reality or is it simply a mirage, an appearance that will at some point disappear? Can I stay and meet this sense of "me" the one who is struggling, until it dissipates?*
- *What does Aware Presence have to say about this person or situation I am struggling with?*
- *Can I see the loving reminder to wake up and remember who I am in this situation?*

Get quiet and look at the questions above and do one of the following:

- *Sit silently, breathe deeply a few times and then slowly and silently ask the question. Then fall silent and just stay with the question; stay with the silent intuition of it, the energy of it. Do that a few times, staying silently with the question for a few breath each times. This is a more intuitive, meditative form of inquiry.*

- *Sit silently, breathe deeply a few times and then slowly and silently ask the question and then fall silent and just stay with the question, stay with the silent intuition of it, the energy of it and then go in your body and look for the answer, the felt sense of it in your body. Explore the question through your body, feel the part of you that is unsatisfied and resisting, meet it, see if it has any independent reality. Look for the one who wants things to be different, can you find this self? Can you hold it and give it love and compassion?*
- *If you like writing and exploring in a more cerebral way, pick up a pen and paper, sit quietly, calm your mind, slowly and silently ask the question, and then fall silent and just stay with the question. See what bubbles up. Every insight that comes up, write down. Everything that arises from your core, that feels absolutely true in this moment, write down.*

~

19.
Love – The Essence of our Being

It is not possible to love the world
Without loving oneself first.
Is one not
Part of the world rather than
Apart from it?
Love the smaller first,
Then the greater.
In so doing, the space between
Oneself and the world disappears;
One becomes the world.
– Wu Hsin

If I had to pick one word that describes the essence of my message, of this book, of this path, that word would be Love. Some of you might be surprised and wonder, why not "Peace" or "Wholeness," as we've talked about both a lot through this journey. That's true, but you see, peace and wholeness are always a natural extension of love. You can't have love without peace or wholeness, and you can't have peace or wholeness without love. All of the mystics throughout time, most if not all of our spiritual leaders, have had one common message: "Love."

Love is your Birthright

Some people are uncomfortable with the concept of Love. For them, it sounds hokey and way too New Age. If you find yourself restless in your seat, or frustrated by this chapter, thinking, "Where is this going?" that is not your intelligence speaking, that's your resistance talking, one of the many voices of the imaginary self, maybe even a wounded aspect of you, wanting to be heard, met and explored, searching for its way back home. Just relax and breathe through this resistance. Keep in mind all resistance is an invitation toward wholeness. What in you is threatened by this little four-letter word, L-O-V-E? Go find that part and give it love. Where does this wounded part, who doesn't believe it deserves love, live in you, and what does it feel like in your body? Go meet it, go connect with it, stay with it, welcome it, open yourself to it, dive into it and through it, and of course love it. Oftentimes what we are afraid of is the very thing we crave and need. Yes, you deserve to be loved; you are worthy of love and completely capable and able to love. Love is your nature.

Just look at your body, does it not love you? Does your heart not beat 24/7, without ever taking a break? What about your immune system? Does it not continually fight for your health until it has exhausted itself? Do your breath and your lungs ever take a break? No they do not, even when you sleep they keep at it. What about your digestive system, or your liver and kidneys, are they not always working to keep your body clean of toxins? Or your feet, will they not walk until they bleed, for you, all of that for you? There is not an organ or a system in your body that will not go to the edge for you; if that's not love, I don't know what is. If you ever question your worthiness or whether or not you are loved or deserving of love, all you have to do is connect to your body. What about your dog, does it ever not love you? Even when you forget to feed it or when you get too lazy to take him on that long walk you promised, doesn't it still love you? Maybe that is why the dogs is man's best friend, because no matter what, no matter our poor choices, our temper, or our moods, dogs remind us without fault that we are loved, lovable and worthy of love.

Love is our very nature, but what exactly do I mean by this word? When I refer to love, I don't mean the jealous, clinging, filled with expectation kind of love that human beings are prone to give one another. I mean a pure warm openness that tenderly and intimately cares for, appreciates and regards another just as they are, without any expectation or wish to control, change or benefit. This kind of warm open love is an automatic natural response of a healthy and whole human being. As we saw in the Deep Dive exploration, all experiences, all sensation and emotions lead back to our Essence, to love. Don't forget that darkness is not the absence of light, but the veiling of light. Love is what you are made of and if you can't see it, feel it or express it openly and easily, it is not because it is not present, but because it is veiled. When your baby is born, you don't have to learn how to love it, your love is a natural extension of you, without expectations or demands, freely felt and freely given. You might have to learn how to feed your child, how to hold her or change diapers, but loving is spontaneous. All you have to do is walk in a pet shop or go to your local animal shelter and you will see how much love naturally lives within you, and how it innately pours out of you.

The newborn fish does not learn to swim. It swims. The swimming arise from the natural state of things. Abiding in what is natural, One cannot make mistakes.
– Wu Hsin

The Sweetest Remembrance
Love is your natural state, you have just forgotten it,

veiled it. So how do we remember it? All of us know love, at one point or another we gave or received unconditional love. At some point in our lives, we felt true, genuine love from and for another, for and from an animal or for and from life. Who do you freely and openly love in your life, alive or deceased? Part of unveiling our natural and spontaneous loving nature is to live that love in our body, in the depth of our being. Remember what it feels like to be truly and unconditionally loved, as the recipient, how does love feel and taste in your body, in your mind, in your heart? How does love perfume your life, your very experiences? Feel that love, stay with that love, awaken what is already inside of you. What about love from the giver's point of view? How does love feel inside your body, your mind and your heart when you love someone, an animal, an object or life itself, freely, openly, tenderly and without any expectations, restrictions or demands? How does that color and perfume your life? This love is within you, draw it out, taste it, feel it, sense it, love it. The more you do this, the more in love with love you become, the stronger it becomes, and the wider it reaches. Suddenly nothing is beyond your love, not the birds, not the trees, not the anger, sadness or fear running through you, not the guy who just cut you off and not the dog who just took a shit on your front lawn, all is deserving of love.

In the poem at the beginning of this chapter, Wu Hsin tells us that before we can love the world, we must first love ourselves. For some, that is the hardest thing to do and it may be much easier to love the world, to love others, life itself, than it is to love ourselves. But as he states, aren't we part of the world? How can we love the world and not ourselves, who are part of it? How can we love our children and not what made them? Is your child not 50 percent you and that's without accounting for all the things that you are teaching him or her that are not included in their genetic makeup. So how do we learn to love ourselves? For starters, this entire book has been a love affair, a meeting and embracing of you; a call back to your wholeness and your own divinity. It cannot be done without some degree of love. Every time you sense a discomfort, a strong emotion or a resistance and you allow yourself the space, the time, the patience and the warmth to meet and explore that anger, that resentment, that sadness, that anxiety, that fear; openly, authentically with curiosity and compassion, that's an act of love! In these moments you embrace the darkest parts of you and remind yourself that even those are worthy and in need of love. You give yourself the gift of love. Giving yourself the gift of love is not self-centered, self-involved or narcissistic; on the contrary it is a generous act that you give the whole world. As you awaken your inner heart and rekindle the natural flow of love within you, it spontaneously overflows into your environment, unto every person and experience, journeying wider and wider, until the whole universe is included in a sea of love. Suddenly your whole being, all of your responses, all of your choices, all of your actions are bathed in love and spring out of love.

Love, our Most Generous Act

The Essence of your being is love, and love never leaves its own behind. It is love that goes back into the body and the soul to heal and make whole all our wounds, all our knots and fragmented parts. It is love that digs deep into our core to meet, receive, hold and free all that is still bound. Without Love, there is no awakening, no transformation. Even resistance is no other than a misguided form of love, which attempts to protect and shield us from the pain of being human. All suffering is a call for love, a call for it to find its way to that part within you that is lost. Love will transmute all fears, judgments and resistance into itself, all fragmented parts into the wholeness that they are. Love is the final blessing, the sweetness of our soul and the grace of transformation into the full realization of the essence of our Being. Love is the beat of the heart, the movement of life, all of life springs out of love, without it nothing is. Without love we remain in ignorance. A spiritual path without love is impotent and fragmented. In the final analysis, all true paths, even the ones that can seem very cerebral at first, are always a movement back to Love, to the opening of our hearts, and to the raw and wholehearted embrace of life. When I was working through what seemed like a mountain of blockages and knots, trying to stay open and compasssionately connect to the tenderness and vulnerability deep in my heart, I would often do these silly love meditations, sometimes sitting down, sometimes before bed or before getting up, and sometimes while walking the dog. They are very simple and a little hokey, but you know what? It worked. So whenever your natural spontaneous love seems veiled and your heart feels closed, practice one of these for a few minutes and see what happens. It should awaken your already ever-present inner love and allow you to open your heart.

~Experiential Adventure: Silly love Meditation #1~
1. *As you breathe in, say to yourself quietly "I love my self."*
2. *As you breathe out, say to yourself quietly "I love my life."*

You will find that after a few minutes, the words don't

matter, but the feeling of love permeates your being and easily extends out of you.

~

~Experiential Adventure: Silly love Meditation #2~
This practice, which is equally simple, involves being more direct about what you love. As you breathe deeply, every in breath represents an aspect of yourself, whether you actually love that part of you or not is beside the point. The truth is that there is nothing about you that is not deserving of love and that is not loved and supported by the universe. Everything, every aspect of you, is an aspect of life, of the Absolute, so if you can find any aspect of you that is not worthy of love, you are in fact saying that the Divine, that God is not worthy of love.

Here is an example:
In breath – I love my body.
Out breath – I love my mind.
In breath – I love my heart.
Out breath – I love my toes.
In breath – I love my worry.
Out breath – I love my colon.
In breath – I love my fear.
Out breath – I love my eyes.
In breath – I love my liver.
Out breath – I love my depression.
In breath – I love my struggles (you can also name each struggles individually).

And so on...You get the point. There is not rhyme or reason to it, and you don't have to get to every emotion or every parts or organ in your body. Just when the love is flowing naturally and freely through and out of you, just let go of the thoughts and stay with the love.

~

~Experiential Adventure: Silly Love Meditation #3~
This mediation is for those of you that are more visual. It is hard to do with your eyes *open so, it is not recommended to do while walking or driving.*

Think of a color that represents love, for some it is pink, for others red, for some just a transparent bright shimmering white light.

Think of someone that you love and feel the love inside your chest, once you clearly feel it, visualize the feeling as the color of your choice. Visualize this color; for this example, let's use pink. See this pink cloud of love emanate from your heart, see it expand and slowly emanate from your organs, from your blood vessel, from your cells, from your bones, your brain, from all your pores, out of your hands, through your feet, see this cloud of love permeate your entire body and slowly emanate from you. You are made of this cloud of love, it is the foundation of ever cell of your body, of the marrow of your bones, of the blood that flows through your body. See this cloud of love start to ripple out of your body, first permeating the room you are in, enveloping and loving every object or person in that room, then the neighborhood you are in, then your city, then your state, country, your continent, the world. See your love touch all life forms, soothe all suffering and heal all illnesses. Then continue to expand your love through our solar system and beyond, allow it to expand until there is nothing but this cloud of love that exist and it permeates everything. Make sure that before you close the mediation, you allow yourself to feel this love inside of you and throughout your body. And then slowly come back to your body and this present moment.

~

~Experiential Adventure: Not so Silly Love Meditation #4~

This practice is based on the open field of awareness. It is one of my favorite of the love meditations. Take a comfortable position. Allow your breath to come in and out, relax your body and your mind and just become aware that you are aware – not aware of anything in particular, just aware. Allow your aware attention to be open, spacious and unqualified, like a screen, waiting to receive whatever might be projected on it, let go of thoughts and just allow yourself to be wide open and present. When a sensation, sound, feeling or even a though arise on your screen of awareness, notice it, allow it to arise and dissipate naturally and on its own. Whatever it is, pleasant or unpleasant, whether it is a sensation, thought, sound or emotion, doesn't matter, your only job is to stay open and present to it and give it love. You might give it love by just saying in your head "this too, I love," or "this too is love," or "I love you," or "you are love," or "you are loved," or simply by saying "love" for every perception that arises. You also can do it from a sensory point of view by feeling love in your heart, that sweet warm sensation and by intentionally directing it to the sound, sensation, thought or emotion that is arising, or even by sending, directing and enveloping whatever was noticed in the color you associate with love. The trick is to just be aware of nothing in particular, to just stay in an open receptive state and allow any and all forms to arise and come to us on their own. Once you have received them fully, send your love, embrace them and bless them with love, realizing that no matter what life brings to you, that too is love, nothing is ever left out.

Here is an example of a relatively common practice for

me. The word love is simply named quietly in my head. I always start my practice by thinking of someone I love, awakening my natural inner love and opening my heart so that all senses are experienced from the heart:

- The sound of traffic in the distance – love.
- A dog barking – love
- An ache in my knee – love
- The thought "I wish this ache would go away; I wonder if something's wrong with my knee" – love
- The air conditioner turning on – love
- A sudden knot in my stomach, anxious feeling – love
- An itch on my nose – love
- The thought "Darn, I forgot to put the clothe in the dryer" – love

On and on it goes for 5, 10, 15 or even 20 minutes – thoughts appear, sensations appear, emotions and feelings appear, sounds appear and then they dissipate. We do nothing, we don't resist any of it, we don't hang on to or entertain any of them either, the moment they come into our awareness we recognize them as love, we name and feel them as love and we gift them love. If a thought, sensation or emotion grabs us, the moment we come back to the simple Awareness of Being, we simply give it love. And if we feel frustrated at having been high-jacked by a thought or emotion, we notice our frustration, our resistance and we give that love and allow it to dissolve in its own time. If we feel something strong and painful showing up from the depth of our being, we just stay present to it, experiencing it, welcoming it, we might even name it love and give it love and then widen our awareness to include whatever else is entering our perception. The goal of this exploration is to stay open and indiscriminately *receive whatever comes into our awareness. Some sounds, feelings or sensations will stay with us for only seconds, others might be present through the entire exploration, multiple things might be happening at once in our Awareness. All we do is stay vast and open, without focusing on one particular perception, however grabby it might feel and we feel and send love to the whole parade.*

~

Do all of these practices once or twice for 5 to 15 minutes and see if one or two resonate more with you than the others. This isn't science, so if your intuition guides you to change the wording or the process to make it more comfortable for you, don't hesitate to play around and find the best fit for you. These explorations are offered to help you find the love within and help it flow naturally. Love is the goal, not doing the practices perfectly. Sometimes something as easy as focusing your attention on your chest and feeling into the heart is enough to open it and allow the love to flow. Do what works and feels good to you; you are your own teacher.

As we discussed earlier, we operate out of an emotional and mental program that was created through misunderstandings and repetition. Our thoughts and feelings create grooves in our brain that corresponds to mental and emotional loops. These quick and easy meditations are just a way of remembering that love is a natural aspect of our wholeness and that when freed up, it flows through us and out of us naturally. The more we do these simple practices, the more we remember and feel that love is our true nature.

As we explore and taste our own Essential Beingness, we find that the veil becomes more and more transparent, allowing us to experience as well as give love more openly, freely and more often, until the veil is completely lifted.

20.
Forgiveness – The Spontaneous Movement of Awareness

The Infinite has no preferences.
It kisses both the darkness and
The light equally.
  – Wu Hsin

When most people think of forgiveness, or the act of forgiving, they employ the term in such a way as to indicate the pardon of another's wrongdoing or mistake. Forgiveness viewed in this fashion makes three false assumptions: first, that there is such a person as an "other": second, that this other person could actually harm or wrong you, and; third, that mistakes exist. From the point of view of the separate imaginary self, these three assumptions are very real, they define how we live, perceive and experience our lives. They also define all our interactions and relationships. But from the point of view of the Absolute Self they have no more reality than a dream.

There is Only You

First, let's explore this notion that there is a "me" in here and a "you" out there who is separate from me. This belief, upon which our life revolves, is not as bullet proof and certain as we first assume. As we discussed earlier, science now shows that we are all evolving out of and connected to each other and to the rest of life by a conscious field. Everything arises out of the same aware substance; all matter is made of it, regardless of its shape, density or sentience. Think of ice cubes in water. The ice cubes seem to have an independent shape and life of their own, to be different and separated from each other and from the water in which they float, but in the end, whether you look at H2O in the form of ice, water or vapor, they are all one substance, regardless of the form and density they seem to take. Can we truly know where we end and the other begins? Is there even such a separation or are we one seamless movement and happening of Totality? Similarly, we cannot say where one wave ends and another begins, as all waves are movement of the totality that is the ocean.

Another finding that emerges out of scientific studies is that whatever we experience and however we make sense of it is not an accurate reflection of reality; it happens in our head and is never the absolute Truth. All that we perceive, see, hear, understand, interpret of the world out there, including of other people, actually happens inside us, as a construction of our mind. Everything that we experience is experienced not only in us but through us, we can't ever take ourselves out of the equation to know what truly exists out there, what is actually true and real independently of us. This goes for all human beings. Reality out there is perceived and experienced through each individual human brain and body, other organisms experience a vastly different world than we do, and it is very likely that each human being also experiences a very distinct and personal version of the world. As I stated earlier, there isn't one world but as many worlds as there are beings. Sometimes our version of reality seems to match someone else's version and sometimes we might as well be living on different planets. We are not unlike the projector through which the light passes and out of which images on the screen appear. Without the projector, nothing is viewed on the screen. The light is awareness which shines through the projector of your body and mind instrument. As the light of awareness passes through your singular and subjective projector, the images that are within you are projected onto the screen of space and time, which becomes your lived experience of a world out there. The Light is prior to it all, it is Awareness itself, without a second, out of which a body, a mind and a world arises, this body / mind creates and projects out a sense of space and time in which to live, have experiences and evolve.

The world that we see and engage in is our own projection and construction. Let's use the example of a heated discussion with your boss. What you see of your boss –even her appearance, who you believe her to be, how you interpret her actions and motives – this all happens in you, and is seen and experienced through you, it is not real in and of itself. How you interact with her, your lived experience of it, as well as your interpretation of her and her actions, is not her, it is you. That entire experience is a construction of your mind. You are the common denominator of all your experiences, they all happen in you and through you. If your boss, had the same exact exchange with someone else, this someone else would potentially view, live and interpret the interaction and your boss in a completely different way than you did, because the whole thing would be experienced from and within them, and from their beliefs, assumptions and current mood. Similarly, your boss is interacting, responding and making sense of your exchange through her own filters. It is like two worlds clashing and interacting with each other rather than two people. So this is the first false assumption we make in forgiveness, that this other person and the experience we are having with and of them is the Truth, when in fact it isn't the Truth, it is just a projection of our own self. The situation has no validity independently of us, it is experienced, understood and made sense of in us and through our own biases and conditioning.

Self-realized beings will often say that there is no separation between the subject (you) and the object (the world, another person, a state of mind, thought or emotion) you perceive and experience. The object emanates out of and is an extension of you. One of my favorite teacher, Rupert Spira, often says that "all we know of the world out there, of objects, people, situations and experiences, is the knowing of them. All we know of the world is the experience of sensing, seeing, hearing, tasting, smelling and touching of it. All of these senses and experiences occur in and are made of our Awareness, of the knowing of them through our awareness. So when we experience the so called world out there, we are only experiencing ourselves."

All of existence emanates out of this One Conscious Knowing, which includes every sentient being and all of life. At core we are all this One awareness, appearing as the many, just like ice cubes in water. The subject and the object are one. David Bhodan writes, "Awareness is all there is...Liberation is the spontaneous cognition and remembrance that separation and individuality are both illusory...Those who have fully comprehended the nature of Reality without a shred a doubt, know that division and boundaries are mere mental constructs created in the mind – and therefore are unreal." Just like the many waves are no other than the One Ocean. There are no clear boundaries between one wave and the other, their seeming separateness and distinctiveness is illusory, only a movement within the One Ocean that they are and out of which they emanate.

There is not and never was two, only the One in all its many shapes and forms. There is no "Other" that could hurt or harm you. There is only you, as Aware Presence, engaging, playing and fighting with yourself. Loving and forgiving, at core, is the collapse of a separate subject and object. It is the collapse of a "me" that loves or needs to forgive a "you." It is the understanding that there is no "me" and "you" but simply two seemingly separate wave in the movements of the Aware Field of existence. The self-realized being never has to forgive another, forgiveness is spontaneous, since nothing happened and there never was another to begin with, just an extension of herself, of Oneness. When there is no "other," who is there to forgive? When there is no "other," who is there to love? Loving and forgiving are not an act done by one person toward another; they are the state of our being, the core of our Absolute Nature. In the absence of a "me" and a "you," only the spontaneous natural emergence of loving and forgiving remains.

Infinitely Untouched and Pristine

Even if there was an "other," which in Absolute term there isn't, he or she could never harm or diminish what you are in any way. The second false assumption we make in forgiveness is the belief that we could ever be harmed or hurt in some way. From the point of view of the separate imaginary self, that is a very real experience, but from the Absolute Self it is an illusion. As we discussed earlier, whatever bump we run into, whatever hurt we feel, is actually our greatest teacher, it is our map to freedom. The person you believe hurt you is no other than yourself showing up in your life as a guide, exposing where you are yet to be free and what is still stuck or wounded within you. Those very parts of us that are seemingly hurt by another are the very aspects of us that have yet to be seen through and healed. To feel hurt, disappointed, angry, ashamed or whatever else a supposed other person could make you feel, is actually an opportunity to see where you are still blocked and bound. This hurt is an opportunity to meet the parts of you that are wounded and trapped in delusion. It is not us who are hurt by others or the world, but the remnant identification of the imaginary self. These fragmented wounded aspects of us have yet to be explored, restored and freed by the Light of our Aware Presence. All pain is a nudge from life, a loving reminder that you have once again forgotten who you are and identified yourself with the false. The idea that your enemy is in fact your greatest ally is not a new concept. It is the very people that challenge us, sometimes to the brink of our sanity that are our greatest teachers. They are our guides to freedom. Those who offend you are in fact not hurting you, they are giving you a clearer picture as to what parts of you need to be healed and integrated back to Wholeness. They are your map and your guide, without them you would not know your way home, you might be trapped in illusion, eternally misidentified. This is why transformation and true freedom usually needs direct connection with the entirety of life, including its seemingly messy and nasty side, to be complete. The person who lives by themselves in nature or in an ashram or monastery and never has to deal with monetary problems, a nasty coworker, traffic, a draining job, the end of a relationship or the death of a loved one, cannot ever truly know if they are fully free because they are never confronted with the necessary people and circumstances to show them where they still have blind spots and buttons that have yet to be explored, seen through and dismantled.

As I discussed earlier, life is messy and distressing at times, regardless of how Awake you are. The self-realized being is not a robot, he feels sadness, she feels disappointment, but there is no true identification to it. Their pain is the pain of being human, of living in this form, it is beautiful and natural and as such it flows right on through them and out. The Awake person feels hurt and anger and fear, but it is permeated by the peace, love and openness of their own recognition. To be Awake is to give others and ourselves full permission to feel and be everything that we are in every moment.

That which you are, at core, your Essence can never be harmed; it is only illusion that is hurt, not Truth. Your Absolute Self is eternally at peace, regardless of what is going on out there and regardless of your misidentification. The Light that you are is boundless and infinite. It has no age, no gender, no body, no story, preferences, beliefs, moral guideline, religion or sense of personal self to protect. It cannot be hurt, it cannot die, it is never sick, and it could never be wounded or damaged. It allows for all of the above to arise within it, as they are necessary to the play of human experience with its game of evolution and growth, with its experience of disentangling the Truth from the false and of remembering of the Essential Self. But to think that we could actually be harmed is a delusion; that which we are – our Aware Presence – is ceaselessly unaffected, at peace and whole. Just like the depth of the ocean that is eternally still, regardless of what storm might be brewing on its surface. Your Absolute Self is also ceaselessly open and in love with life as it is, nothing is denied and nothing is rejected. This other that you feel harmed you, that you feel you need to forgive is no other than yourself, the Absolute Self, in a different package. What is going on between the seeming two of you is not injury or insult, in the end there is not other to injure or insult you, we are all the same One in different shapes and forms, playing the human game, interacting with ourselves, seemingly pushing and shoving, in an effort to remind ourselves who we are and point ourselves back home. There is no other, there is no enemy. There is no harm done and nothing and no one to forgive.

Flawless Wholeness

This brings us to the last false assumption that is necessary in creating the idea of forgiveness, that there are any such things as mistakes and wrong doings. The background of reality is this Open Boundless Aware Presence. Everything that is, every action, every reaction, every thought, every emotion, every form and perception emerge out of this Presence, every experience is an aspect of this Awareness, of the Absolute. To say that there are mistakes, that an action, a thought, a feeling, a person should not be, is like saying that this Aware Field is a mistake. It is also a denying of the absolute nature of Reality, what is the purpose of saying that what is should not be, it is! And if it is, then a knowing and Aware Presence, greater than our mind, allowed it to be and embraced it as it is. Our suffering, our disappointment in someone else, our anger and blame is a sure sign that we are identified with the imaginary self and resisting reality. Our Absolute Nature is at peace with all life, all people and all events. Forgiveness is a spontaneous and instantaneous arising out of Presence, which cannot conceive of such a thing as a wrongdoing. What we are in Essence is complete and whole as it is and does not see or experience any harm or conflict. It is never a victim, it cannot suffer or ever be less than it is. If you are hurt, if you feel harmed or victimized, you are only a victim of your own illusion, nothing else.

Do Unto Others

On a more human and less esoteric level, I am going to ask you to be kind to yourself, to give yourself a break when you mess up, laugh at whatever stupid things you do, and forgive yourself when you fall short, get caught up in life and forget who you are at core. That which you are, your Aware Presence is beyond fault and sees no fault, but our mind and our body can be caught up in illusion, perceive fault where in fact there are none and act from that false viewpoint. Please realize that you are on a journey and that you will make mistakes. You deserve to give yourself another chance and to love yourself no matter what, because that which you are is love and forgiveness itself, and Awareness loves all of life, including this body and mind, with all its perceived shortcomings. Every mistake, every slip is an opportunity to remember, to love, to come back to yourself. I am also going to ask you to do the exact same thing when others fall short, give them a break and forgive the fact that they are human and probably still bound and living from the point of view of the imaginary self. Seeing the light, becoming free from the darkness that permeates us is not always easy and everyone gets to it on his or her own time. Your job is not to judge yourself or someone else or to punish, but to always come back to yourself and lead by example. As you go through life, keep in mind that making mistakes and messing up is part of the process of growth and of that experience we call being a human being.

This is important because I am betting on the probability that if you can realize that you, too, forget who you truly are sometimes and act out of illusion, you might allow others the space to do that as well. If you accept that sometimes you get caught up in nonsense, screw up, act dumb, selfishly and hurt people's feelings, and yet beyond all of that, your essence remains pure, you will see that all people's Essence are as pure as your own, regardless of their choices, because their Essence is your Essence, you are one Beingness appearing as the many. Beyond all illusion and all faults, your essence is loving and at peace with all of life. If you realize that, then maybe you will give others another chance and you will recognize that beyond their behaviors, beyond their mistakes, beyond their faulty programs, they are the same as you, you share the same pristine Wholeness. When you come to embrace this understanding, your very core will be patience, kindness and forgiveness. You will expect people to be on this journey from confusion to Truth, from lack to fulfillment and part of that journey, part of what leads us to seek what is real, to seek the peace we long for is chaos, perceived imperfections and flaws. You will expect people who are still struggling with their imaginary self to create chaos, to create suffering for themselves and others and you will let them be, while you remain seated in the Truth and peace of your own Being.

We must forgive ourselves for being human.
We must forgive ourselves for being imperfect.
Because when we judge ourselves we automatically
judge others. And what we do to others, we also do
to ourselves. The world is a mirror of our

> *internal selves. When we accept ourselves,
> and forgive ourselves, we automatically
> accept and forgive others.*
> *– Debbie Ford*

In the end, if you are able to cut yourself a break, to forgive and love yourself no matter what, to never abandon yourself or cut yourself short, regardless of what chaos you or others have created, then you might give others a break, you might love and forgive them despite their shortcomings and you might be willing to not give up on them and give them a second chance when appropriate and kind to yourself.

From a relative point of view, this understanding in no way prevents you, as a human being, from protecting yourself and making the changes that need to be made. Obviously if you are in an abusive relationship or job, regardless of whether your Absolute Self is harmed by it or not, as a human being you need to love, respect and preserve yourself as best you can. Awakened beings have very clear boundaries; they care for and appreciate all of themselves and their entire life. This human self is no other than the Absolute, your life and the time you have to live and experience it is no other than the Absolute, to not honor yourself and your life is in fact to not honor your Essential Self and life itself. This body and this human journey is a gift and needs to be treated as such. This path is a graceful integration of our realization as Aware Presence in this human form and this messy life. This life is a paradox, we are both eternally whole and unharmed and vulnerable, it is our work to fall in love with it all. To honor others or see past our seeming separation is never about betraying ourselves.

From the point of view of The Divine, there is no such

thing as forgiveness. Your Absolute Self does not know the word or act of forgiving since it is open to all of life, since it is life. It never has anything to forgive. To forgive assumes a resistance, which life and Awareness does not know. Forgiveness is always and only done by an imaginary self, in an effort to let go of some gripe and find peace, because being angry and holding on to a grudge is miserable. Where the act of forgiveness can be useful is not in forgiving another for his or her supposed wrong doing but in freeing them of the guilt we have unfairly laid on them, based on our own illusory interpretations and false beliefs in right and wrong. As Peter Russell writes in *From Science to God*, "When we forgive others we let go of the judgments we may have projected onto them." In the end it is not their mistakes we forgive but our own; we forgive our own illusions, our own trappings and our momentary lack of clear seeing.

There is nothing more painful than walking around with bitterness in your heart.
– Hugh Prather

~Experiential Adventure: Spontaneous Forgiveness~
This experiential adventure's aim is to allow a more profound connection to your Absolute Self and to help you slowly unwind and let go of any resentment by seeing that what you are is forgiveness itself. Close your eyes, take a few deep breaths, and bring your focus within. Allow your thoughts to pass by, without getting caught up in them. Shift your focus inside and find that Aware Presence within that sees through your eyes, hears through our ears and witnesses the totality of your experience. Allow each exhalation to loosen your body and expand your spirit. Focus on the vastness that you are, your consciousness

without a beginning or an end, without boundaries, without a shape, age, gender or any defining stories, ever present, ever free. As you shift your focus to that still and silent space within, notice how vast and open you are. Now, from that place, remember an experience or event that caused you deep disappointment, sorrow or betrayal, something you have yet to let go of. Feel the energy of the emotion and sensations you are experiencing at this moment that are directly related to this other person, the situation and your disappointment or anger toward them (Whether the event was in the past or is happening now, the feelings you are experiencing while practicing this exercise are rooted in your present experience, they are alive in you now.). Drop any label, story or judgments you have about the circumstance and the people involved, and just stay with the energy of it, the emotion of it as it arises and lives in your body. Allow it to flow, to move, to express itself, stay open without abstraction or resistance. Come back to your Aware Presence and ask yourself these few questions (Don't forget to come back to your Essential Self for a few seconds between each question.):

- *Is this vast Aware Presence that I am, affected by this emotion, this sensation and its energy? Or does it just stay open, untouched and free?*
- *Does my Absolute Self have a point of view about the circumstance and the people involved, does it take sides, or is it just clear and open, without judgment and sense of wrongness?*
- *Is the Clear Wide Open Presence that I am hurt, damaged or pushed off kilter in any way by this hurtful event? Is it affected at all, or is it complete, peaceful and whole in itself regardless?*
- *Does the Aware Presence that I am resent, condemn or*

blame anyone or anything in this situation? Or is it wide open to all of life, without judgments, labels or preferences?
- *From the point of view of my Absolute Presence, is forgiveness necessary? Is there anything to forgive? Or is forgiveness spontaneously arising moment by moment? Does Awareness have to work at forgiving or is the hurtful event or person automatically and instantaneously forgiven?*

Find the peace and freedom that you are beyond the hurtful experience and the emotions and sensations that arose from it. Realize that this Aware Presence that you are spontaneously and instantaneously forgives, as it sees no harm done. You are that wide-open, complete, unaffected and whole loving Presence. Can you experience both at the same time, the self that is caught up and hurting, as well as the peace and openness in the background, through which the event and emotions are experienced and known and into which they dissolve? Allow the story of this event and the energy around it to flow through and out of existence and dwell in the vast knowing space that is your True Nature, feel its transparency, its underlying peace and joy, regardless of what shows up in it. Experience the freedom and peace of being ever present, without a gender or an age, without a story, open to and genuinely okay with all of life, including all hurtful events, disappointments, anger and sadness.

~

After this exploration, if you still feel emotionally caught by this event and betrayal, don't hesitate to explore the feelings of grief, disappointment, resentment, anger, betrayal or whatever else you might be feeling, by doing the Deep Dive exploration in Chapter 18.

21.
Acceptance – The Deepest Trust

When vision and compassion
Expand to include the opposition,
The opposition ceases to oppose.
         – Wu Hsin

Jeff Foster, in his wonderful and highly recommended book *The Deepest Acceptance,* writes that freedom can only exist in "a deep and fearless acceptance of whatever comes your way." If this chapter moves you, then please do yourself a favor and read his book, it is an absolute jewel. Beyond the everyday idea we have of acceptance, beyond the new age cliché of "Let Go and Let God" there exists a peace beyond measure. This radical, fierce acceptance lies in the depth of our being, in the essence of what we are, and in the full receiving and allowance of our humanity.

Love in Disguise

Our reactions to life's circumstances are not always very logical, rational or helpful. Resistance to what is inevitable is futile. How do we know it is inevitable? Because it is happening and unfolding in this very moment; if it is, if it exists then we cannot make it un-exist, we can't escape from it, it is inevitable. How does it make sense to resist what already is? What benefit do we get by saying "No" to a circumstance, sensation or emotion that has already appeared into our awareness? Does resisting make whatever we wish wasn't, go away? Do we suddenly feel better? Does the bill or lump or anxiety we are fighting against, actually disappear? No, regardless of what the mind says, what already is cannot change or disappear solely because we wish it to; what is, IS. So what sense does it make to fight, to worry, to resist? How do we benefit, outside of giving ourselves headaches and ulcers and building walls between our experiences and ourselves? We don't benefit at all, but the choices of the imaginary self, which are based on fear and control, rarely make sense and they rarely bring us joy or relief.

Being in the moment, at ease with whatever comes one's way, becomes contentment...When your mind is quiet, you enter into the flow of love, and you just flow from one moment to the next as naturally as breathing.
– Ram Dass

As we've explored in detail, the imaginary self is the one who is in conflict with life, who resists life as it is and wants it to be different. Consciousness, our Absolute Essence is undefended, simply pure unconditioned allowance, acceptance and love. The universe doesn't know the word "No," everything is accepted, allowed, welcomed. It is pure inclusiveness, nothing is ever unworthy or excluded from it. Even hatred, judgments, sadness, anger, anxiety, depression and any other form of violence, fear and resistance are allowed. Your Essential nature is the boundless capacity to receive and welcome all that is. Our suffering is solely an outcome of our deep misunderstanding and resistance to life, but even that is included by what you are. These negative states and emotions are here as a reminder that you have forgotten who you are. They point to the recognition that who you truly are exists beyond this current state and that at any point you can choose to wake up from this dream and step out of the sticky illusory web that the imaginary self weaves through your thoughts, beliefs and stories. All seemingly negative states, moods and emotions have their place and purpose; they are our road map to freedom since they remind us that we have lost the present moment and gotten stuck in the sticky web of the deceptive mind. These states emerge out of a field of love; compassionate guidance is the impulse behind all movements. By definition, we can then deduce that all states, especially the seemingly negative ones, are nothing else than love itself in disguise and as such are fully embraced by what we are. Don't forget that in absolute terms, everything, including these states, is the Divine.

Beyond Our Control

For most of us, when we think of acceptance, our efforts focuses on trying to accept life, even when life is difficult, painful and in many ways unacceptable to our mind. How can we surrender to what is and stop fighting this current that seems so beyond our ability to accept and control. The thing is, it is not in the imaginary self's makeup to be able to surrender, just like a drowning man fights the one trying to save him. In our panic, in our resistance, in our effort to gain the upper hand, we find ourselves fighting even when we wish not to. That is the way this mind / body instrument functions. It is basically impossible for the imaginary self to accept and surrender to what it deems to be unacceptable, and so the struggle continues. In the example of drowning, it is this very fight, this very resistance and effort that exhausts the swimmer and leads to his possible death or at the very least to his surrender. On our path to freedom, it is this exhaustion at our inability to accept and control our environment that leads to the metaphorical death or surrender of the illusory separate self and to our transformation. Trough this exhaustion, through this giving up the idea of control, we come to see the failing of this imaginary self for whom and from whom we have been leading our lives. It is only then that we are ready to step off the crazy wheel, the wheel of suffering, and recognize that a deeper Reality exists. A Reality that has been here, right with us all along, closer to us than anything else we could think of or imagine. This Reality has been here with us, in us, seemingly hiding in the quiet background of our crazy making, waiting for us to be tired enough and to stop long enough to realize that another way has been here all along.

I used to think that peace and surrender was something I had to 'do' – and that they were states I could reach.
However, what was discovered was that peace and surrender was already present before I went in search for it. They were both present realities that went overlooked. The knowing or seeing of this is the peace that surpasses all understanding.
– David Bhodan

An Absolute 'Yes'

The Absolute Self has no concept of anger, pain, depression, hate, anxiety or any other so called negative emotions because the All is everything. The reason the Absolute Self does not know negative emotions is because its main characteristics is inclusivity. The Absolute says "Yes" to everything and is everything. Through this deep acceptance of all that ever does or could arise, all traumatic or seeming negative emotions are transformed into peace and love. The negativity that we encounter, the suffering we feel and associate with these states only arise as part of the conceptual resistance we emit. Without conceptual abstraction and resistance to what is, to others, to life, can hate, anger, anxiety or even the wish for things to be different remain?

What would happen if you said an all-resounding, open hearted "Yes!" to every state, sensation, event, situation or person you encountered, no matter what? Under such circumstance, where would the resistance, anger, resentment, fear or worry come from? How could it even come into being? Negative emotions can only come out of and strive in a "No." The moment we say "No" to any part of life, we reaffirm our belief in our separateness, our limits and our fallibility; out of that "No," fear and all other negative emotions erupt. What is mind blowing is to realize that even our "No" is a "Yes" to our Essential Nature. All "No," all seemingly negative emotions are a side effect of the illusory self; when we see that these emotions emerge out of these false thoughts and beliefs we identify with, we realize that all these states are as illusory as the self they belong to. But even the illusion, the negative emotions and our false identification to them are embraced by the Absolute; nothing is left out. As we are saying "No," the depth of our Being has already said, "Yes."

Before we can say "yes" and "welcome" to any aspects of life, we must first be willing to say "yes," "welcome" and fully receive our "No" and the part of us that is resisting, because that fragmented wounded aspect of our personality is also part of life and it too is effortlessly welcomed by our Absolute Nature. We cannot receive life if we cannot commit and be open to receiving the parts of us that are afraid and in pain. That is the first movement in acceptance, to notice and fully receive all of ourselves. By opening to, meeting and exploring our inner knots, we stop fighting life and enter into its flow.

> *The dawning of a willingness*
> *To accept the unacceptable.*
> *Produces the cessation of worry.*
> *In a world without worry,*
> *The empty man is an emperor.*
> *– Wu Hsin*

Becoming Whole

As we know, the imaginary self strives on fighting the current experience, it even resists its own resistance; this is the way it maintains its sovereignty. All experiences, including our emotions, are maintained by the energy and attention we give them, including the energy of resistance and denial. As we inquire, we come to recognize that the experiences, sensations, circumstances and feelings we enjoy, are allowed to pass through us, happily, without any type of denial or resistance, allowing them to arise as well as dissipate effortlessly. On the other hand, the experiences, emotions, states and sensations that we judge as painful or negative, we resist, deny and become stuck in them. Our rejection of them traps them in our being rather than keeping them at bay as we had hoped. By allowing old unfelt, denied and unexplored feelings and traumas to rise up to our consciousness, to be explored and embraced by the Aware Presence that we are, we become acceptance and openness in action; allowing all wounded parts of us to be healed and released and simultaneously liberating us from our confines. All parts of us are then brought back into Wholeness. All those knots are undone and the string attaching us to our illusion is unraveled. Freedom, fearlessness is only found in allowing all that has been repressed, resisted and shunned inside and outside ourselves to come to the surface and be reintegrated in the fullness of life. There cannot be any freedom as long we live as fragmented beings in a fragmented life. It is essential that we meet, explore and include these disowned and fragmented parts so that we may live whole and undivided, with an open heart and in complete intimacy with life. The Deep Dive practice described in chapter 18 is a great way to do that. The embracing of our disowned and fragmented parts, carries forth this deep and fierce allowance that is the reality of our True Nature.

The imaginary self, believing and feeling that it is separate and disconnected from the world, automatically identifies with and attaches to everything that it thinks, feels, owns and experiences. Our imaginary self takes everything personally; the joys are personal, but so are the sorrows and disappointments. The more the imaginary self attaches to its own individual world, the more disconnected from the whole of life it feels. Because the imaginary self is unwilling to receive the pain that is natural to a full life, it lives in a jail of its own making and creates separation and aloneness. This resistance to life and the compulsion to control and protect itself lead to suffering and a deep sense of hollowness that can never be filled. Our identification, our attachments, and our habit of taking everything personally, keeps us from recognizing that life is not personal. Things come into our life and then dissolve out of it, that is the ebb and flow of life, the way the tides rise and fall or the moon waxes and wanes. The painful moments are not a personal affront, and the wonderful moments are not a reward, they are simply life unfolding as it does, for all beings. Life doesn't play favorites; it just plays the game of life.

The Pain that Connects Us

Everyone has to live through hard times and through pain. Even very spiritual people, rich people, and giving, compassionate people bury their loved ones, lose everything they have, or end up with cancer. All of us get a taste of it, one way or the other. The heartache we experience is not our personal pain, it is simply pain and it is the pain we share with all beings. As Jeff Foster tells us, "Beyond the personal story of my own suffering, I discover that pain is not really my pain. It is humanity's pain. When I lose my father, the grief I experience is not my grief, but every son's grief...I become anyone who has ever lost someone they love. In the most intimate recesses of present experience...I discover that I am the others I long so much for connection with." If we were to surrender to and gracefully receive difficult times as well as find the courage and willingness to sink into and embrace the ache in our heart, we would be broken wide open. Hearts don't just break from the weight of our suffering; they break open. Our pain, when embraced and allowed in, is our way to oneness, connection, compassion and love. It is our way to unconditional love and acceptance, both of ourselves and of all other beings. If we could openly receive our pain, we would find ourselves in a profound closeness with all life and all people; our pain would be their pain and their pain would be our pain. This openness and connection would be an unfolding of love and intimacy with all beings, with all of life. The pain that is received and embraced does not make us suffer, it makes us fall more deeply in love with ourselves, with life and with each other. In welcoming life as it is, with its up and down, we find ourselves naturally surrendering to this paradoxical loving pain, allowing life to blow us open. When we are wide open, we find that we are in fact one with all things and live beyond fear. Freedom is not about being beyond or free of pain, untouched by life, never dealing with any difficulties. Freedom is being at peace, in love and open to all of life regardless of pain and in spite of whatever difficulties comes our way.

> *The amazing paradox is that there is nobody*
> *here separate from this moment, and yet,*
> *a deep surrender of this moment is already occurring.*
> *All thought, sensation, sound and experience*
> *are already being allowed in*
> *the impartial Space that you are.*
> *– David Bhodan*

The Sweetness of the Whole

If we trust that life evolves and emerges out of Wholeness, out of the deep peaceful knowing space of Awareness, then we can trust that it unfolds as it is meant to, even when it doesn't seem or feel like it. When we rest in that trust, we find that every experience, whether it is joyful or miserable, is permeated and enveloped by a subtle sweetness. This sweetness is the after taste of the Absolute, out of which every experience arises. If we trust this loving thread which is the background and essence of all of life, we can let go of our need to control, let go of our need to know what the future holds and let go of our desire to understand why things are as they are. With this trust comes the understanding that the relative can never understand and know the Absolute, we can only be it and live it. With this trust, we can just dive without reservation into the mystery that is life. Acceptance, in many ways, is the greatest form of trust. As long as we resist, as long as we fight, we do not trust. As long as we hold the view that life is broken, we cannot ever be one with it and live in the peace that lies at the center of its flow. Acceptance, surrender is nothing else than the deep willingness to stay open, no matter what life brings. Do you want to be on your death bed, resisting and pushing away what is coming, tense and afraid or do you want to be on your death bed wide open, embracing each moment and at peace with passing through this next threshold. A well-lived life is the prerequisite to a well-lived death. Life is no other than a constant unfolding of thresholds and our great work is in passing through these doorways with growing grace, our heart filled with love, trust and allowance. Living life and crossing threshold as the Aware Peaceful and Loving Presence that we are, we realize that death is no other than another gateless gate to cross on our journey to infinity.

When I die, I want my heart and soul fully seeded with rich stories and experiences. I want to be moving forward, falling upward, leaving my body well worn. I want to know presence, staying with what is hard until it softens, staying with what is narrow until it expands. I want to know how to lift above and sink below the flow of life, to drift and dream in the currents of what cannot be known. It is not so much about being prepared for death as it is being full of life. I want to be so well practiced in crossing thresholds that dying is merely another step in the dance.
– Dawna Markova

The Little Self Made of Thoughts

Who is it that says "No" to life, that resists particular circumstances, states of mind, emotions or sensations? Is it The Absolute Self or is it simply thoughts from the imaginary self? Obviously it is not our Essential Self that rejects our experience since our Aware Presence is an open all-welcoming and accepting Spaciousness, which only says "Yes." What happens when you take away the thoughts, "I don't like this" or "that is not the way it should be" or "I want this feeling/situation to go away or be different" or "what am I going to do, what's going to happen to me now?" When you take away any of the resisting thoughts, what happens to the resistance? When you drop all the mind stuff, where is the problem? Is there even still a problem? Is the suffering we feel truly in the experience we resist or is it actually in the resistance itself? In the conceptualization and mental formations we build around the uncomfortable state? Who says "No" to life? It cannot be our Absolute Self, but just to be sure, explore it. The next time you find yourself suffering, fighting life, worrying, wanting a situation or emotion to be different than it is, ask yourself, "Who wants this situation/emotion/sensation to be different?" and "Who is it that struggle with this?" Quiet down and find the one in you that is vast, infinite and still, that sees through your eyes and is everlastingly aware of all experiences, does this One wants things to be different? Is this one worried? Or is it the imaginary self that wants things to be other than they are? Can you actually locate this imaginary self inside you, or is it simply made up of thoughts? As we explore our resistance, we find that the Aware Presence that we are, our Absolute Self is completely open and accepting of whatever experience or emotional energy is showing up in any moment. It has no agenda, it is at peace with everything. It is our thoughts, our beliefs, and our mind program in the shape of this imaginary self that says otherwise. Once we remember who we are, then every experience carries with it the after taste of peace and all efforts to make what is other than it is, fall away. David Bhodan in his book, *The Lazy Man's Way to Enlightenment,* describes his life while living from the position of the Absolute self, "There is always an abiding sense that all is well, even if it doesn't appear that way. A deep and tangible peace is still felt, regardless of what's happening on the periphery."

The Wide Open Nature of Reality

Our Aware Nature is like space; it allows everything to come into it and has no preference or judgment as to what does. It is wide open. The space of a room doesn't reject certain people, sounds, smells or objects while allowing others; no, all is welcome. The same can be said of paper; it is the background upon which words and images are laid, but it has no preference as what the words say or which font is used, the color of the ink, or the image printed on it. The paper doesn't say, "I am sorry, only pieces of literature are allowed on me, not this crap, I am too good for grocery lists – write of love, and I am all yours." No, the paper is naturally open, clear of judgments, and allows all forms of writing and all images to appear on it. When you think about it, our body is the same. Take our sense of hearing, for example; all vibrations that our body can hear, are openly received, the sound of distant traffic, or birds singing, or a dog barking, sweet words are allowed in, hateful words are allowed in. You don't have to do anything, you don't even have to be aware of the sounds and yet the moment you shift your attention to your hearing, you realize how many subtle and not so subtle sounds have been naturally allowed to flow in, un-judged, without negotiation or control, just the natural ease of hearing. It is the mind, our imaginary self that superimposes itself on the natural accepting ways of hearing and goes to war with the different sounds: "Could someone get that dog to shut up, already?"; "I can't believe they start construction before 8 am"; "I should have chosen an apartment on the other side of this complex, away from the road"; "God, my neighbor has the worst taste in music"; and on and on it goes. But prior to our attention being shifted to the sounds, prior to our judgments and thoughts of resistance, all sounds were equally and peacefully received and welcomed in the quiet Awareness of our Being. If you explore, you will find that this is true of all our senses – smelling, seeing, tasting, sensing – everything is effortlessly allowed in and welcomed prior to any thought or judgments about them.

Our Aware Presence is at ease with all that is, partially because it is all that is. What we are at core, our Essence, by saying yes to all things, resists nothing and indulges in nothing except in its own Being. It allows everything to move at the speed it desires to move, to appear, evolve and disappear as it wishes. The Absolute, Awareness is the background of all experiences, it is the unwavering reality of all that exists. It is vast, open and fluid and all experiences are created in its image. Just as waves are not separated or different from the very ocean out of which they emerge, so are every event, thought, feeling, sensation and experience, no different or separated from the life out of which they emerge, regardless of the tone or shape they take. The ocean accepts all it waves, it doesn't resist any wave regardless of how big or powerful or even destructive it might be. No wave can harm the ocean and no wave is ever separate from the ocean. Similarly all experiences are just waves of energy and aliveness in the shape of feelings, sensations, actions, perceptions, sentient beings and objects they emanate and arise in and out of the Aware Presence that we are. We, as our Absolute Self, are prior to any of the waves and hence can never be destroyed or even harmed by any of the waves of life. Jeff Foster writes in *The Deepest Acceptance*, "from the strong, violent waves to the soft, gentle waves – they are all water. And so, on the deepest level, the ocean does not have a *problem* with any of the waves...There is, therefore, a deep okayness with all the waves, a peace beyond understanding, which comes from recognizing their basic inseparability from the ocean."

Awareness is not separate from life, it is Life. Our Absolute Self is naturally welcoming; acceptance, allowance and receptivity are its nature. We are not separate from life, so how can we resist and not accept aspects of life, in many ways when we oppose life we are actually denying aspects of ourselves. No wonder we feel fragmented and alone. As Jeff Foster writes, "The ocean accepts every wave because it is every wave...The ocean's acceptance of its waves is beyond the conceptual opposites of acceptance and non-acceptance. The acceptance is the inseparability of the ocean and the waves, and as such, it has no opposite. Every wave is *already accepted* by the ocean." Acceptance is not something we do or can do as an imaginary self; it cannot be forced. Acceptance is our Nature, we cannot influence it, but only spontaneously be it. If we try to force ourselves to accept what the mind cannot or doesn't want to, then acceptance becomes a deceptive and refined form of resistance, a subtle form of violence. We only have to realize and understand, that no matter how the mind feels on the surface, at the depth of our being, our Essential Self has already accepted the specific even or state as well as our initial non-acceptance of it. We don't need to "do" anything; life is whole as it is and it is already at peace with all its shapes. As we understand and taste the depth of this realization, we find ourselves naturally resisting less and less. We find ourselves spontaneously in harmony with life as it is, regardless of how it might look or feel, and we realize that we didn't "do" or work at this harmony, at this peace, it imperceptibly grew out of our understanding, exposing the natural and authentic expression of our deepest Self.

The mind, the imaginary self, cannot accept and see the goodness in all experiences and all situations, if it did, it would literally be committing suicide, since a full acceptance and openness to all of life is equal to its undoing. By definition, the imaginary self sees and experiences life from a position of polarity, judgment and opposition, it cannot see the wholeness that is beyond the division. It cannot see that all polarities, all seeming divisions, are simply an authentic expression and emergence of the completeness and oneness of Life. Even though our conditioning, our fears and our sense of lack keeps us from seeing the wholeness of our experience, Reality lets us know that everything is welcome, that everything belongs. How do we know this to be true? Well if it wasn't so, then this moment wouldn't be as it is. If it is, then it belongs; if it is, then it is already welcome by life. We can deny many things, but we cannot deny Reality, what is IS!

You cannot accept – for what you are is acceptance itself. You are not really a separate person – you are an effortless yes to this moment.
– Jeff Foster

Acceptance is not a Doing but a Being

We do not need to accept what the mind is not able or

willing to; all we have to do is realize that allowing and accepting is already taking place beyond the mind, beyond this imaginary self and whatever resistance it feels and start to relax into this moment. What we are in our deepest nature is allowance itself. We cannot do acceptance, we can only be it, it is an effortless Beingness, the way sounds are naturally heard. We can Be acceptance by realizing that whatever is, is one with us; that it has already been allowed and welcomed into our experience by us. Our Absolute Nature has already accepted it, or it wouldn't exist and we wouldn't be experiencing it. There are no mistakes, this emotion you feel, this sensation you feel, this experience you are having is part of you and it is here because Life said "yes" to it, because you, as your Absolute Self, already said, "Welcome, come on in." It is only an afterthought that says, "No, I don't want this, I don't like this, it should be different." In the end, all our resistance is superficial and late to the dinner party. It only exist in the form of a few passing thoughts with no independent reality of their own, with no more power than what we choose to bestow upon them. As Jeff Foster writes, "By the time a wave appears, it has already been accepted by what you are. The arrival of a wave *is* its acceptance. When you see that what you are trying to escape is deeply okay – that recognition, in itself, is the end of seeking." That recognition is also the end of resisting. Even the thoughts of resistance and judgments are accepted and embraced by what You are. Your pain and your distress are fully embraced by the deep ocean of your Aware Presence, and so is the fear that you might have toward that pain. Your wish to be done with it, to be free of it, that too is embraced. It is all accepted and welcomed by the wholeness, completeness and greatness that You Are. In the end, even when it doesn't feel that way, it is all okay. All you have to do when you find yourself in the grip of suffering, in the grip of a deep resistance to this present moment is to take a few deep breaths, relax and remember that whatever is happening has already been allowed by your deepest Self or you wouldn't be feeling it and experiencing it, this is the only Reality there is. Jeff Foster explains the importance of this realization, "knowing that, in the moment, even your non acceptance is deeply accepted is something that can crack even the most hardened suffering at its core...your pain is okay, your dislike of pain is okay, your wanting to be free from it is okay...You could say perhaps that *all* suffering is simply our blindness to this deepest acceptance."

Our Path is to take our stand as that Self that we are, as our Aware Presence, and see all resistance as a movement of thought emanating from the illusory self, with no true reality. In recognizing who we are and in being willing to soften and rest in this moment just as it is, we become the acceptance we seek and allow the mind, the imaginary self to do what it does, while staying firmly seated in the still open space of our Being. You have one choice, in every moment, you can choose to misidentify yourself to the one who resists and its divisive thoughts or to rightfully identify to the One who is prior to the resistance and is the great allowance itself.

~Experiential Adventure: Saying "Yes" to Life~

This is a simple practice. It can be done sitting down with your eyes closed in a formal meditation practice, or it can be done while taking a walk, driving around or even while doing chores around the house. This can also be done whenever you find yourself in some type of opposition with life.

Take a few deep breaths and bring your focus within. Allow your thoughts to pass by, without getting caught up by them. Shift your focus inside and find that Aware Presence within that witnesses your experience. As you shift your focus to that tranquil, peaceful and silent space within, notice how vast and still you are.

Feel every in breath expand you, literally open you up. With every in breath say to yourself "Yes." As you open up and expand physically, the quiet or silent inner "yes" invites the mind to still and the body to open up. Allow yourself to melt and rest in your "yes" to life. As you exhale stay silent, allowing each out breath to loosen your body and act as a release of any constriction and resistance that still exists within you. With every out breath make the conscious choice and the silent prayer for the love and courage to let go of resistance and desires and just allow yourself to be intimately one with this moment.

- In breath – Expands and opens you up to all of life as you say "Yes."
- Out breath – Silently and naturally loosens the remaining knots of resistance and whatever contractions still exist in your body, as you choose to relax, release and let go.

~

*Why do you offer
Such resistance to life?
Has not Wu Hsin told you
That resistance
Only extends and intensifies
Your pain and discomfort.
There is a secret word
Which, when used
With sincerity,*

> *Aligns you with all of life.*
> *That word is*
> *Yes.*
> *– Wu Hsin*

~Experiential Inquiry: Locating the One who Resists~

Whenever you are struggling with and resisting a circumstance, sensation or an emotion, ask yourself these few questions:

- *Where in this moment am I stuck in illusion?*
- *Where in my body does this resistance lie? Can I meet it, with warmth and openness?*
- *What are the thoughts associated with this feeling of resistance?*
- *Can I find the thinker of these thoughts? To whom do these thoughts belong? Can I locate this person that is resisting, or is that person only made up of thoughts, with no real reality of its own?*
- *From whose point of view am I living this moment? Who am I identified with right now as I resist? Am I identified to an imaginary self that is made of thoughts or to the Aware Presence that is beyond it?*
- *Who is troubled, who is resisting? Is the vast peaceful Aware Space that I am, the one that sees through my eyes, upset?*
- *What does Aware Presence have to say about this situation, emotion or sensation I am struggling with?*
- *What does Aware Presence have to say about my resistance?*
- *From the perspective of the Wholeness that I am, is there anything that is not okay, that is not welcomed?*
- *Can I remember that I am acceptance itself, untouched and wide open, regardless of how I feel?*

Get quiet, look at the questions above, and:
- Sit silently, breathe deeply a few times and then slowly and silently ask the question and then fall silent and just stay with the question, stay with the silent intuition of it, the energy of it. Do that a few times, staying silently with the question for a few breath each times. This is a more intuitive, meditative form of inquiry.
- Sit silently, breathe deeply a few times and then slowly and silently ask the question and then fall silent and just stay with the question, stay with the silent intuition of it, the energy of it and then go in your body and look for the answer, the felt sense of it in your body. Explore the question through your body, feel the part of you that is unsatisfied and resisting, meet it, see if it has any independent reality. Look for the one who wants things to be different, can you find this self?
- If you like writing and exploring in a more cerebral way, pick up a pen and paper, sit quietly, calm your mind, slowly and silently ask the question and then fall silent and just stay with the question see what bubbles up. Every insight that comes up, everything that arises from your core, that feels absolutely true in this moment, write down.

~

After these explorations, if you still feel caught in the grip of suffering and deeply resisting what is real for you in this present moment, don't forget to use the Deep Dive exploration of Chapter 18. Use the feeling, thoughts and sensations of resistance as the subject of the exploration, Dive Deeply in them, meet them, hold them and find out that Spaciousness resides on the other side of any opposition. Resistance is the act of closing, while Deep Dive is its exact opposite, the act of deeply unconditionally opening.

22.
The Art of Meditation: The Embrace of What Is

Make no effort to meditate
Make no effort to not meditate
Make no effort to make no effort
Being is not something
One does
Being is what
One is.
– Wu Hsin

Whether it is love, forgiveness or acceptance, the ego, the imaginary self always think of them as actions, states of mind that need to be worked on, cultivated, mastered and maintained, but from the point of view of our True Essence, all of these are just natural unfolding in what we are. Love, forgiveness and acceptance are not acts that we do, but qualities that we are. The same is true of meditation. Meditation is not an action, it is literally the cessation of all actions, it is Beingness pure and uncluttered, open to and aware of all that is.

Staying Open and Vast rather than Focused
We are not used to staying with the vastness of our Awareness. Usually our mind takes this open field that we are and turns it into a condensed beam of attention that focuses on one or two things at a time, seriously limiting

our experience of reality. It may be because of this function of the mind to automatically focus that many of the traditional meditation practices start out by having the meditator focus on a particular object such as our breath, a picture or a sound. This is not the kind of meditation we will practice here. That being said, when we find ourselves caught up in a stream of thoughts, coming back to our breath or to a mantra or a word that represent a quality of awareness we would like to emulate, such as Yes, Open, Love or I am, can be a useful anchor back into Awareness and Beingness. The goal of meditation in this book is not to reinforce the habit of the mind by turning our awareness into a focused beam of attention, but on the contrary to allow us the opportunity to shed the habits of the imaginary self and connect to the qualities that are intrinsic to our Aware Presence.

The natural state of awareness is to be wide open, clear and vast. Life emerges out of this Aware Field. Our Absolute Self, which is no other than Awareness, recognizes that all that exist is simply an expression and extension of itself. From that point of view Awareness turns away from nothing and resists nothing. Aware Presence takes in everything equally, it attaches to nothing in particular and denies nothing in particular either. It is intimately open and one with everything that arises. Meditation is the art of consciously dropping into and becoming that aware field. When we get lost in a thought or a sensation, then we have simply referred back to the focusing habit of the mind and the expansiveness of Awareness has been condensed to a single point of attention, rather than staying open to the totality of our experience. When awareness gets focused down and grabbed by a thought or an ache, everything else is dismissed. The felt sense of being the vast open space of

Awareness seems to be lost, all the sounds, all the smells and the more subtle sensations are also absent from our experience. Suddenly we become this thought, this ache, and forget the expansive reality of our Being. As we explained earlier, this directed attention isn't bad or wrong, it can actually be very useful in living our lives. We need to be able to focus our awareness on specific tasks or situations to maneuver through life successfully. Fear is a great example of that; it is part of our survival mechanism that allows us to condense all of our awareness and focus on a particular sound in the bushes, or image in the distance. This ability allowed us to survive and strive as a species and is still very useful today. We use it when concentrating on a project or consumed in a good book or driving a car in bad weather. This ability to focus is just another aspect of Aware Presence. It can be likened to the sun. We can see the sun by looking straight at it, in which case the energy of the sun is condensed in one fiery ball, which blinds us to the world around us. Or we can see the light of the sun all around us, reflected in every object, every tree, every person and in the warmth and light that surrounds us; the whole world is aglow, lit up and warmed by the vast open light of the sun. When we look at the sun the only thing we can see is it, when we back up and widen our focus, we see that the sun is vast; it is everywhere and shines on all of life, the good, the bad, the beautiful as well as the ugly. In fact, the light of the sun has no concept of good or bad, pleasant and unpleasant, it shines on it all evenly. It is our mind that wants to differentiate and label, but the labels are as illusory as the imaginary self out of which they emerge.

Both the condensed light of the sun as well as the soft, warm, vastness that shines and permeates all of life, are true aspects of the sun, one is focused and intense, the other open, soft and spacious. The problem is that this focused mode of functioning has become our way of life. We live as if staring at the sun and have become blind to what we are and to the completeness and beauty that exists in the vast totality of life. We seem to have lost, except for small moments here and there, the ability to be present and open to all of life, not just one small aspect of it. To make matters worse, our focused attention is put on the very things we find disturbing in our lives like our constant pesky thoughts, our traumas, our disappointments, our fears, our resistance, our discomfort and our desires.

Is it really all that surprising that we are unhappy, unhealthy, stuck in our suffering, lost and blind to the way home? All we have to do is move our eyes away from what blinds us, widen our stance, let go of the focus and see that there is so much more to us and to life than previously believed, that home is right here and now, that we've, in fact, never left, but were blinded by the intensity and direction of our focus. In this type of meditation, we learn to take a step back, to widen our stance and to open our senses and our heart. In meditation we come back to our vastness over and over.

Most of the explorations of this book have included widening our focus and connecting to the spaciousness of our Essence, which is no other than meditation. In this form of mediation practice, we come back to the qualities of our Absolute Self over and over: boundless, present, aware, open, still, welcoming, authentic, primary and unaffected.

In meditation, we learn that we don't need to stare at the sun to feel its warmth and see its light, we can relax, ease back, and discover that warmth and light is everywhere and in everything.

~**Experiential Adventure: Being with What Is**~

Close your eyes, take a few deep breaths and bring your focus within. Allow your thoughts to pass by, without getting caught up by them. Shift your focus inside and find that Aware Presence within that witnesses your experience, sees through your eyes and hears through your ears. As you shift your focus to that spacious, peaceful and silent space within, notice how vast and still you are

Stay spacious and open and keep your eyes closed while allowing your in-breath to open you up, expand you and your out-breath to release and melt away all constrictions. Relax your body and your mind and just be aware that you are aware. Not aware of anything in particular, just aware, alive; that beyond any doubt, you know that you are, that you exist effortlessly. Allow your Aware attention to be wide, spacious and unreserved, like the space of a room, just open, vast and welcoming. Let go of thoughts and just allow yourself to be still and present. Keep your focus and attention wide and open to all that seems to be happening within you and around you, without grasping on to anything in particular. Whatever enters your awareness notice it, welcome it and allow it to pass through and disappear whenever it wishes to and then simply stay present to the next moment and the next apparition, the light filtering through your eyelids, the noises around you, the feeling and sensations happening in your body, the though passing by. Revel in your senses, if you are outside feel the sensuous feel of the wind running through your hair and the warmth of the sun kissing your face. If you are inside, sense the ground, the chair or your bed holding your body safely and lovingly, feel the melting of the edge of your body with whatever surface it connects to, listen how the walls, furniture sound and creak, having their own language, or the sounds of the birds and cars in the distance. See how all of life is connected to you through your aware senses and how life continuously and intimately communicates with you. Just quietly notice all of these happening. Try to stay without judgment of them, without label, as if you had no thinking mind, simply the ease of noticing, sensing, feeling and experiencing. Feel the joy and stillness of allowing life to be as it is, of being with what is, completely and authentically, without resistance or requirements, without opposition or grasping. When a sensation, sound, feeling or even a thought arise on your screen of awareness, notice it, allow it to arise and dissipate naturally and on its own. Throughout this meditation stay with the awareness that you are. If you find yourself resisting something or being sucked in by a pattern of thoughts, sensation, perception or emotion, just whisper 'yes' silently and allow your exhale to dissipate the resistance or attachment and to bring you back to the eternal now and the vast, open and unqualified nature of Awareness. Allow the world to flow in, around and through you, while staying as the Aware Presence that you are, without judgments, labels or stories about the movements that enter your perception. Notice that you cannot clearly say where you end and where the present movement in your awareness begins, just one seamless intimate connection. Just allow the natural, spontaneous unfolding of creation to dance and move as it wishes. You remain yourself, open, present and spacious, while connected and one with life as it is, complete and whole.

Dwell in this vast knowing space and the sensuous movement of your senses and of life; feel the peace, the stillness, the intimacy, the completeness and oneness of fully experiencing, fully being present with what is. Sense and be the freedom and peace of being without a gender or an age, ever present, without a story, open to, one with and

genuinely okay with all of life.
~

There is a place where words are born of silence,
A place where the whispers of the heart arise.
– Rumi

Fall in Love with Silence

I would be remiss if in the chapter on meditation I did not talk briefly about silence. Mediation can also be a simple appreciation and movement toward silence. Silence is the gateway to our own intimacy with life and with our own Self. We cannot enter in communion with this silent inner movement and with our intuitive guidance when our mind and entire being is caught by the sound of the television, of the radio's blasting, the kids calling for our attention, the phone ringing or the incessant stream of thoughts running through our mind. Our Peaceful Aware Presence and the aliveness that flows in, through and around us cannot be known through all this noise. Our Essence, the peace we seek, is most alive in the silence that exists beyond the noise of everyday life. This is why most if not all great religions and spiritual traditions have recommended making time for silence every day, even if it is only for a few minutes here and there. As we sit in silence, doing nothing in particular but being open and one with the silence that permeates and surrounds us, we begin to hear the silent voice of our being, a slow kindling of a knowing Presence deep within us. As we continue to remain with this inner spirit and learn to recognize its subtle voice, ways and movements, over time, this quiet voice and felt Presence becomes stronger, deeper and clearer. Over time we find ourselves permeated in silence and stillness even in the midst of commotion. Silence is no other than the opportunity to steep in yourself, to taste yourself and come to know yourself beyond any doubt and any distractions.

23.
Awake to the Sweetness of Life

Sooner or later on this journey, every traveler faces the same question: Are you a human intending to be a god, or a god pretending to be human?
– Eric Micha'el Leventhal

Flipping the Switch

Awakening or the remembering of who we are, can be equated to turning on the light. Imagine that you are living in a dark room, only using a flashlight to illuminate the things around you and find your way. You do your best, but the light of your lamp only gives you a partial view of the room you live in, not your whole environment. You can only see the things you focus the light beam on and so you live in a dark and fragmented world. You seem not to know or maybe you've forgotten that the room is wired with electricity and that there is an on and off switch at your disposal. All along, all you've had to do was find the switch and flip it on. The realization of our True Nature is the remembrance that there is more light available to us then the small flashlight we have been using to light our way. The choices we make to turn toward and explore our Absolute Nature, to meet and release our pain and the blockages that veil us from our Wholeness and finally to continuously live our life from that wisdom can be likened to searching for and flipping on the switch, so that we may live in light, be illuminated and know the completeness of life.

Instantaneous and Progressive Path

For some, this understanding is instantaneous, a shock of grace to the system, a sudden realization of our own inner light. In one clear instant, sometimes unexpectedly, who we are at core is known, felt and experienced. One moment we are living as an imaginary separate self, the next moment, a shift happens and it is clear that we are not and never were this illusory self. We realize that this false self is just a movement and a network of thoughts and beliefs, with no validity of its own and that we are prior to it.

For others, the knowing and experiencing of who we are is a much more gradual process, almost like someone is opening the blinds very slowly allowing more and more light to shine in. My individual path started with a curiosity and wonder of the world and of what lies unseen. In my early teens, I was already reading metaphysical texts and meditating in an effort to understand what life is about and to know the nature of God. This continued throughout my teens and into my early twenties, culminating into a relatively formal Buddhist practice for quite a few years. In my mid-twenties, I read Leo Hartong's book *Awakening to the Dream*; I didn't understand everything I read and rejected parts of it outright, but I still felt drawn to the teachings, something about the author's view of reality resonated with an unknown part of me. I knew deep down that this was my way home, and so began a love affair with Self, with this Aware Presence that had been here all along while I searched for it in so many different directions. At first, my understanding was completely theoretical and conceptual, but I could always taste the Truth of it, right in the background, just like the way a word hangs on the tip of your tongue but you can't quite remember it. Through explorations, not only could I understand this Truth, but slowly I began to recognize it, know it and feel it in the depth of my being and all around me. This knowing seemed to move in me and I in it and this inner wisdom began to permeate my life. Through numerous insights this understanding became much more than a beautiful concept, it became my reality, an intimate dance with the Divine, with myself.

A Never Ending Exploration of Love

At first, I experienced this Stillness deep within me, in fleeting glimpses and then slowly just like the tea that gets stronger by simply steeping in itself, I could feel Absolute Presence and this subtle peace and sweetness in the background, infusing every moment. Even in the grip of anger or sadness, the aware stillness is still there silently waiting to be recognized. I can feel the subtle movement of love and wonder in the wind rustling the leaves, in the rays of the sun touching my face and in the space that seems hold yet separate you from me. Somewhere deep in me slowly, gently and over time the remembrance and recognition that we are all this stillness and this love, that it is our essence and our birthright sprout into being. This Peace is in the back of my eyes, in the seeing, hearing, touching, smelling and tasting of all my experiences and in the beat of my heart. This still sweetness lives in the depth of my body and all around me as the backdrop of all life. All beings and all life forms are alive with it. This Presence permeates all people, all plants, trees, animals, insects, lakes, rivers and oceans and it is even in rocks, mountains and in the space that seems to separate and connect all things. The entire universe, the earth, the sky, the clouds and the stars are made of it. It is the divine breath of creation.

For a while, this realization was enough. I explore and lived in this peace, but slowly I come to intuitively know that there is still more to discover and that this love and wisdom is in everything, even in the places that feel nothing like peace and love. I now find myself propelled back into my life, into my body, into the realm of feelings, of pain and past suffering, yet this peace, this knowing of who I am never quite leaves me. On the contrary as I willingly open to entirety of myself and the totality of my experience, with its ups and downs, this inner wisdom and trust expands. I find that this is true for many if not most people who are willing to stay and intimately connect with what is present. A great journey of unfolding and deepening begins in which we discover, that all the states, sensations, emotions, memories and situations that we distanced ourselves from, judged as being wrong or bad are also the Divine and in some way want to be known and recognized as such. We discover that it is only though meeting them, exploring them, owning them and loving them that we come to fully know and embody the totality and fullness of who we are. Openness and inclusiveness becomes our path. Through this undefended and full embrace, we also come to realize the wholeness and completeness of Reality just as it is. Michael Singer writes, "What does it mean to drift upward? It's an experience of being drawn further back inside yourself... You used to walk around feeling anxiety and tension; now you walk around feeling love...Your backdrop is love. Your Backdrop is openness, beauty and appreciation." This initial encounter with the limitless, infinite and eternal peace that we are, that is the background of life, becomes our anchor, or the buoy that allows us to safely and freely dive to the depth of the ocean, to the depth of our Being; into our pain, our shame, our guilt, our sadness, our rage, our loneliness, our traumas and into the suffering of humanity, but also into our passion, our kindness, our joy, our love, our beauty and sensuality and into the magnificence and the richness of the world. We dive into the wholeness, fullness and completeness that is life.

The sweetness of Presence never leaves me completely. My greatest disappointment, my moment of deep sadness or seething fury are always subtlety permeated by this sweet vastness. Even the most bitter pill is easier to swallow; with willingness and the courage to stay put, I discover that its aftertaste is always sweet. As you delve and dive further in to your Being and allow life to open you up, you find that no matter what comes your way, you can enter in an intimate dance with it, trusting and fearless. You discover that you are everything, including the Dance itself. Life is complete and graceful; it flows naturally, spontaneously, and lovingly. The Divine is seen and experienced everywhere and in everything, including your most wounded places. Every moment, every experience and every aspect of yourself holds the beauty, wholeness and sweetness of life.

I thank you for going on this exploration to the depth of your own Being and for trusting me to be your guide. I hope that this book is the beginning of a joyful and ever deepening journey into Wholeness. If any parts of this book have been helpful to you in any way, then please take a few minutes to shoot me an email, write a review or even share the book with a friend. I leave you with a final quote by Michael Singer and wish you the peace and sweetness of the world:

Imagine what would happen if you started feeling tremendous love for all creatures, for every plant, for every animal, and for the beauties of nature. Imagine if every child seemed like your own, and every person you saw looked like a beautiful flower, its own color, its own expression, shape and sounds. As you went deeper and deeper, you would start noticing a phenomenal thing – you are no longer judging...There is just appreciating and honoring. Where there used to be judging, there is now respecting, loving and cherishing. To differentiate is to judge. To see, to experience, and to honor is to participate in life...You feel open and light. You feel love. You see beauty...And when you begin to feel this joy, that's when you'll know God's nature. Then nobody will upset or disappoint you. Nothing will create a problem. It will all appear as part of the beautiful dance of creation unfolding before you.

About the Author

Since the earliest time she can remember, Ilsa has been intrigued by the deeper aspect of life. As a child and teenager, she was an avid reader, always wanting to find answers to the big questions: "Why are we here?"; "Who am I really?"; "Why do people seem so unhappy?"; "How do we create peace?"; "What would make life easier?"; "Is there a God?"; "What is God?" to find her answers, Ilsa delved deeply into philosophy, spirituality and finally psychology.

Having studied and personally explored the process of personal healing and transformation for over twenty years, Ilsa brings an abundance of professional and personal knowledge and wisdom to her work. Her life-long search for Truth and transformation, has led her to discover that healing, peace and happiness is always available in every moment and for everyone. Her life's work now focuses on writing and helping people find their own way back to their essential Wholeness. Through open discussions, potent inquiries and deep explorations, Ilsa guides and supports people in releasing and integrating all the limitations, pain and traumas that keep them bound, while helping them to rediscover their Essence and reclaim their most authentic Self.

Over the years, Ilsa has worked with many teachers and mentors to deepen her own experience as well as to develop her skill as a therapist and mentor. Spiritually and therapeutically, Ilsa has been greatly influenced by Joan Ruvinsky and Richard Miller and their teachings in non-dual work and the release of trauma, by Rupert Spira's poetic Wisdom, Adyashanti's no-nonsense clarity, June Konopa's embodiment teachings and her invaluable guidance in learning to listen and connect to the wisdom of the body, Jeff Foster and his teaching on radical openness and acceptance, and lastly Richard Sann and his heartfelt and compassionate presence.

Ilsa was born in Geneva, Switzerland, and spent her childhood in the south of France. She moved to South Florida with her family in 1993. Ilsa received a Bachelor's Degree from The University of Miami and her Master's Degree from Nova Southeastern University. She is a Licensed Marriage and Family Therapist and works mostly with adults on a many areas of support in the mental health and spiritual field. She lives with her husband, Patrick, and their two dogs, in Boulder, Colorado. Ilsa works with people face to face, over the phone or through Skype. For more information about Ilsa and her work, please visit her website at www.ilsacomte.com.

Reading List

- A New Earth: Awakening to Your Life's Purpose by Eckhart Tolle

- As It Is: The Open Secret of Spiritual Awakening by Tony Parsons

- Awareness: The Perils and Opportunities of Reality by Anthony De Mello

- Awakening to the Dream by Leo Hartong

- Consciousness Is All: Now Life Is Completely New by Peter Francis Dziuban

- Dancing Wu Li Masters: An Overview of the New Physics by Gary Zukav

- Disillusionment: The Doorway to Present Moment Clarity by Roy Melvyn

- Doorway to Total Liberation: Conversations with What Is by Scott Kiloby

- Falling in Love with Where You Are by Jeff Foster

- Falling into Grace: Insights on the End of Suffering by Adyashanti

- From Science to God: A Physicist's Journey into the

Mystery of Consciousness by Peter Russell

- God Is Not Dead: What Quantum Physics Tells Us about Our Origins and How We Should Live by Amit Goswami
- I Will Not Die an Unlived Life: Reclaiming Purpose and Passion by Dawna Markova PhD

- Infinite Potential: What Quantum Physics Reveals About How We Should Live by Lothar Schafer

- Live Your Truth by Kamal Ravikant

- Love Yourself Like Your Life Depends On It by Kamal Ravikant

- Mysticism and the New Physics by Michael Talbot

- Nothing to Grasp by Joan Tollifson

- Passionate Presence: Seven Qualities of Awakened Awareness by Catherine Ingram

- Perfect Brilliant Stillness by David Carse

- Polishing the Mirror: How to Live from Your Spiritual Heart by Ram Dass and Rameshwar Das

- Presence: The Art of Peace and Happiness - Volume 1 by Rupert Spira

- Quantum Enigma: Physics Encounters Consciousness by Bruce Rosenblum and Fred Kuttner

- Simply Notice: Clear Awareness is the Key to Happiness, Love and Freedom by Peter Francis Dziuban

- The Deepest Acceptance: Radical Awakening in Ordinary Life by Jeff Foster

- The Essential Laws of Fearless Living: Find the Power to Never Feel Powerless Again by Guy Finley

- The Field: The Quest for the Secret Force of the Universe by Lynne McTaggart

- The God Theory: Universes, Zero-Point Fields, and What's Behind It All by Bernard Haisch

- The Lazy Man's Way to Enlightenment: What You're Looking for Is What Is Looking by David A. Bhodan

- The Lost Writings of Wu Hsin: Pointers to Non-Duality in Five Volumes by Wu Hsin (Author) and Roy Melvyn (Translator)

- The Power of Now: A Guide to Spiritual Enlightenment by Eckhart Tolle

- The Self-Aware Universe by Amit Goswami

- The Ultimate Key to Happiness by Robert A. Scheinfeld

- The Untethered Soul: The Journey beyond Yourself by Michael A. Singer

- What Am I? A Study in Non-Volitional Living by

Galen Sharp

• Why Materialism Is Baloney: How True Skeptics Know There Is No Death and Fathom Answers to life, the Universe, and Everything by Bernardo Kastrup

www.ingramcontent.com/pod-product-compliance
Lightning Source LLC
LaVergne TN
LVHW051543070426
835507LV00021B/2374